Deer Hunters
1997 Almanac

FROM THE PUBLISHERS OF DEER & DEER HUNTING MAGAZINE

Published by:

krause
publications

700 E. State Street • Iola, WI 54990-0001
Telephone: 715/445-2214

Please call or write for our free catalog of outdoor publications.
Our toll-free number to place an order or obtain a free catalog is
800-258-0929. Please use our regular business telephone
715-445-2214 for editorial comment or further information.

Library of Congress Catalog Number: 92-74255

ISBN: 0-87341-475-6
Printed in the United States of America

Deer Hunters' 1997 Almanac

FROM THE PUBLISHERS OF DEER & DEER HUNTING MAGAZINE

FEATURES

Dan Schmidt

Your success at trailing and recovering a wounded deer begins with proper shot selection. For in-depth information on tracking and trailing techniques, turn to Page 9.

turn to Page 9.

FAST FACTS

FIRESIDE STORIES

Can You Put it Down?

We're hoping that you can't.

One look and you'll see that we've revamped your *Deer Hunters' Almanac* into this information-packed 1997 edition. We've included everything a deer hunter could want in a camp-side companion: helpful how-to articles, state-by-state deer hunting statistics and harvest records, weather information, and easy-to-reference venison recipes.

Don't miss these new features for '97:

✓ Two landmark articles on tracking and trailing: "Practice and Precise Shots Ensure Easy Tracking," and "Secrets to Tracking Success." These articles will define the most critical factors to hitting and recovering deer. Both are loaded with helpful charts and firsthand testimonials.

✓ Fresh "Deer Browse." A new supply of interesting facts and stories about white-tailed deer and the world they live in.

✓ "Shot Placement for Whitetails." This six-page section features sketches that show gun- and bow-hunters proper shot placement for whitetails in different positions. Also included are full-page anatomy charts that show the location of a whitetail's organs, muscle groups and skeletal system.

✓ An in-depth "How-To" section. Learn how to better estimate distances; become a better bow-hunter; select camouflage; and determine arrow length.

✓ "Tactical Tips & Tricks." From the pages of *Deer & Deer Hunting*, these are some of the best deer hunting tips and tricks we received from readers since the column first appeared in March 1995.

✓ Deer harvest records. State-by-state histories of bow- and gun-hunting white-tailed deer harvests.

✓ Boone & Crockett record whitetails. The most up-to-date listing of bucks in the Boone & Crockett Club. They're all here, listed state-by-state for your convenience!

If you have articles, stories or original photographs that you would like to have considered for publication in next year's almanac, write to us at Deer & Deer Hunting, *700 E. State St., Iola, WI 54990.*

Deer Hunters' 1997 Almanac

Patrick Durkin
Editorial Director

Dan Schmidt
Associate Editor

Cover photo by Robert Franz

The Meeting Place

■ *Joel Spring*

The faint sound came from above. Clip-clop. Clip-clop. Like horses on a dusty trail.

I couldn't believe it. A deer was crossing the road above. I heard twigs gently snapping as the deer entered the woods, yet could still hear hoof-falls on the blacktop. More than one! It had been five years since I hunted this spot, and six since I had seen a deer here, yet here they came, five minutes before sunset.

I hoped Dad was in place. Please let him see this, I thought.

We had spent the first day of our first deer hunt together trudging through the swamps and dense conifer stands of the Adirondack Mountains in northern New York. We would stop and set up in a good-looking area, and I would rattle the big 6-point antlers and blow my grunt tube. This was Dad's first deer hunt since he was a teen-ager, and I wanted desperately for him to think I knew what I was doing. But from the sideways glances I sometimes got, I'm sure that's not what he was thinking. Inside his camo face mask he was probably laugh-

ing. We covered lots of territory that first day but saw nothing besides red squirrels and moss-covered trees.

I slept fitfully that first night in the iced-over cap of my truck. I plotted as Dad snored peacefully.

The Adirondacks are rough to hunt, and not so loaded with whitetails that seeing even one a weekend is guaranteed. But I wanted to get my father close to deer and excited enough so I could talk him into taking vacation in two weeks for a bow-hunt in the Catskills. I figured once he had seen deer up close, he would get hooked on hunting as quickly as I had.

When dawn broke Sunday morning, both of us were sore, and I wasn't well-rested. After a miserable breakfast hastily prepared over a propane burner, we headed into the woods. The icy morning turned quickly into a sticky, uncomfortable day as we headed along another unexplored ridge. To the right the ridge angled suddenly and steeply upward. Straight ahead lay a small draw that looked like a natural funnel from the mountains to a swamp below. We hiked into the draw, letting the towering beech trees and smattering of hemlocks swallow us.

"Let's set up to call here."

Dad agreed, but I swear he had a look of weary amusement dancing across his face. Even so, he climbed a little farther up in the draw and sat on a log that leaned against the base of a massive, gnarled tree. I had trouble picking him out from the lush surroundings when he donned his camo mask, but the white tips of his recurve eventually betrayed his presence.

I began to rattle. A warm breeze had picked up, and so I rattled louder to make sure the sound would carry. I banged a small hemlock with the antlers, and stomped the ground with my right foot. I tried to picture an old buck on that hillside hearing the noise and reacting to it. I stopped after rattling only about five minutes. I gave the antlers a gentle tick about 15 minutes later, and blew two short, deep "uuughs." I then tucked the grunt call back into my shirt and hung the antlers on a branch.

Ten minutes later, Dad looked in my direction and I decided it was time to move. A year had passed since a buck had come to my rattling, and my confidence on this warm September day -- with the rut still so far away -- was low. I stretched and hefted my compound, thinking how much nicer it would be to carry the light, graceful recurve my father balanced so effortlessly.

"Did you hear that," he asked in a hushed voice as we reached each other.

"No," I said, puzzled.

"Maybe it was nothing."

I suggested we sit a few more minutes. I blew gingerly on the grunt call a couple more times, and strained to see into the midday shadows of the huge woods. After 30 minutes, we began climbing the steep draw to see what was over the ridge. We went about 100 yards until I spotted the tracks. A single dark line was visible in the draw's damp leaves, and it stopped in a small clump. I moved the leaves to reveal a huge hoof print gouged into the black earth. Obviously, a deer had been coming down the hill into our ambush when we decided to move. If he had stayed on course he would have passed within yards of Dad.

We didn't exchange words. None were needed. It had been my decision to move, and we knew I was the more impatient of the pair. Dad would have sat there all day.

We followed the buck's tracks back up the mountain, finally losing them when the damp earth gave way to rock. Suddenly I was cool. We had climbed a long way — several hundred feet — and the wind was blowing harder up here. We spent a couple of hours exploring this mountain with no name, stopping occasionally to try to call our buck back. We knew it was futile. As we neared the road, Dad finally asked, "So, are you ready to go home?"

"No, let's take a ride and sit until dark," I offered.

When we parked the truck we had less than 30 minutes of light remaining. Dad, being a good partner, didn't give me much of an argument when I had him sit against a tree, not 50 yards down the edge of the roadside. I took my bow and sat about 70 yards away. I couldn't see him through the thick wall of chest-high hemlocks.

When the deer crossed the road and stepped into the woods, I prayed they would go his way. I could see them momentarily silhouetted against the sky as they stepped off the pavement. Picking leisurely at the vegetation, they slowly came in my direction. The lead deer, a huge doe that would surpass 200 pounds, passed broadside at 10 yards. Instinctively, I drew as she neared, but let her pass, hoping she would work toward Dad. After she passed, I looked around and saw the other deer, all smaller does, facing away from me. I silently let my bow back down. However, I had failed to see a small button-buck watching me from about eight yards away.

"Whoosh!"

His loud snort signaled the end of a promising bow-hunt. The big doe blew a return warning, and I think I heard a hoof stomp in the wet leaves. In seconds, the woods were alive with crashing, snorting deer and their bobbing white tails.

When I eventually found Dad, sitting stock-still in the darkening woods, he said he hadn't seen the deer but had heard the whole thing. I started to apologize for the day's second blown chance, but then noticed his smile. The tremor in his voice made me realize he was having as much of an adrenaline rush as me.

He looked hooked.

On the way home we relived the day's hunts, and the excitement of being surrounded by deer at sunset. I told him about the first time I hunted the spot we had just left, and how an 8-point buck had strolled into the middle of the road at dark to watch me put my gear away, and how that incredible experience hooked me on deer hunting.

He then began telling stories about hunting these mountains with his older brother when they were boys. I had never heard these stories, and I hung on his words. I could see by the gleam in his eye and the excitement in his voice that I had found a new hunting partner.

Practice & Precise Shots Ensure Easy Tracking

■ *Patrick Durkin,
with Jay McAninch*

I can clearly remember the first deer I shot at with my bow and arrow, though it happened nearly 25 years ago. Maybe that's because it was also the first deer I missed.

I was 16, and standing atop a large limb in a white oak. Portable tree stands weren't legal in those days. Shortly after dawn, an 8-point buck walked down a nearby trail, turned to his left, and stopped broadside seven yards from the base of my oak. A leafy branch one yard from my toes partially obscured his lower chest, so I aimed slightly above the leaves and turned loose the cedar shaft from my 43-pound recurve. You can guess the rest. The buck coiled and crouched at the bow-string's slap, and the Bear Razorhead zipped cleanly

Factors Affecting Whether Deer are Hit/Recovered

13% Practice	5% Hunting method (tree stand, still-hunt, etc.)
13% Distance of the shot	5% Shooting aids (scopes, sights, etc.)
13% Experience in hunting and taking shots	3% Hunting pressure in the area
12% The deer's position	2% The deer's size or sex
11% Movement of the deer	1% Time left in the season
8% Weather conditions	1% Hunting with a group or by yourself
7% Type of bow or firearm	
6% Type of hunting terrain	

above his back, never clipping a hair.

I replayed that shot nightly for the next year, and can still see the red blur of my fletchings as the arrow burrowed into the ground. The buck leaped forward about 15 yards, looked back down his trail, and then disappeared.

I practiced more earnestly than ever during the next year, and cleanly killed my first deer, a doe, four days into the following bow season. Since then, I've never forgotten the importance of practicing with bows and firearms. When coupled with knowledge of the deer — which is also gained through experience and persistence — steady practice instills the confidence needed to become an effective bow-hunter.

I imagine most deer hunters have formative experiences similar to mine. Therefore, I wasn't surprised to see that shooting practice was ranked as one of the most important factor in determining whether hunters hit and retrieve deer they shoot at.

That fact was one of many that arose from the *Deer & Deer Hunting* Readers' Survey on trailing and tracking. In fact, nearly 50 percent of the responses given by readers suggest they know success hinges largely on preparation and decisions made before taking a shot. Besides practice, these factors include hunting experience, weapon type, hunting area selected, hunting method used, and shooting aids used.

Evidence of this preparation is seen in the type of shooting aids being used today. Respondents showed a strong tendency for using sophisticated shooting aids such as scopes, string peep sights and special slug barrels to improve their chances for success.

Work to Prevent Long Tracks

Most respondents reinforced the importance of practice in their shooting decisions. "It all comes down to one thing," wrote Shaun Bumedes of Richlandtown, Pa. "Make the shot placement good on the first shot.

Shooting Opportunities and Success Rates

	Passed	Shot At	Hit	Kill/ Recovered
Bucks	Bow 2.0	1.0	0.6	0.5
	Gun 1.9	1.2	0.71	0.67
Does	Bow 8.0	0.7	0.4	0.3
	Gun 9.8	1.0	0.6	0.57
Fawns	Bow 6.0	0.1	0.1	0.1
	Gun 5.6	0.1	0.1	0.1

Analysis: The recovery rate of deer in the *D&DH* survey was based on the average number of deer killed and recovered as a proportion of the deer hit. For bow-hunters, the recovery rate was 83 percent for bucks and 75 percent for does. For gun-hunters, the recovery rate was 94 percent for bucks and 95 percent for does. The bow-hunting recovery rates were similar to those reported in the Camp Ripley, Minn., study, which found an average of 87 percent of deer hit by bow-hunters were recovered.

You won't have to track the deer if you see it go down."

Steven Artz of Schofield, Wis., spoke for many readers when he wrote: "If you cannot consistently place your arrow in a 6-inch circle at a given range while under pressure, don't shoot. Shooting at ranges beyond your level of confidence is unsportsman-like, and the animal deserves more than this." Tom Balestrieri of Sussex, Wis., added: "You must have confidence or you don't belong out there. Confidence comes from practice and years of hunting experience."

Another common response was the need for thorough knowledge of deer anatomy. As Ross Bulgrin of Akron, Ohio, wrote: "I only shoot when I know I can place my bullet or arrow in the vitals for a quick, clean kill. Practice with a 3-D target at various ranges is crucial for bow-hunting."

Bob Martino of Hubbard, Ohio, stressed that while practice is important, knowledge of the deer itself is the most important factor. "We need to develop a deep knowledge of its movements, positions, attitudes, anatomy and its psyche. It is not until we totally understand deer that we will become proficient and successful."

In studying the factors that readers deemed important in hitting and recovering deer, we grouped the responses and assigned a percentage between 1 and 100. In brief, 52 percent of the factors are important before the shot, 40 percent are important at the time of the shot, and 8 percent are related to the weather. Two of the top three reasons are based totally on preparation for the shot. Further, the only factor hunters don't have some control over when shooting is the weather, although the weather can affect decisions they make about when or if they shoot. The table that follows shows how these factors ranked:

Decisions made at the time of the shot include the shooting distance, position and movement of the deer, and — to a lesser degree — the sex and age of the deer, and time left in the season. Those final two responses, although uncommon among our respondents, represent pressures that are self-imposed or brought on by peers or other hunters. This suggests that outside pressures can produce poor shot selection. Why? In these situations, the overriding factor appears to be whether to take or pass the shot, not the quality of the shot itself.

A small number of respondents also mentioned the "Now or Never" approach to shot selection, another form of self-imposed pressure. As one of them wrote, "Shoot when you see them, because you might not see them again."

Elmer C. Haley Jr. of Warren, N.H., claimed the deer population is too low in his state, and said low deer populations cause hunters to be less choosy. "This philosophy influences the hunter to take difficult shots that he might not otherwise take if the deer population were higher," he wrote.

A more common view among our respondents, however, was voiced by Ken Gravois of Louisiana. Gravois said it's important not to give in to external pressures. "Shooting is only a small part of the experience," Gravois wrote. "I think hunters would get more enjoyment if they hunted only to please themselves, and not try to match up to peer pressure."

The type of bow or firearm hunters choose was considered an important factor by 44 percent of the respondents. This suggests hunters have substantial concerns

What Techniques or Shooting Aids are Used?

✔80 percent of the respondents used a scope on their firearm.

✔78 percent practice judging distances in the field.

✔54 percent pace off distances before hunting from a stand.

✔53 percent shoot with pins and a peep sight on their bow.

✔46.5 percent shoot only at deer that are standing or walking slowly.

✔45 percent shoot with a pin sight on their bow.

✔38 percent use a slug barrel on their shotgun.

✔37 percent hunt so much that they feel confident judging distances.

✔29 percent use an open sight on their gun.

✔24 percent use a bead sight on their shotgun.

✔21 percent use binoculars to check the line of sight or judge distances.

✔18 percent fire several shots if they're sure it's safe.

✔17 percent use a range-finder to judge distances.

✔16 percent use a lighted sight pin on their bow.

✔11.5 percent shoot their bow instinctively.

✔11 percent shoot their gun only when they can find a solid rest.

✔8 percent use a peep sight on their gun.

Analysis: More than 99 of 100 respondents had used one or several of the above techniques or shooting aids. For ease of reporting and comparing responses, the data were grouped and assigned a percentage between 1 and 100. Nearly half of the responses (46 percent) indicated hunters depend on some type of mechanical shooting aid (riflescopes, bow sights, range-finders or binoculars) to improve their chances of hitting a deer.

---

about recovering deer hit with various sporting arms, and that some believe this factor is important in the outcome of their shooting decisions.

Shooting, Hitting and Recovering Deer

When *D&DH* readers decided to shoot a deer, the proportion of shots that hit the animal are remarkably similar between bow- and gun-hunters. Regardless of whether they shot at a buck or a doe, archers and gun-hunters, on average, hit about 60 percent of the deer at which they were shooting.

A caution regarding the rate at which hunters miss shots: This rate is difficult to assess because the only evidence of a hit or miss is a report based on the split-second observations of a hunter watching the deer after shooting. That's particularly true as the distance of the shot increases, such as with shotguns or rifles. Adding to the difficulty is that a shooter's view of the projectile's impact is usually obscured by recoil, and seldom can the bullet or slug be recovered for analysis. Further, the ability of hunters to judge the outcome of shots varies between individuals. More importantly, each situation involves conditions that can significantly

> **The survey's recovery rates for bow-hunters were 83 percent for bucks and 75 percent for does**

affect how hunters assess each shot.

The recovery rate of deer reported in the *D&DH* survey was based on the average number of deer killed and recovered as a proportion of the deer hit. For example, if 10 deer were hit and eight were recovered, the recovery rate would be 80 percent.

On average, gun- and bow-hunters in the *D&DH* survey killed and recovered all the fawns (4- to 6-month-old deer) at which they took shots. While this statistic suggests a 100 percent hit-and-recovery rate on fawns, the reality is that some fawns were missed or hit and not recovered. Regardless of the actual number of fawns hit and recovered, the *D&DH* survey indicates recovery rates are extremely high for this age group.

The survey's recovery rates for bow-hunters were 83 percent for bucks and 75 percent for does, while the recovery rates for gun-hunters were 94 percent for bucks and 95 percent for does. The recovery rates for deer hit by bow-hunters were similar to those recently reported in the Camp Ripley, Minn., study of more than 6,000 bow-hunters. (See *Deer & Deer Hunting*, August 1995, "Camp Ripley Research: New Insights Into Bow Wounding.") The Ripley study found an average of 87 percent of deer hit by bow-hunters were recovered. The statistical limits of the recovery rates reported for the four Camp Ripley hunts were 76 percent to 98 percent.

Recovery rates in the *D&DH* survey were slightly lower than reported in the Camp Ripley study, but were likely a better composite average of most situations in which readers bow-hunt. Camp Ripley's hunts take place over a two-day period on a 53,000-acre military site, and involve hunter densities of more than 20 per square mile. Consequently, a portion of deer recovered by Camp Ripley's archers had been hit previously by other hunters, which increased recovery rates. In most hunting situations reported by *D&DH* readers, hunter densities were likely much lower than at Camp Ripley, thus reducing the chances of other hunters recovering a deer hit by a particular bow-hunter.

The high recovery rates for gun-hunters were similar to earlier studies. These findings also reflect increased recovery rates, which are likely caused by more group or party hunting; the ability of hunters to shoot more than once at a single deer, which might reduce the quality of shot selection; and the higher hunter densities typical of gun seasons, which would promote more recoveries of deer.

Shooting Decisions

What factors helped respondents decide which shots they would take or pass? The survey's findings demonstrated that bow- and gun-hunters passed 3 to 4 times more does and fawns than bucks. Hunters reported passing more does than fawns, but those data were likely biased by the difficulty of distinguishing fawns from other antlerless deer as autumn progresses. That factor is especially pronounced in late October and November, when most hunters are afield.

On average, bow- and gun-hunters passed about the same number of bucks, does and fawns that they could have shot and killed. At first glance, that might sound surprising because the distance at which hunters typically shoot deer with a bow or firearm would not be similar and, in some cases, substantially different. For example, the average bow-hunter would be passing shots at deer that were certainly within 40 yards and, more likely, between 10 yards and 20 yards. On the

> *At least 50 percent of bow- and gun-hunters did not pass up a shot at a buck, while only 14 percent of bow-hunters and 10 percent of gun-hunters passed shots at five or more bucks.*

other hand, gun-hunters likely could have considered shooting deer at least 40 yards away and, more likely, 75 yards to 150 yards.

However, the high number of deer passed by bow-hunters could have resulted from substantially more days spent hunting. Bow seasons in most states and provinces are several weeks or months long. Gun seasons, of course, often run from only a few days to several weeks.

At least 50 percent of bow- and gun-hunters did not pass up a shot at a buck, while only 14 percent of bow-hunters and 10 percent of gun-hunters passed shots at five or more bucks. These data confirm what deer managers have known for years: Many hunters are happy to shoot the first buck they have an opportunity to kill, and most will not pass many bucks before shooting.

Wildlife managers have also realized that many hunters pass up antlerless deer largely to ensure they can continue hunting, and because they want to shoot a buck or a bigger doe. These observations are based on the timing and rate at which deer appear at check stations during the season. Typically, the percentage of does and fawns in the daily harvest increases as the season progresses. In the *D&DH* survey, more than 20 percent of bow- and gun-hunters passed at least 15 or more does. Meanwhile, about 12 percent of both groups passed 15 or more fawns.

> *Wildlife managers have realized that many hunters pass up antlerless deer to ensure they can continue hunting, and because they want to shoot a buck or a bigger doe.*

Why are Shots Passed?

When asked why they passed shooting opportunities at deer they could have hit and killed, hunters reported they didn't have a good shot, 18 percent; they were hunting for a buck, 16 percent; they were hunting for a bigger, older deer, 13 percent; they were hunting for a trophy buck, 11 percent; they were not ready to fill their tag, 9 percent; or it was too dark, 8 percent. What were the least common reasons? The respondents reported it was before or after legal shooting hours, 5 percent; they didn't have the right tags for the deer, 5 percent; they already filled their tag, 4 percent; the

weather was bad and the deer might not be recovered, 3 percent; and it would have gotten too dark to recover the deer, 3 percent.

In all, 50 percent of the passed shots occurred because of the hunter's selectivity, 32 percent because of shooting conditions or the quality of the shot opportunity, and 14 percent because the shot would have been illegal.

A condition of a "passed shot" was that the hunter believed he could have shot and killed the deer, but chose not to shoot. An interesting twist occurred when comparing this condition against the most common reason for passing a deer, namely, a poor shooting opportunity. As Stephen Gerlach of Illinois wrote: "There are enough variables to consider in good shot placement without adding to the problem by taking a less-than-ideal shot. ... I would rather let the animal pass, and get a better shot later, one that creates a swift, clean kill."

A gratifying result of the survey was that hunters typically didn't risk hitting and losing deer because of poor shot opportunities, even though they considered the deer to be within their effective killing range.

Still, the fact that hunters considered these to be passed shots was confusing. Perhaps peer pressure makes some hunters feel the need to report an opportunity as "passed shots." Maybe they've heard other hunters talk about passing shots, and felt the need to make similar reports.

> *Perhaps peer pressure makes some hunters feel the need to report an opportunity as "passed shots." Maybe they've heard other hunters talk about passing shots, and felt the need to make similar reports.*

Summary

The results of the survey confirmed demographic and background characteristics of hunters that were established in previous studies, such as scientific market research conducted for *Deer & Deer Hunting*. The shooting aids and techniques used by hunters represented a mixture of attitudes, ranging from those who spent considerable time and money to obtain an edge in marksmanship, to those who worked with simple equipment and basic techniques to shoot deer.

The similarities between the gun- and bow-hunters in passing shots, taking shots, hitting deer and recovering deer were surprising. Many factors could have influenced these results, including the fact that many respondents hunted with both a bow and firearm. Regardless of the reasons, the factors most related to the recovery of deer are directly or indirectly related to judgments made by the hunter before, during or after a shot opportunity presents itself.

Patrick Durkin is editor of Deer & Deer Hunting *magazine. Jay McAninch, who designed the questionnaire and provided analysis of the results, is a deer research biologist with the Minnesota Department of Natural Resources. McAninch was one of the principal researchers in the Camp Ripley bow-wounding study.*

Are We Training Top Trackers?

Secrets to Trac

18

ing Success

*The 1995 Readers'
Survey indicates that
deer-trailing lessons are
rarely taught by
hunting mentors, even
though we know every
hunter will have to trail
many deer they've shot.*

■ *Patrick Durkin,
with Jay McAninch*

Shortly after dawn on Sept. 19, 1973, three of my teen-age friends and I wandered around a woodlot looking intently but erratically for a doe I had shot with my bow and arrow the night before. In our excitement to find the deer, we had forsaken almost everything we had read or heard about trailing deer after the shot.

After 45 minutes of futile searching, the one member of our group whose father hunted deer took charge. He directed me to climb back into my portable tree stand and point out where the doe had been standing when I shot. Moments later, Vic found the first blood

drops. After that, the search became easier, even if a bit haphazard. About 15 minutes into this second attempt, I found my first bow-kill about 90 yards from where I had shot. The newfangled Wasp three-blade broadhead had cleanly sliced its heart. As my friends gathered to congratulate me, they were amazed by the blood trail the deer had left. How we missed it earlier still baffles me, but it demonstrated to the four of us that we needed to slow down and trail every deer as if we were detectives piecing together evidence at a crime scene.

And now, 22 years later, after analyzing the results of *Deer & Deer Hunting's* 1995 Readers' Survey, I see my friends and I were typical of beginning deer hunters: We were relying mainly on common sense and our limited experience to recover deer we had shot. That was before the days of videos and special deer hunting TV shows, but we had read many articles and books, and attended a few seminars on trailing deer. Still, when we trailed our first deer, our lack of firsthand experience nearly ruined my chances of recovering it until our most experi-

Which of these aids have you used in tracking, and how important was each?

(Results given in percentages)

Rank	Item	Never Used	Very Useful	Useful
1	Flashlight	12.8	56.4	29.0
2	Material to mark trail	13.0	68.5	17.8
3	Battery lantern	52.1	25.7	21.1
4	Gas lantern	48.0	40.2	10.7
5	String-tracker	82.0	5.7	7.6
6	Hair ID booklet	83.9	5.7	9.4
7	Tracking dogs	86.8	6.9	5.3
8	Blood-activated spray	88.1	5.0	5.5
9	Infrared detector	96.8	0.4	1.1
10	Radio devices	97.4	1.1	1.1

Analysis: Most respondents believe a light — either a flashlight or lantern — and material to mark the trail are the necessities in tracking equipment. The above ratings do not necessarily mean that respondents thought other tracking devices were ineffective. Rather, our data indicate most hunters simply had not tried them. However, many respondents included strong letters of support for the use of tracking dogs, even when they had never seen one in use.

enced member — the one whose father took him deer hunting — got us organized.

The *D&DH* Readers' Survey proved eye-opening when we analyzed how hunters learn their trailing skills. This survey indicates that deer-trailing lessons are rarely taught by hunting mentors, even though we know all hunters will have to trail most deer they shoot. Consider that statement's implications. Many sociological studies by universities and wildlife agencies have found that hunters are usually introduced to hunting, and trained to hunt and shoot, by

family or friends. Despite the traditions of initiation into hunting, more than 86 percent of our survey's respondents said they learned their trailing skills on their own.

In fact, almost half of the survey's respondents received no training from a friend or parent, either on an actual trail or a practice trail. Further, more respondents, 64 percent, said books and magazines helped teach them how to trail deer. In addition, 23 percent said they learned with the aid of videos, and 13 percent said they were helped by TV shows.

Stephen Salkaus of Mass-

How long would you wait before tracking a deer you think you hit?

(Results given in percentages)

Location of Hit	Heart/Lungs	Abdomen	Legs	Unknown Hit
Bow				
Wouldn't wait	16.0	4.6	27.8	15.0
Wait 1-9 minutes	15.4	2.3	8.1	5.0
Wait 10-19 minutes	26.4	5.2	7.0	10.7
Wait 20-29 minutes	21.1	9.0	5.9	13.8
Wait 30+ minutes	21.1	78.9	51.2	55.5
Rifle				
Wouldn't wait	45.7	20.3	44.3	34.4
Wait 1-9 minutes	27.8	7.9	11.5	13.1
Wait 10-19 minutes	16.0	15.8	10.7	14.4
Wait 20-29 minutes	5.0	10.5	6.5	8.7
Wait 30+ minutes	5.5	45.5	27.0	29.4
Shotgun				
Wouldn't wait	44.1	18.5	42.1	33.3
Wait 1-9 minutes	24.8	10.1	12.2	11.0
Wait 10-19 minutes	17.1	12.6	9.4	11.5
Wait 20-29 minutes	7.0	12.2	6.4	10.5
Wait 30+ minutes	7.0	46.6	29.9	33.7
Muzzleloader				
Wouldn't wait	40.6	15.8	39.6	31.0
Wait 1-9 minutes	29.8	10.2	13.9	14.1
Wait 10-19 minutes	16.0	11.0	9.2	9.3
Wait 20-29 minutes	7.5	9.7	5.3	9.0
Wait 30+ minutes	6.1	53.3	32.0	36.6
Handgun				
Wouldn't wait	43.0	14.0	42.1	33.1
Wait 1-9 minutes	25.5	10.9	16.5	15.3
Wait 10-19 minutes	18.8	10.3	8.5	9.2
Wait 20-29 minutes	7.9	10.9	6.1	7.4
Wait 30+ minutes	4.8	53.9	26.8	35.0

Analysis: As expected, bow-hunters tended to wait longer after a shot than firearms hunters. Still, most hunters tend to take a conservative approach to trailing deer, meaning that, whenever possible, they prefer to wait before trailing.

achusetts spoke for many when he wrote: "I didn't learn too much from my dad, but he is the one who got me into the woods to hunt. Thank God, and Dad, for this opportunity. But I'm making my own luck. I read a lot. I read good deer hunting articles numerous times so the information really sinks in."

Wendell Mayes of Iowa was like many readers in that he said his trailing skills were self-taught, but he also learned from a parent or friend, and magazines and books. "I use any information I can find from every source available," Mayes wrote.

A surprising conclusion is that the most critical aspect of hunting — what happens after the shot — is learned from books and TV rather than in the field. As a result, it follows that our trailing skills will only improve with each deer we track and recover.

Clearly, our survey suggests that experienced hunters are not working enough with inexperienced hunters who need insights to improve their tracking skills. If more trailing assistance were available, perhaps fewer hunters would report they learned tracking on their own.

Another explanation for the high number of self-taught trackers is that while reading, watching and listening can aid in learning trailing tactics, the best lessons are taught in actual tracking situations. In that case, firsthand experience is the most critical factor in developing trailing skills.

Bob Stinson of Michigan stresses the importance of taking responsibility to learn trailing skills.

"I realize that in our modern, urbanized society, most deer hunters have not had many opportunities to develop tracking skills," Stinson wrote. "Therefore, it's necessary that hunters make an effort to practice tracking skills whenever they go afield."

Experienced Hunters
This apparent shortcoming in teaching tracking skills is

Trailing Myths

✔ Deer never go uphill.
✔ Deer always go to water when wounded.
✔ Deer always circle. This won't likely happen unless the cover is limited, and the deer doesn't want to leave it.

particularly surprising, given the experience level of *Deer & Deer Hunting's* readers. How experienced are *D&DH's* readers? As you will recall from Part 1 of this series, the average respondent had been bowhunting 13 years and gun-hunting 21 years. *D&DH* readers can also be characterized as multiple-season hunters. More than 91 percent of them have hunted with a bow, more than 86 percent have hunted with a rifle, 61 percent have hunted with a shotgun, more than 50 percent have hunted with a muzzleloader, and a little less than 25 percent have hunted with a handgun. People with that kind of deer hunting devotion likely read and discuss every aspect of hunting year-round.

Given the many comments respondents submitted with their questionnaires, we believe our survey represents a thoughtful summary of the behavior and skills of experienced, dedicated hunters.

Larry Ryland of Alabama emphasizes the importance of experience. Ryland considers himself self-taught, and he also studies books and magazines. Still, it would appear he ranks his 35 years of hunting experience as the most crucial factor in developing his trailing skills.

Some readers went out of their way to become schooled in trailing wounded deer. As Dan Lander of Pennsylvania wrote: "I would ask friends to call me if they were going back to trail a deer. Going along with good, experienced trackers is like going to school. It's very helpful."

Ensuring Success

While our survey uncovered an apparent lack of training in trailing skills, it's obvious from Part 1 of this series that most deer shot by our readers are recovered. To review, *D&DH's* bow-hunting readers recovered 83 percent of the bucks and 75 percent of the does they shot. The recovery rates for gun-hunters were 94 percent for bucks and 95 percent for does.

Is this a contradiction of the apparent gap in trailing lessons? Not necessarily. Again, our respondents stressed the importance of practice, knowledge of deer anatomy, and shot placement in ensuring their trailing was successful.

Another important aspect of recovering deer is being in position to observe deer before, during and after the shot. Most respondents had excellent vantage points because they use tree stands, 61 percent; or ground blinds, 14.5 percent. Still-hunting was next in popularity at 12.6 percent, while drives and pushes were rare.

Where Trailing Dogs Are Legal

Alabama	New York
Arkansas	North Carolina
California	South Carolina
Florida	South Dakota
Georgia	Texas
Louisiana	Virginia
Mississippi	Wisconsin (If
Nebraska	on a leash)

After the shot, hunters in stands are more likely to see how the deer reacts, hear noises the deer makes, and pinpoint where the deer was standing at the time it was shot and where it was last seen. Simply said, more information will likely lead to more retrieved deer.

Ross Bulgrin of Ohio knows the importance of staying quiet on his stand after shooting. "I am always very still after my shot to watch and listen," he wrote. "I always wait at least 30 minutes, depending on my shot and what I see afterward."

Shooting Decisions

In Part 1 of this report, we covered most aspects of the shot, except the deer's position at the instant the arrow is released or the trigger pulled. The deer's position and its motion can't be controlled by hunters, but these factors dictate the outcome of shooting decisions. With good teaching and firsthand experience, hunters learn to spurn tempting but risky shots. Those who haven't learned should listen to

Readers' Input: Trailing and Tracking Tips

Greg Hanson, Michigan: "As an instructor in the International Bowhunter Education Program, I find the trailing and tracking portion of our classes to be an important part of the instruction. Not only is this segment received well by the students, but they have a great time blood-trailing. They also learn it's not as easy as it might seem.

"We teach what to do after the shot, such as shot placement, direction of travel, marking the last sighting, listening, etc. ... Veteran hunters might think there is nothing else to be learned. I found out otherwise by taking and then teaching the IBEP class."

Claude E. Fernandez Jr., Georgia: "If you don't see the deer lying dead on the ground after shooting, mark where you're standing with orange tape or spare orange clothing before taking another step. ... Make a detailed mental picture of the spot where the deer was standing. Find reference points. Make another mental picture of where you last saw the deer as it ran off. Finding these exact locations quickly is critical, because the sign there will usually tell more than any other spot about what happened and what to expect."

Kevin Klute, Wisconsin: "After I shoot at a deer, the first thing I do is look closely at the deer's hoofs, and pick out landmarks that help me pinpoint where the hoofs had been. I've found that if I look at the deer's back or head, I'll walk past the spot where the deer was standing, and miss the blood trail. Pinpointing the hoofs' location puts you right on the blood trail."

Shaun Bumeder, Pennsylvania: "Make sure your first shot is properly placed. If I find myself tracking a deer farther than 200 yards, something went wrong with the shot. ... Tracking dogs should be legal for trailing wounded deer, as long as they're used in a tracking party, not a hunting party."

Roger Soletske, Wisconsin: "My partner and I use a 50- to 75-foot strip of surveyor's tape that we tie to our jacket and drag behind us as we unravel the trail. The tape follows the blood trail and helps mark the deer's direction of travel. If we temporarily lose the blood trail, we remove the tape from our jacket and leave it on the ground. We then go back to the tape's mid-point, squat down to the deer's eye level, and try to see what the deer was seeing. Look for openings in the brush, trails that split, etc. Return to the last blood spot, and then look for blood in areas you noticed while looking around at the deer's eye level. After locating blood, retie the tape and continue tracking. After finding the deer or finishing the track, roll up the tape and save it for the next hunt."

John J. Mazur, Florida: "Use a gas lantern. It seems to put out a white light, which makes blood spots shine more than light from a flashlight."

Gary Roseman, New Jersey: "When my hunting partner and I lose a blood trail, one of us gets down on his hands and knees to look for blood specks. The other stands over him, looking ahead and on the higher brush for any sign. When you're looking intently at one distance, it is hard to stay in focus at different heights. Any time we crawl over any brush, we are careful not to miss anything, for fear of ruining the trail. We keep going back to the last sign and starting over until we find something. Usually, signs are there if you take the time and look hard enough. What doesn't work is to go in the direction you think the deer went and look for a dead deer."

Wayne L. Kiernan, Wisconsin: "If the deer isn't recovered quickly, let it bed down in a swamp or thick cover. Next, get out a map of the site and place standers around the cover to watch likely escape routes. If a map isn't available, draw one. Make sure the standers know each other's locations, and determine safe shooting lanes. Once the standers are in position, the tracker slowly follows the deer into the cover."

this advice from Claude Fernandez of Georgia:

"A hunter who is willing to take a 'high-risk' shot also takes on an increased obligation to follow up the shot to prevent needless waste of the animal."

As might be expected, bow-hunters made shooting decisions based on relatively short distances. When a deer was standing broadside, the average bow-hunter was comfortable shooting at 31 yards and less. When the deer was walking, the average bow-hunter was comfortable shooting 22 yards and less. When the deer was running broadside, the "comfortable" distance shrank to four yards. In fact, nearly 75 percent of bow-hunters would not shoot at any running broadside deer, no matter what the distance. Of those who would shoot, nearly all would limit it to 20 yards or less.

After standing and walking broadside shots, the angling-away shot was the next most comfortable shot for archers. All but 6 percent would take this shot at an average distance of 21 yards. The other shooting scenarios we presented were not popular with bow-hunters. About 71 percent wouldn't shoot at a deer that was head-on or head-away, while 46 percent wouldn't shoot at a deer angling toward them.

Despite the conservative shooting behavior of most bow-hunters, about 2 percent to 4 percent would take 40- to 50-yard shots at deer moving at any speed in any position. A handful of respondents, 1 percent, would even shoot at a deer running broadside at 50 yards or more. Clearly, such archers are extremely confident or, possibly, overrate their shooting skills. Either way, the possibility of them finding much evidence of the deer's location at the moment of impact and its condition after the shot is remote.

Firearms Findings

The four most comfortable speeds and deer positions for bow-hunters were identical to almost all firearms hunters. Rifle hunters listed few shots they didn't like. The least popular position was a deer facing head-away. In such situations, 44 percent of rifle hunters wouldn't shoot. After that, the least popular shots were a deer running broadside, 17 percent wouldn't shoot; a deer coming head-on, 14 percent wouldn't shoot; and a deer angling toward the hunter, 8 percent wouldn't shoot.

Comfortable shooting distances for rifle hunters ranged from an average of 200 yards for deer standing broadside, 153 yards for walking broadside, 132 yards for angling away, 114 yards for angling toward, 102 yards for head-on, 83 yards for running broadside shots, and 58 yards for head-away shots.

At distances of 250 yards or

more, the only popular choice was a standing broadside shot, favored by 32 percent; followed by walking broadside, 15 percent; angling away, 10 percent; or angling toward, 8 percent. Despite the difficulty, about 5 percent of rifle hunters would shoot at deer coming head-on or running broadside.

Many respondents stressed the importance of practice and preparation at various distances. Hiram Hallock of Wisconsin, for example, has equipped his permanent stand with a shooting rest in every direction. Besides practicing regularly, he has calculated a table that tells him how far to lead deer moving at four different speeds at ranges of 100, 200 and 300 yards. He keeps this lead table in front of him when shooting at deer with his custom-made .308 rifle.

Meanwhile, the average comfortable shooting distance for standing broadside shots with a shotgun was 81 yards; walking broadside, 71 yards; angling away, 58 yards; and angling toward, 51 yards. The least popular angle with shotgun-hunters was the head-away position, where the average maximum distance was 25 yards. Further, nearly 50 percent of the shotgun hunters wouldn't take this shot. Also, few would take shots other than a standing broadside opportunity past 100 yards, and less than 2 percent would take a shot beyond 150 yards.

> ## The least favorite shot for handgun hunters was head-away, where 55 percent wouldn't shoot.

The responses of muzzleloading hunters were similar. The average maximum comfortable shooting distance at a standing broadside deer was 89 yards, followed by walking broadside, 74 yards; angling away, 62 yards; and angling toward, 53 yards. Again, more than 50 percent of muzzleloaders would not shoot at a deer head-away, and slightly more than 25 percent would not shoot at a running broadside deer.

For handgun hunters, the average maximum shooting distance for standing broadside shots was 56 yards; walking broadside, 46 yards; angling away, 40 yards; and angling toward, 34 yards. The least favorite shot for handgun hunters was head-away, where 55 percent wouldn't shoot; followed by running broadside, where 46 percent wouldn't shoot. As few as 2 percent and as many as 20 percent of handgun hunters would take shots past 75 yards, depending on the deer's position and movement. For hunters not familiar with scopes and shooting aids for handguns, such distances might be greater than expected. Still, more than half of the handgun respondents wouldn't shoot past 60 yards regardless of the deer's position and movement.

Tracking the Deer

Although hunters using bows and firearms showed a wide variation in their shot selection, we detected few differences in the circumstances under which they decided to track deer. Not surprisingly, almost 91 percent of all hunters said they would track every deer until convinced it had not been hit. This result is a measure of the responsibility *D&DH* readers feel toward the deer, and it reflects their concern for determining the outcome of their shots.

As Tim Rutledge of Alabama wrote: "I take trailing/tracking very seriously. If I shoot, I plan to recover the deer. They're too valuable to waste."

The next most common circumstances for tracking deer were based on tangible evidence. This included finding blood and/or hair, believing the deer was hit, seeing the deer act as if it were hit, and seeing the arrow or a wound in the deer. The respondents showed lower confidence in tracking deer with less solid evidence, such as believing the deer was mortally wounded, hearing the arrow or slug/bullet hit, being uncertain about where the shot hit, being unable to locate the arrow or evidence of the slug,

or having a hunting partner report the hit.

Based on these responses, hunters operate under the rule that they will track deer until they're satisfied they know its fate. However, if they don't have hard evidence or strong feelings of a hit, they are less inclined to get on the track.

Tracking Decisions

After an arrow, bullet or slug strikes a deer, how long do hunters wait before getting on the trail? Respondents to our survey base this decision largely on where they think the deer is hit. Bow-hunters generally wait before tracking, and they tend to follow accepted tracking ideas for deer. For example, 80 percent will wait at least 30 minutes before tracking gut-shot deer, and they're more cautious about beginning the track than they are when carrying firearms. In fact, 56 percent will wait 30 minutes or more to track deer when they're uncertain where the hit occurred, 51 percent wait that long on leg hits, and 21 percent will wait that long on heart/lung hits.

Rifle hunters — as with all firearms hunters — tended to track animals immediately. Most wait less than 20 minutes on deer shot in the heart/lungs, 89 percent; and almost half will wait less than 20 minutes on deer hit in the abdomen, 43 percent. In fact, only on gut-shot deer do 46 percent of rifle hunters wait before tracking.

19 Tips on How to Find a Wounded Deer

✔ Deer seldom leave a good blood trail when going up or down embankments of 10 to 30 feet. Look at the embankment's top or bottom for blood. This includes stream banks, ditches and railroad beds.

✔ If tracking with a companion, one hunter should always stand beside the point of last blood. He should mark the spot with a stick with flagging or a handkerchief, and look ahead for the deer or other sign. The other hunter should track the deer from the side of the trail.

✔ Bend over or squat beside the trail, if needed. Don't get down on all fours. That will disturb too much ground, and cover your hands and clothing with debris.

✔ Always carry the bow or gun in a safe position. Because you could trip, do not keep an arrow on the string or a shell in the chamber while unraveling the trail. Once the deer is spotted, move in slowly, gun or bow poised, ready to fire a finishing shot.

✔ Work closely together with your hunting partner(s). Don't range far from the last blood spot. On a tough trail, you have a better chance of finding more blood near the last spot than 40 yards away.

✔ Don't shout or make loud noises.

✔ Have or get permission from landowners before following deer onto another person's land.

✔ If it's raining or snowing, push ahead as best you can while maintaining the trail. But remember, most gut-shot deer won't die any sooner.

✔ Warm weather is only a problem if you must leave a deer overnight. Although the rumen will bloat within an hour of death, the rest of the meat will be good for a few hours in hot weather.

✔ If you gut-shoot a deer at dusk, and the temperature is expected to be 40 degrees or lower overnight, leave the deer until morning, if possible.

✔ When tracking at night, a small flashlight or hand lantern is excellent. The small direct beam gives the best possible light for searching the ground at close range.

✔ As you search, listen carefully. You might jump deer or hear them moving ahead. When you see other deer, watch them carefully. Unless you see a wound, do not shoot.

✔ Base all your judgments on the evidence found. Don't try to "think like a deer." Many hunters have lost deer because their "deer logic" was more human than they realized.

✔ Follow only the tracks or blood trail and, if you lose both, begin a systematic search of the areas you believe the deer might have gone. Conduct ever-widening circles from the point of last blood. If that fails, gather some friends, and use a line of walkers to fully cover the search area.

✔ When tracking with one or more hunters, first decide on a signal to alert each other that the deer has been sighted, and who is to shoot. Too many guns and/or overanxious people will cause safety problem, and possibly, more wounded deer.

✔ If a wounded deer is spotted, watch it carefully and try to determine what it's about to do. If it's close enough and you have a clear shooting lane, take a safe shot. If it's too far, use good still-hunting techniques to get close enough for a shot.

✔ If the deer is down, approach carefully to see if a final shot is needed. Generally, a deer that can hold up its head even partially can get back on its hoofs. Carefully watch it for balance and weakness.

✔ If the deer is down on its back or side and not moving, approach it from behind. With a stick, or the end of an arrow or gun barrel, touch the deer firmly between the shoulders. If it's not dead, it will move or jerk in response to the touch.

✔ Be ethical. Just because your buddies voice other plans, or tell you the deer will be fine, follow your own judgment. Shoulder the responsibility that comes after taking a shot.

In analyzing the data on shotgun, muzzleloader and handgun hunters, we found most would track the deer immediately or within 20 minutes, unless it was hit in the abdomen. In that case, they typically would wait more than 30 minutes.

Another factor in the decision to wait is that it allows hunters a chance to calm down and gather their thoughts. Typically, their heart and mind are racing after shooting, and they've learned to sit tight until the emotions and adrenaline ebb.

"I usually wait a few minutes just to get my head together and gather my wits," wrote Peter Nicholas of New York. "I stay put until the shakes are gone!"

Ada Klute of Wisconsin also uses these minutes to calm down. In addition, she uses this time to plan.

"I try to replay in my mind what just happened," she wrote. "I'm very careful to recall every detail possible about every step he took so I can relate where he was to landmarks. This makes the 30 minutes go fast."

Other readers pointed out that their decision on when to track will also vary depending on the weather, time of day, and other forces they can't control. John Lippincott of Vermont wrote:

"I might start to track a leg-hit deer immediately, but then back off. Or, conversely, if rain is threatening, I follow a gut-shot deer right away. The presence of coyotes is also a factor. My tendency is to track almost immediately (after 10 to 15 minutes to collect myself), and see how the deer reacts to the pressure of being trailed."

Analyzing the Tracking Data

As expected, firearms hunters seemed to believe waiting would have little effect on their chances of recovering hit deer. Our survey found far fewer will wait long before pursuing deer they shot. Ironically, however, the distances at which most firearms hunters reported shooting suggests they begin many trailing jobs with scant evidence of the shot's outcome. Did their slug or bullet hit the deer, and if so, where? Bow-hunters, on the other hand, because they're watching the shot at short distances and are using a more obvious projectile, tend to know more about each shot's outcome. Perhaps gun-hunters believe they need less information because they can shoot at longer distances and take more than one shot. For instance, if they jump a wounded deer, they have a much better chance than a bow-hunter at putting it down.

An interesting twist many firearms hunters pointed out was that competition influenced their trailing decisions. That is, if they didn't get after the deer immediately, they feared it might end up being fitted with someone else's tag. Competition is most keen during firearms seasons, and it tends to make hunters less conservative about when to begin trailing.

Of course, competition might have the opposite effect in some cases. Ed Michaelson of Michigan hunts in farm country, and doesn't want a deer he shoots to be pushed to leave the property he hunts.

"I normally might wait longer for some situations, because if the deer crosses the boundary, I might lose it to another hunter."

Conclusion

We could interpret the trailing and tracking information reported by our readers several ways. First, nearly all hunters — whether they use a bow or firearm — reported tracking deer according to the accepted and popularly reported techniques. That is, they tended to wait the longest before tracking gut-shot deer, and wait the shortest for heart/lung-shot deer. Based on a simple analysis, hunters could be merely telling us what they have read and heard.

Whenever possible, most respondents take a conservative approach to trailing wounded deer. Nearly 91 percent said they track every deer they shoot at until they're sure of its fate, which could mean most hunters, when facing a trailing job, can't be sure where they have hit a

> *Based on these responses, hunters operate under the rule that they will track deer until they're satisfied they know its fate.*

deer. If that's the case, their answers to the questions about how long they wait before tracking deer might merely reflect their knowledge of accepted thinking on when to track. That would mean they weren't necessarily using their firsthand knowledge of dealing with various types of wounded deer. Instead, they're relying on what they've read and heard more than what we might think.

However, given the profile of our survey's respondents, an equally likely interpretation is that many hunters are confident in their tracking skills. They could be relying on time-tested skills and observations in developing logical, consistent plans for recovering deer. Many always prepare for the worst, and cautiously plan each search to ensure they can unravel even the most difficult trail. The many circumstances they've encountered help make the difference in recovering deer.

Deer Browse

For as long as there are hunters there will be a fresh supply of hunting stories. Trouble is, most stories told at deer camp include a grain of truth and a lot of imagination.

Well, the "Deer Browse" section in every issue of *Deer & Deer Hunting* includes some pretty remarkable deer stories. There is a difference, however, between the magazine stories and deer camp stories: The "Deer Browse" stories are based on 100 percent fact.

Did you hear about New York's 13-point doe? How did a white-tailed deer stop a train headed to Chicago? Why did a Wisconsin buck attack a cement lawn ornament? Those are just a few of the subjects of Browse stories that appeared in *Deer & Deer Hunting* since the last *Deer Hunters' Almanac*.

Browse stories, however, do more than entertain; they inform. Who shot Saskatchewan's king of non-typical bucks? How can a flu shot make you a better deer hunter? What role did a deer play in the 1995 U.S. Women's Golf Open? And, what are some communities doing to ease the strain caused by bulging deer herds?

Whether it's intriguing stories or helpful tips, we're sure you'll enjoy every page of this collection of "Deer Browse."

Roger Scales bagged this 13-point hermaphrodite deer while hunting in New York's Southern Tier in November 1994. The 3½-year-old deer had both male and female sex organs. Its rack had an unofficial Boone & Crockett score of 129⅝.

Dave Henderson

■ New York Hunter Bags True Non-Typical

Roger Scales couldn't help but chuckle as he completed the carcass tag for the 13-pointer that lay before him in a central New York woodlot.

"Points, left antler: 6."

"Points, right antler: 7."

"Date of kill: Nov. 21, 1994."

"Sex: Both."

It was a day that Scales, a veteran of 35 hunting seasons in New York's Southern Tier, will never forget.

He dropped the 13-pointer with one slug from his 12-gauge shotgun. All he could think of as he readied for field-dressing chores was, "I've got the biggest buck of my life."

As he began field dressing the animal, Scales quickly realized the 13-pointer was, well, not really a buck.

"There were no visible male organs, and it had a vaginal canal that really didn't lead anywhere inside the body," said wildlife biologist Lance Clark, who examined the carcass. "It definitely wasn't reproductive," Clark said.

After closer inspection, Clark determined the deer to be a hermaphrodite — having both male and female organs. While continuing to field dress the deer, Scales found undeveloped testes inside its body.

Clark said he had never seen a hermaphrodite deer in his five years as a deer biologist.

Besides being rare, antlered does typically carry small, undeveloped racks, he said.

Scales' deer was aged at 3½

years and had an unofficial non-typical Boone & Crockett score of 129⅝ points.

Antler growth among does is attributed to hormone deficiencies. In these cases, the animal usually doesn't have enough male hormones to carry out the shedding process, so it carries the velvet antlers until shedding them in winter.

Comparing Scales' deer to an antlered doe, Clark said it is extremely rare to find such a deer without its velvet. "This deer's antlers had almost completely shed the velvet, although the antlers weren't polished like a buck's would be at this time of year," he said.

C.W. Severinghaus, a former New York wildlife biologist and researcher, once estimated there was one antlered doe for every 2,600 antlered bucks in the state.

Ironically, a polished-antlered doe was killed less than 25 miles from Scales' deer one month before. That 124-pound 5-pointer was taken in Brooktondale, N.Y., by a local bow-hunter.

— *Dave Henderson*

■ Village Hires Military Snipers to Kill Deer

Residents of an affluent Milwaukee, Wis., suburb will pay military snipers $31,000 to kill 200 surplus deer in their community.

The Village of Chenequa, a community consisting of wooded estates, has a bulging white-tailed deer herd. With a lack of predators and a no-hunting ordinance, the village's deer herd has risen to a density of 75 animals per square mile.

Residents want the herd reduced by more than 70 percent because the deer have caused extensive damage to their gardens, wild flowers and other greenery. In addition, 73 auto/deer accidents occurred in the village in the first seven months of 1995.

Early next year, Chenequa will pay two snipers $150 per hour to kill 200 deer. The snipers hope to complete the job while shooting from tree stands positioned near bait stations.

The snipers will also be paid $25 for each deer they kill. In addition, the village will pay about $35 per animal to have the meat processed. The venison will be donated to food pantries.

After considering trapping and relocating, and birth control methods, snipers were chosen "because of the cost-effectiveness and humaneness to the animals," according to a report from the village's deer task force.

Some residents believe hunting would effectively control the herd. "We created this problem by not controlling it in years past," said one resident. "We must start a procedure. Hunting should be implemented."

— *Lake Country Reporter*
Hartland, Wis.

■ Button Buck Seen Rubbing Bark Off Saplings

Antlered bucks are not the only whitetails that rub their heads on saplings and trees as a form of marking.

One fall, I watched and photographed a 5- or 6-month-old button buck rub his head on a young aspen tree. The hair-covered buttons were hard enough to scar the tree's bark, but did not peel bark off, as would an antlered buck.

Once the immature buck was done rubbing his head, he licked the damaged tree, much as a mature buck would do.

More recently, I observed an antlerless adult buck rub his head briefly on two saplings that had been marked the previous fall by an antlered buck.
— *Richard P. Smith*

When interpreting signs in the deer woods, don't believe everything you see. Some rubs, for instance, can be made by button bucks.

■ Buck Mistakes Own Reflection for a Foe

A white-tailed buck was rutting, and ready to defend his turf earlier this year when he strolled past a Huntsville, Ala., home.

While walking past one of the home's picture windows, the buck saw his reflection. Thinking it was a rival, he lunged toward the image, shattering the window. Once inside the home, the buck thrashed violently, causing an estimated $15,000 damage.
— *Herm Albright*

■ Lobbying Pays Off for Indiana Bow-Hunters

Some Indiana gun-hunters were allowed to hunt in state parks in 1995, thanks to a grassroots lobbying effort by the Indiana Bowhunters Association.

The IBA also helped squelch legislation that would have given farmers an unlimited bag limit on deer. Instead, the legislation was reworded to promote cooperation between farmers and hunters.
— *Wildlife Legislative Fund*

■ Illinois Whitetail Endures Odd Death

While on a business trip to Peoria, Ill., in July 1995, I found a big buck that endured a strange, horrible death.

While driving through an upper-class neighborhood, I noticed a 9-point buck hanging from a wrought iron fence. Sometime the night before, the buck had bounded toward a wooded area when he tried to hurdle the fence.

He landed short, and the spikes atop the fence cut him like razors, splitting him open from his chest to his hind leg.

Ironically, the buck could have avoided the fatal fall. The fence ended 20 feet to his right.

— *Mike Pattillo*
Columbus, Ga.

This 9-point buck split himself open when he jumped and fell on the pointed ends of a wrought iron fence in Illinois.

■ Don't Travel Without Gun, Bow Information

I learned a valuable lesson about traveling with firearms by airplane: Always make sure you have a record of the serial number for your gun or bow before checking it with an airline. The same advice applies when flying to a bowhunt.

Most airlines and police agencies can trace the missing weapons to you if you provide the serial numbers.

I recently learned my lesson on the return trip from a Texas deer hunt. When I reached my destination, my suitcase and locked gun case, containing my scoped Remington Model 700, were missing. I wasn't concerned because I've had luggage delayed before. The items, however, never showed up.

When making a claim, I discovered that it helps to keep receipts or canceled checks to prove ownership and value of lost possessions. Most airlines will pay up to $1,200 for lost or stolen items.

To provide extra security, guns and bows should be packed in hard cases secured with padlocks.

— *Richard P. Smith*

■ Whitetail Stops Passenger Train in its Tracks

An Illinois whitetail might not have been able to leap high buildings, but it somehow managed to stop a speeding locomotive on Sept. 24, 1994.

Shortly after midnight in Abbott, Ill., the deer ran from a wooded area and into the path of a commuter train.

The train was headed from Milwaukee to Chicago when the deer leapt in front of it. The train traveled over the animal, but received major damage to brakes on two of its four cars.

No passengers were injured, but their trips were delayed by 1 hour and 35 mintues.

— *Milwaukee Sentinel*

■ Flu Shot will Keep You in the Woods this Fall

Don't head into the deer woods this season without first getting a flu shot, advises the Immunization Practices Advisory Committee of the Centers for Disease Control and Prevention.

Flu season usually begins in December and lasts through March, peaking in January and February. The flu shot, which is a vaccine made from the inactivated influenza virus, is one of the most effective tools used to fight the illness.

The center suggests getting the shot sometime between mid-October and mid-November. It is necessary to get a flu shot every year because the virus can change yearly, and the vaccine is reformulated annually to fight these new strains. However, you should not get the shot if you are severly allergic to eggs or suffer from an acute illness and fever.

Influenza spreads by direct contact or through the air, via an infected person's sneeze, for example.

■ Rutting Buck Attacks Lawn Ornaments

A white-tailed buck demanded attention when it entered the front lawn of a Chippewa Falls, Wis., residence. And it became a little upset in the process.

The buck apparently charged into the yard Oct. 31, 1995, after spotting two concrete deer — a buck and a doe — on the lawn. The real deer tried to get the attention of the fake deer and, when that failed, it attacked both statues.

The homeowner found the doe tipped over with its ears broken off.

— *Milwaukee Journal Sentinel*

■ Saskatchewan's 'King' of Non-typical Bucks Lingered in Obscurity for more than 38 Years

Although the Canadian province of Saskatchewan has produced such recent record whitetails as the world-record Hanson Buck (213⅝ typical) and the Swistun Buck (200⅝ typical), the province is hardly a newcomer as far as trophy whitetails are concerned.

In fact, Saskatchewan's No. 1 non-typical whitetail is a relatively unknown buck killed more than 38 years ago.

As noted in Henry Kelsey's Big Game Records, most trophy Saskatchewan whitetails were killed during the late 1950s and the 1960s — when deer densities were higher, deer hunter densities relatively low, and ideal habitat in great abundance. Saskatchewan held nearly 500,000 whitetails in the late 1950s. The 1995 herd was estimated at 350,000.

One of these early bucks was shot Nov. 1, 1957, by Elburn Kohler. The buck was a massive 33-pointer with a Boone & Crockett score of 265⅝.

In studying this buck's configuration, with an all-time B&C rank of No. 12, it is easy to understand why many call Kohler's deer "The King of White-tailed Bucks." The antlers alone weigh an incredible 11¼ pounds. By comparison, the rack from

Saskatchewan's largest non-typical whitetail was shot by Elburn Kohler on Nov. 1, 1957. The true size of the buck's rack was not realized until it was purchased in 1979 by antler collector Charles Arnold. Its Boone & Crockett score of 265⅝ ranks No. 12 on the all-time list.

the Jordan Buck, the former No. 1 B&C typical, weighs 10¼ pounds.

In addition, the Kohler Buck's antler circumferences average 7 inches, with 54⅛ total inches. The antlers consist of 67⁴⁄₈ inches of abnormal points.

The exact details of how Kohler shot this massive buck might never be known, because he died in 1961. Kohler bagged this buck in the Northern coniferous forest near the small village of White Fox (population 264) in northeastern Saskatchewan. There, Kohler shot the buck in an area where most travel was done by float planes, and where white-tailed deer densities remained low.

According to antler collector Charles T. Arnold, Kohler shot the buck near "the last road to wilderness."

The year Kohler bagged the buck, 1957, is one of the best in deer hunting history. Eight other bucks joined the Saskatchewan record book that year.

When Kohler died, his mother gave the antlers to his half-brother, Colin Bishop, who resided on Vancouver Island. Bishop had the antlers scored in British Columbia; they appeared in the 1971 B&C record book with a score of 246⅞.

In 1971, Arnold began to research the whereabouts of this unique rack. His search led him to a home in Vancouver, and he eventually bought the rack in 1979. Arnold had it rescored by a panel of B&C judges, who tabulated 265⅜ non-typical points. The right antler scored 95, and the left, 91⅔.

> *The Kohler Buck's antlers alone weigh an incredible 11¼ pounds. By comparison, the rack from the Jordan Buck, the former No. 1 B&C typical, weighs 10¼ pounds.*

In 1986, Arnold asked taxidermist Joe Coombs of Loranger, La., to sculpt a new headform for the mount. Arnold then commissioned Joe Meder of Solon, Iowa, one of the world's premier whitetail taxidermists, to remount the head.

— *Rob Wegner*

■ Maine Co. Shuffles Work Plans for Deer Season

When it comes to work and recreation, the latter won out in October 1995 at a Maine home-building company.

Officials at Burlington Homes decided to reschedule a company-wide inventory count when they discovered the task was scheduled for the week of the state's deer hunting season.

The company estimates that 70 percent of its workers are hunters.

— *Wall Street Journal*

■ Wood-encased Antler Dates Back to 1800s

For years, Les Stueber viewed a chunk of wood in his gun cabinet as a by-the-way conversation piece.

It wasn't until he took the relic to work that he realized he owned a piece of white-tailed deer history.

Stueber, a North Fond du Lac, Wis., resident, said the piece of wood — which encases a 4-point deer antler — has been in his wife's family at least 100 years. Stueber isn't sure how old the antler is, but guesses it could have come from a buck that lived sometime in the mid-1800s.

"I didn't think much of it at first," Stueber said. "I took it to work one day and everybody said, 'You really have something there.'"

Stueber said he has yet to find the answer to the most-commonly asked question surrounding the artifact: How did the 4-point antler get inside the wood?

"We have a couple of theories," he said. "One, the buck shed its antlers and the tree grew around them.

"Two, the buck was hung up in a wye of a tree to be field dressed. After skinning and taking the meat, the head and antlers were left in the wye, and the tree grew around them."

Stueber said his wife's grandfather, John R. Coon Sr., found the wood-encased

This wood-encased white-tailed deer antler was found in northern Wisconsin near the turn of the century. It's likely the buck was hung in a tree and the tree eventaully grew around the antlers.

antler in northern Wisconsin near the turn of the century. Coon's father made wood shingles, and probably found the antler while splitting wood.

The antler measures about 14 inches from base to tip. Stueber is working with the University of Wisconsin in trying to obtain more information on the age of the wood and the antler.

— *Dan Schmidt*

Greg Schultz of Wisconsin shot two unusual bucks within five days in November 1994. The bigger buck sported a rack that scored 172% Boone and Crockett.

■ Wisconsin Hunter Bags Two Unusual Bucks

Greg Schultz waited 10 hunting seasons before bagging a buck, then waited just a few days to repeat the feat.

What's more, Schultz wound up taking two impressive bucks and he didn't even own a rifle.

Schultz, of Oconomowoc, Wis., shot his first buck on opening day of Wisconsin's 1994 firearms season. Hunting in Juneau County, Schultz was in a tree stand overlooking a thicket when he noticed a buck stand up and cautiously walk toward him. He downed the buck with his father's .308.

To his surprise, Schultz discovered it only had three legs. Its right rear leg was a mere stump. The deer's injury had healed and scabbed. The left side of the buck's rack sported four points, including a drop tine that jutted straight out from the base, no doubt a result of its injury.

Five days later on Thanksgiving morning, Schultz was group-hunting when his friends pushed a 14-point non-typical buck toward him. He dropped the buck in its tracks, this time using his brother's .308 carbine.

The buck field-dressed only

148 pounds, but its rack had an inside spread of 20½ inches. It tallied a Boone & Crockett score of 172⅝ — the largest non-typical buck taken in Juneau County in 40 years. In 1955, Maurice Sterba bow-killed a buck that scored 195 points on the Pope & Young scale.

Because he was still reeling from his first buck, Schultz wasn't aware the second buck was of record-book proportions.

"I looked at the rack and my eyes popped open a bit, but I didn't realize how big it actually was," Schultz said. "After all, this was only the second buck I shot in my life."

— *Dan Schmidt*

■ Well-Traveled Rack Finally Comes Home

It took nearly 35 years and several thousand miles, but the antlers of the largest typical white-tailed buck taken from Michigan's Upper Peninsula have come home to stay.

The antlers were recently obtained by Dave Wellman of Bark River, Mich. Wellman, however, had to search the country for the rack.

The antlers, which score 185⅞, came from a 16-point buck killed in Iron County in 1960. Unfortunately, more is known about the rack's journey than who it originally belonged to.

The buck was shot by a

■ Whitetail Spooks Professional Golfer

It might not be noted in golfing history books, but a white-tailed deer played a role in the 1995 U.S. Women's Golf Open.

During the first round of the tournament, a doe ventured so close to the 12th tee that it caused pro golfer Tammie Green to back away from her shot to the 199-yard par 3. Her caddie, Chuck Parisi, yelled, "Hold it," just as Green was ready to begin her backswing.

The wind was gusting into Green's face when the deer appeared, but died down by the time she made her shot. As a result of the calm conditions, Green's shot flew over the green, causing a bogey.

— *Rollin Moseley*

Grand Rapids man who died a few years after bagging it. News of the antlers possibly being a state record spread after the rack was sold at a garage sale.

Wellman tracked down the antlers when they were sold again, this time to a collector in Montana. He obtained the rack and had it scored, but the antlers had shrunk considerably.

Michigan's largest typical buck in the Boone & Crockett listings was killed in 1986 by Craig Calderone. That buck scored 193⅝.

— *Richard P. Smith*

■ Police Have 979 Suspects in Hunter's Death

Alabama authorities face a monumental "whodunit" after a hunter, who was found gasping for breath on a logging road, died of a bullet wound to the back.

Law enforcement officials say they have at least 979 suspects.

In autumn 1994, a hunter on the Oakmulgee Wildlife Management Area found Ronald G. "Bubba" Snyder Jr., 35, lying in the road at daybreak gasping for breath and attempting to stand up. The hunter tried to get Snyder to tell him what was wrong, but Snyder was unable to talk.

The man left Snyder to contact authorities. Paramedics found him dead, listing the cause of death as an apparent heart attack.

It was only later, after removing Snyder's clothes, that Coroner Kevin Crawford realized the man had been shot. "The bullet entered the back near the armpit on Snyder's right side and did not exit the body. There was almost no loss of blood," Crawford said.

Hale County Deputy Sheriff Donald Rainey said he believes someone shot Snyder, thinking he was a deer, and panicked and fled.

A .30-06 shell casing was found about 100 yards from the body, but Rainey said the shell could have been fired during a previous hunt.

The victim was participating in a state-organized hunt in a 44,500-acre management area. Hunters are required to purchase a daily permit to participate in the hunt, but are not required to register by name. Records show 980 hunters purchased permits to hunt that day.

"Everybody that was there is a suspect, and I've got an armload of suspects," a deputy said.

Deputies arrived on the scene quickly after paramedics were called and took down the license plate numbers of all vehicles in the area. Several hunters were questioned and some were asked to turn over their guns to be tested.

Any hunting fatality in Alabama automatically goes to a grand jury.

Snyder's death was the first hunter-shooting-hunter fatality in any of the state's 22 WMAs since January 1974.

■ Pennsylvania Motorists Kill 42,000-Plus Deer

More than 42,000 white-tailed deer were killed by automobiles on Pennsylvania highways in 1994.

Total out-of-season deer mortality for 1994 was 48,323, including 2,206 illegal kills; 1,761 for crop damage, and 478 by dogs.

The leading counties were: Allegeheny, 2,343, and Westmoreland, 1,925.

■ Injury/Infection Deforms Whitetail's Hoof

Injuries to a deer's hoofs can cause the animal to grow odd-shaped hoofs.

I recently found an abnormal hoof while working with an agent from the Virginia Department of Game and Inland Fisheries. Instead of growing straight, the toes of the hoof were curled in, nearly touching each other.

One of the department's biologists said this hoof deformity probably resulted from a cut that became infected.

Also in my collection is the skull of a deer that had double molars occupying the

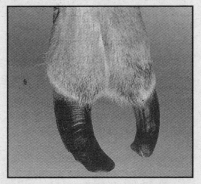

Deer can grow odd-shaped hoofs if the hoof becomes infected.

same socket on both sides of the jawbone.

— *Tom Barnett*

■ Warden Does His Job, Gets Trophy Buck

The efforts of two poachers last fall didn't stop Gordon Wood from doing his job and hunting a trophy whitetail.

Wood, a conservation officer in southern Indiana, had spotted a massive-antlered buck on several occasions while rabbit hunting in a brushy area of Pike County. He had decided to hunt for the buck but, because of his duties, could not begin his pursuit until the third day of the firearms season.

However, his hopes for bagging the trophy were all but dashed when he heard a few days later that two men illegally shot a big buck in the same area.

To the poachers' surprise, another hunter was in the area when they killed the deer. He told Wood who they were, which led to their arrests.

The deer was confiscated after the men confessed to shooting it from the road. The driver was fined $125 and the shooter $650.

As is turned out, the poached buck was not the same buck Wood saw earlier in the year. He shot that buck — a 15-pointer — on the fifth day of the deer season. It had an unofficial Boone & Crockett net score of 163⅜ inches.

— *John Trout Jr.*

■ Conflict Erupts When Deer Meets Cat

It's not uncommon for white-tails to wander close to buildings on our hunting club's land in Michigan's Upper Peninsula.

One doe, however, made it a routine to hang out near our garage, and a conflict erupted when the deer encountered a stray cat.

The doe devoted her attention to harassing the cat. When the feline crossed her path, the doe displayed some odd behavior. With her hair bristled, the doe fanned her tail, pawed the ground, and extended her long slender neck. She did all of this in obvious anger while advancing toward the cat.

The cat ran into our garage to escape the irate deer, but matters grew worse. The doe hung out near our garage and would not leave. Knowing the cat was inside, the doe hissed while long streams of saliva flowed from her lower lip. This

This Michigan doe harassed a stray cat for several weeks. Here, the doe stood near a garage and hissed as the cat tried to leave the building.

strange behavior lasted about 45 minutes.

At times, the doe laid on the sidewalk where she stayed for several hours. The doe periodically harassed the cat for about a month before finally leaving it alone.

— Betty Sodders

■ Confused Whitetail Sprints into Airport

A white-tailed deer made a surprise visit to Kansas City's International Airport in August 1995, surprising and scaring several people at a busy terminal.

"I have no idea where it came from, but I looked up, and there was a deer running down the hall of the terminal a mile a minute," an airline employee said. "It charged up to the ticket counter and almost knocked

over a little kid along the way."

Witnesses said the doe sprinted into the terminal after walking past an automatic door. After running through the terminal, the deer scampered into an airline office. Employees stopped it by shutting the door to the office.

It was removed by wildlife officers after it became exhausted and laid down.

— Dick E. Bird News

■ Indiana Man Bags Two Bucks With One Shot

David Beste hoped to get an opportunity to fill his deer tag when he left his Posey County, Ind., home on the last day of the 1995 gun-deer season. However, he never dreamed he would bag a large buck that had the head of a bigger buck attached to it.

After an uneventful morning in a tree stand, Beste returned home at 9 a.m. Moments later, his friend stopped by and said he had seen a big buck earlier that morning in a field near Beste's stand.

Beste's friend said the buck was slumped over, and it appeared something was stuck on its antlers.

Beste decided to investigate. While surveying the area, he found fresh drag marks in the field. He followed the strange trail, which led him to a brushy thicket. He eased into the dense foliage and spotted a bedded buck.

"At first I thought he was dead because his head was down on the ground," Beste said. "But when I got within 25 yards of him, he jumped up and took off."

Although Beste had no chance to get a clear shot, he soon realized there was something wrong with the deer. The buck was skinny, did not run at full speed, and appeared to be dragging

David Beste of Indiana bagged this 10-point buck in 1995. The buck had the head and antlers of a larger buck locked to its rack.

something with its antlers.

Beste followed the buck's trail, which led to an open field. He found the buck and killed it with one shot.

He soon discovered why the 10-pointer was lethargic. The buck was carrying the head, neck and antlers of another 10-pointer. The two bucks had apparently locked antlers several days earlier.

All that was left of the dead buck was a portion of its hide and one of its legs.

The buck Beste killed scored 134 on the Boone and Crockett scale. The other rack scored 142⅝.

— *John Trout Jr.*

■ Tuberculosis in Lower Michigan Whitetails Linked to Overpopulation

Tuberculosis is rare in free-ranging whitetails. Before 1994, only one case had been recorded in Michigan. Recently, however, a potentially serious outbreak of TB occurred in northeastern Lower Michigan.

In November 1994, a hunter noticed internal lesions and abscesses on the lungs and rib cage of a buck he shot in the "Club Country" near Alpena. The hunter notified the Michigan Department of Natural Resources. Biologists examined the deer and determined it had bovine tuberculosis (*Mycobacterium bovis*).

In 1995, 15 of 300 deer tested in Lower Michigan were carrying the disease. One additional case has since been verified.

Bovine TB is most commonly found in cattle. It's a strain of TB different from that normally found in humans. It's unlikely a hunter could contract the disease while field dressing an infected animal. However, DNR officials urge hunters to use heavy rubber gloves while field dressing deer. Thorough cooking of venison is also recommended.

TB is primarily spread through the air. Contamination from coughing and sneezing spreads the disease when animals live in crowded conditions. Repeated or prolonged exposure enhances the spread of the disease. The disease is less likely to occur among

> *DNR officials believe crowded feeding areas were major factors that contributed to the TB infection.*

healthy deer living at low densities.

However, in northern Michigan's Club Country, many years of winter deer feeding and inadequate antlerless deer harvests have contributed to overpopulation. The area's deer herds, now at about 60 whitetails per square mile, are at least twice as large as the habitat can support.

DNR officials believe crowded feeding areas were major factors that contributed to the TB infection.

Nutrient-poor soils in the Club Country do not naturally support high deer numbers. Artificial feeding, however, has helped increase herd sizes. In turn, browsing pressure has depleted the habitat. Deer in the region tend to be malnourished. They grow poorly, and mature animals are smaller than normal. In addition, their unhealthy and stressed condition probably makes them more susceptible to diseases other than TB.

According to Ed Langenau, Michigan's big-game specialist,

the primary concern is to prevent the disease from spreading. The disease is believed to be restricted to an area 8 miles by 12 miles.

Aside from continual testing of livestock and deer, the DNR will meet with private clubs to educate them about tuberculosis and to plan strategies to reduce deer numbers.

A heavy winter kill is expected because clubs will be strongly discouraged from feeding deer. In addition, the DNR will support an increased antlerless harvest within 100 square miles of the infected area. The goal is to reduce the herd to about 30 deer per square mile.
— *John J. Ozoga*

■ Buck's Size, History Surprise Hunter

The Virginia deer and fall turkey seasons occasionally overlap. When this happens, Charles Corder, a long-time hunter of both species, puts one round of buckshot in his 12-gauge and a pair of No. 6s in its tubular magazine.

When Corder unexpectedly flushes a turkey while deer hunting, he shucks out the first round to get to the bird shot.

One November morning, while still-hunting through dense honeysuckle, Corder jumped a deer. When he realized it was a large buck, Corder fired his load of buckshot.

Corder found the dead buck after trailing it two hours. He was surprised its rack was immense. The high-tined 12-point rack had an inside spread of 23 inches.

The surprises did not end there. Later, after skinning the deer, Corder discovered the 3½-year-old buck had multiple wounds that had healed. The buck's carcass contained four .22-caliber bullets, a full load of birdshot, and a short piece of

Dinny Slaughter

Charles Corder of Virginia shot this buck while still-hunting with his shotgun. However, Corder's buckshot was not the first the buck had encountered.

barbwire.

A lucky shot? Maybe, but consider this: Using the same still-hunting method, Corder has killed 71 whitetails, all bucks; and 51 gobblers.
— *Dinny Slaughter*

■ Illinois Buck's Antlers Resemble Teardrops

In 1994, I killed a buck that had unusual headgear.

The buck had teardrop-shaped antlers that were only partially hardened. In fact, the left antler was encased with a sheath of dried velvet.

The antlers caused noticeable pressure against the jawbone, and they were so close to the eye sockets that they nearly rubbed against the buck's eyelids.

The buck was in good condition. He field dressed at 150 pounds.

— Lyndall B. Cuba
Downs, Ill.

Lyndall Cuba

Lydall Cuba of Downs, Ill., shot this buck during the 1994 archery season. It sported two antlers that hung down and pressed against its jawbone and eye sockets.

■ Virginians Set Record, Show Generosity

In addition to setting a state record white-tailed deer harvest, Virginia hunters were generous in their support of a welfare food program in 1995.

Last fall, Virginia hunters donated 103,575 pounds of venison to the state's Hunters for the Hungry program, easily surpassing the 82,000 pounds distributed in 1994.

Hunters for the Hungry is a private non-profit organiza-
tion that provides food for the needy. The organization's goal is to eventually distribute 200,000 pounds of venison annually.

Virginia hunters killed 218,476 deer in 1995, a 4.3 percent increase from the previous record harvest of 209,373 set in 1994. The state has eclipsed its harvest record eight consecutive years, beginning with a kill of 135,094 in 1989.

■ Whitetail Drowns in Pennsylvania Flood

A white-tailed deer found itself trapped as melting snow and heavy rains flooded the banks of Pennsylvania's Loyalsock Creek in late January 1996.

LaRue VanZile and Ron Wall of nearby Williamsport were hiking in the area a few days after the flood when they found the doe 12 feet off the ground and entangled in debris.

The wooded, flat creek bottom is located between two steep mountain sides. VanZile said the shallow creek is normally 30 yards wide, but it stretched about 200 yards wide during the flood. Water reached depths of 15 feet during the flood, he said.

It's likely the flood took the deer by surprise, sweeping it away in fast current. As the doe struggled, it became tangled on limbs and

This white-tailed deer drowned after being tangled in flood debris. Melting snow and heavy rains caused the flood in Pennsylvania's Loyalsock Creek area.

brush, and eventually drowned.

The doe was found about 30 yards from the edge of the normal stream channel.

– *Dan Schmidt*

■ Bow-Hunter Kills Three-Beamed Buck

I was hunting on private land in Dodge County, Wisconsin, last fall when I arrowed an unusual three-antlered buck.

With 6 inches of fresh snow, conditions for hunting that day were perfect. I had been in my tree stand for about two hours that afternoon when a small 8-pointer appeared, walking down a corn row about 40 yards away. Turning around, I saw the three-antlered buck following the 8-pointer.

I picked an opening in a corn row about 40 yards out and shot when he stopped in the opening.

When my brother-in-law and I found the buck, we were shocked to discover it had a third antler located just above its right eye. The extra antler measures 17 inches and is 3 inches in diameter at the base.

— *John Figel*

John Figel of Mayville, Wis., shot this buck during the 1995 season. The buck sported a third beam, measuring 17 inches.

■ Swimming Deer Not Bothered by Geese

I was photographing Canada geese near a Minnesota river recently when I saw two white-tailed deer do something strange.

A doe and fawn stepped from the river bank and, for no apparent reason, began swimming toward an island that was about 300 yards away. Although I have seen whitetails swim on numerous occasions, I have never seen deer swimming alongside several thousand geese.

The geese became nervous when they first saw the swimming deer, but the birds eventually calmed down. Oddly, the flock split and formed a wide circle around the deer. The deer reached the island, shook off the water and walked out of sight. The geese came back together as one flock after the deer disappeared.

—*Bill Marchel*

■ Adult Whitetail Still Carried Fawn Spots

A rare whitetail — an adult doe with fawn spots — was killed in northern Wisconsin during the state's nine-day gun season in 1995.

Paul Tofte, *Deer & Deer Hunting's* design artist, said he and Bob Buege were hunting in the Nicolet National Forest when Buege killed the 2½-year-old doe. The doe's spots, though light, were distinct leftovers from her fawn coat.

John Ozoga, *Deer & Deer Hunting's* research editor, said hair color aberrations are among the most common anomalies in white-tailed deer. Ozoga said he has seen a few spotted does in his career as a deer researcher. However, he added that he has never seen an adult whitetail with distinct spots like those in fallow and sika deer.

"Whitetails have been reported from black to white and everything in between," Ozoga said. "It seems that melanistic animals are even more rare than albinos."

Citing early albino research, Ozoga said different genetic causes are responsible for white coats and spots. Albinism is caused by an inability to synthesize melanin — the blackish-brown pigment found in skin and hair.

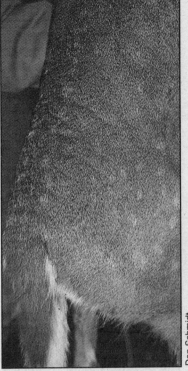

Dan Schmidt

This 2½-year-old Wisconsin doe still had some of its fawn spots when it was killed in 1995.

Conversely, white spots might result from a complete absence of the pigment in the affected areas.

Although some spotting is genetic, it doesn't appear that Buege's deer passed on the trait. The doe he killed had three fawns, but all had normal coats.

— Dan Schmidt

Richard P. Smith

Fawns often lack a sense of danger, which can lead them to come in contact with humans. These twins left their mother and approached the author in Michigan when he stopped his car to take photographs of the pair.

■ Newborn Fawns Lack Sense of Danger

I never realized how trusting white-tailed deer fawns can be until I photographed a pair of twins in May 1995. While driving along a woods road in Michigan, my wife and I spotted the fawns alongside the road with their mother.

Leaving the vehicle to get a few photos, I was surprised by the fawns' reaction. Instead of trying to hide, they stood up and walked curiously toward me. I backed up at first, not wanting to come in contact with them and spook the doe.

When I moved to the spot where they had been with their mother, the fawns followed me and laid down. Based on that experience, it's obvious why it's illegal to possess wild animals. It would have been easy to pick up the fawns and take them with me. Had I done so, I would have deprived those young deer of a normal life in the woods.

After taking photos of the fawns, I returned to my vehicle. One of the fawns later stood up and started walking toward the car, bleating as it came. That prompted the doe to quickly come to its aid. She led it back to the woods, and the second fawn soon followed.

— *Richard P. Smith*

Al Cornell

When melting river ice refreezes, it creates "honeycombed" layers of water and ice. These situations are deathtraps for whitetails that try to cross. The author took this photo in March 1995.

■ Water and Unpredictable River Ice Create Deathtraps for Whitetails

River ice can be unpredictable in late winter, creating a deathtrap for whitetails.

In March 1995, I found a deer that died from exhaustion and hypothermia after it broke through a thin layer of river ice. This happened when warm weather thawed the ice in a channel, then a cold snap refroze a portion of it.

The deer slipped and fell when it tried to cross the "honeycombed" layers of ice and water. The fall probably caused muscle and joint damage, making it difficult for the deer to get back on its hoofs. The whitetail was bleeding from its mouth, indicating it had struggled considerably before dying.

In a similar incident, I approached a motionless deer that had fallen through thin ice. It had struggled a few hours, but it appeared to have lost the battle. However, after noticing me, the deer renewed its struggle and eventually escaped the icy trap.

— Al Cornell

■ Exhibit is Home to Record-Book Whitetails

An exhibit devoted solely to white-tailed deer is so popular it is quickly becoming known as one of the top tourist attractions in Clarksville, Ark.

The exhibit, known as *Whitetail World,* is a collection of replica head mounts of more than 70 of the largest white-tailed bucks in the world.

Believe me, until you see this exhibit, you don't know what a big buck is.

Don't let the word "replica" scare you. I visited the exhibit with kind of a negative expectation. I expected — well I don't know what I expected. But what I saw was unbelievable. I doubt more than one hunter in a thousand could tell he was not looking at the real thing.

Around every turn in the maze-like exhibit hall is a new set of bucks — bigger than the ones before.

Among the replicas are The Jordan Buck, Hole-in-The-Horn buck and Mel Johnson's No. 1 typical bow kill, to name a few. The exhibit also includes a 10,000-square-foot art gallery that is a showcase for numerous wildlife paintings.

Whitetail World is the brainchild of Dayne Phillips, who got the idea after seeing a replica deer head mount at a Shooting, Hunting & Outdoors Trade Show.

Charlie Smith

The Whitetail World Museum in Clarksville, Ark., is home to replica mounts of several famous bucks. The Hole-in-The-Horn buck, shown here, is one of the replica mounts on display.

It took Phillips four years, and the help of his sons, Bruce and Bobby, to make the dream a reality.

"We've seen some mighty fine bucks, but most of us will never see bucks like these in a lifetime, no matter where we hunt," said Bruce Phillips.

The heads were created by Klaus Lebrecht of Wisconsin.
— *Charlie Smith*

Mark Dietz

Nebraska forest rangers used rope and a hand saw ·to free these locked bucks. The bucks became locked after brawling in the peak of the rut. One of the bucks was already dead when the rangers arrived.

■ Nebraska Buck Saved from Death Tangle

As a ranger for Nebraska's Fontenelle Forest, I have seen my share of interesting incidents involving white-tailed deer. This past fall, I learned first-hand what happens when two bucks engage in an all-out brawl.

During the third week of the rut, hikers reported seeing two large bucks locked together. After learning one of the bucks was already dead, I headed to the area with chief ranger Gary Garabrandt and photographer Ken Bouc.

We found the bucks after following a fresh trail of crushed weeds and broken twigs — unmistakable evidence that a large object had been dragged through the woods. We soon heard a loud crash and a snort, so we slowed down and carefully approached the fight scene.

The live buck was a large 12-pointer. His dead opponent was even larger and sported a non-typical 10-point rack.

Even though he was hopelessly tangled, the 12-pointer immediately felt our presence. He backed away frantically, crashing and tripping over logs and throwing the dead buck around as if it were a piece of carpeting.

It was almost dark, and we didn't have the right equipment to attempt a rescue. After discussing our options, we decided to return at dawn.

We decided our only chance at rescuing the buck would be to subdue him with ropes and saw his antler off. We thought about using a dart gun and tranquilizer, but a colleague reminded us that the drug would cause too much stress and therefore kill the buck.

When we returned the next morning, we found the buck several hundred yards from where we left him. He was in good shape, even though he had struggled to fend off coyotes. Amazingly, the coyotes left the 12-pointer alone while they feasted on the hind quarters of the dead buck.

The weary buck thrashed when we approached. However,

> *We decided our only chance at rescuing the buck would be to subdue him with ropes and saw his antler off. We thought about using a dart gun and tranquilizer, but realized it would cause too much stress on the buck.*

we easily caught up to him and lassoed his antlers and hind legs. I pulled the rope tight around both legs to stabilize him.

Garabrandt used a hand saw to cut the antlers loose. The buck laid motionless when we untied the ropes, and, for a moment, we thought he would die. Then, all in one motion, he jumped to his feet and darted into the woods.

The buck was not reported after the rescue.

— *Mark Dietz*

■ Whitetail Uses Hunter's House to Hide

A Pennsylvania man returned home from an unsuccessful day of deer hunting last fall only to find a deer hiding in his basement.

The 100-pound doe apparently ran from a nearby wooded area and crashed through the basement's 16-inch by 36-inch window. The hunter freed the deer by opening a door.

— *Herm Albright*

■ Wisconsin Farmer Bags Buck of Dreams

Vernus Larson has killed numerous bucks in his lifetime, but none compare to the buck he took last fall.

Larson, a 71-year-old Wisconsin farmer, was hunting on his land Nov. 18, 1995, when he placed his shotgun's sights on the shoulder of a large buck. The buck, a 19-pointer with a 20⅛-inch spread, was chasing a doe along a fence row when Larson dropped it with a slug.

The rack unofficially scored 208 non-typical and 178 typical. Either measurement would place the buck within the top 45 in the state's Boone & Crockett standings.

— *Paul Ovadal*

Paul Ovadal holds the rack of a 19-point buck killed by 71-year-old Vernus Larson. Larson killed the buck on his Wisconsin farm in 1995.

■ Coyote Catches Fawn by Surprise

Although their camouflaged markings protect white-tailed deer fawns from most predators, coyotes often find easy meals by scouring meadows in spring.

In early June 1995, I was walking in a meadow near my home when I heard a series of intense fawn bleats. I headed in that direction and found the fawn, freshly killed. It had two puncture wounds in the top of its skull, obviously the work of a coyote.

I also found a small wound on the fawn's hind quarter and a few more wounds on its neck. The fawn was about

Just weeks old, this fawn was no match for a coyote, which killed the fawn in a meadow.

three weeks old. Having witnessed similar incidents, I've found that fawns less than six weeks old usually aren't developed enough to outrun coyotes.

— *Al Cornell*

Al Cornell

The manner in which a deer jumps a fence can determine whether it will get hung up in the wire strands. Running deer typically clear these fences easily. This deer, however, became tangled after attempting a jump from a standing position.

■ Jumping Technique can Doom Whitetails

With millions of miles of fence strung across deer range, it's amazing more deer don't get tangled in the wires each year.

The doe in this photo became caught when she tried to jump the fence while leaving her hind legs extended behind her body. However, she struggled only briefly before freeing herself.

The manner in which a deer jumps a fence usually dictates if it will get snared. I once watched two deer jump a roadside fence on a bank. The fence's height from where they jumped was 6½ feet, and normally would cause no problems. The first deer jumped while running, and easily sailed over the fence. The second stopped at the foot of the bank, and tried a standing jump. It barely made it over. The deer hit the top wire, causing it to snag momentarily before toppling over.

I have seen jumping deer that tucked their rear legs forward, under their bellies. In these jumps, a deer's hind legs come forward, making it easy for them to be caught on wires. If a fence is strong and taut, the deer might not be able to escape.

The results of these jumps can be devastating. Unless it frees itself quickly, a fence-snared deer will usually die from broken bones or severe cuts.

— Al Cornell

■ Injured Bucks Prone to Deadly Disease

Once considered extremely rare for free-ranging animals, a disease that leads to brain abscesses is killing white-tailed deer. The abscess can eat a hole the size of a pencil eraser through a whitetail's skull.

After studying the disease for several years, researchers fear it could affect today's quality deer management practices. The disease is caused by bacteria that erode the skull, pit the cranium, and destroy cells and tissues.

The spread of the disease was studied by William R. Davidson, a professor at the University of Georgia in Athens, and other researchers at the Southeastern Cooperative Wildlife Disease Study. From 1971 to 1989, the researchers compiled and examined records of 683 infected whitetails. They found that 24 of the 683 deer, or 4 percent, had brain abscesses. All but three were bucks, and their median age was 3.2 years old. Most of the deer were free-ranging animals.

The researchers concluded the disease can reduce quality deer management goals because prime-age bucks are more prone to abscesses. Of the deer studied, 21 were alive. Their symptoms included blindness, weakness, emaciation, poor coordination, profound depression and lack of fear. The abscessed areas were inflamed and surrounded by yellow and green pus.

The abscess usually starts from another injury, such as an infected wound, Davidson said. "What appears to be the most frequent and most common scenario is that there's a bacterium that starts around the antlers," he said.

The bacteria — actinomyces — is found on plants. It can enter a deer's bloodstream various ways, including through skin lesions, previous diseases, and from carriers such as ticks and ear mites. However, bucks seem more vulnerable than does because bucks often receive open wounds while sparring. Only three does were studied, and each had other diseases before forming brain abscesses.

The disease can also enter a buck's bloodstream when his pedicle areas are raw during the velvet- and antler-shedding periods.

Davidson said older bucks might attract the bacteria easier because their pedicle holes are typically larger than those of young bucks. Most older deer in the study contracted the disease in February and April.

Yearling bucks were vulnerable during the rut because of the increased incidents of broken pedicles. About 80 percent of the yearlings studied contracted the disease in October and November.

To the dismay of QDM proponents, brain abscesses tend to kill prime-age bucks. For example, Tom Indrebo, a western Wisconsin hunting guide, said he watched a 4-year-old buck die in his backyard in February 1996. He said the buck's left antler was broken at the brow tine, and was porous and covered with pus.

A month later, Indrebo noticed the buck pacing in a field, his head hung low and a bloody, pus-covered spot on his left pedicle. The buck was disoriented and acted like he had the flu, Indrebo said. When he approached the buck, Indrebo noticed a small hole near the pedicle. He said the buck might have developed a brain abscess after fighting or rubbing during the rut. "It must happen fairly fast when it happens," he said.

Davidson said quality deer managers should not be surprised if the disease kills some of their older bucks each year. "(The disease) is competing with hunters and the product you are trying to produce by deer management," he said.

However, researchers say the disease is not the main cause for high buck mortality during late fall and winter. "Percentage-wise, you're going to lose deer one way or another," Indrebo said, adding that older bucks can die from a number of causes. "This is nature's way of taking care of some of them."

This type of brain abscess was first documented in domestic sheep in 1941. Since then, the disease has been confirmed in horses and cattle. Unfortunately, a cure has not been discovered, and Davidson said he doubts one will be found anytime soon.

Davidson is seeking more examples of white-tailed deer skulls that have been damaged by skin lesions. Contact him by writing: Dr. William R. Davidson, c/o School of Forest Resources, University of Georgia, Athens, GA 30602.

— *Kathy Dugan*

Katie's Deer

■ *Mike Moutoux*

Kapow! The shotgun barked, rocking the 14-year-old girl on the shooting bench. "Ow," she said, turning to the man beside her. "Did I even hit the paper?"

He grinned.

"Oh yeah, just missed the bullseye, Katie. You want me to sight it in the rest of the way for you?"

Even he hated shooting at paper, and he knew the 12-gauge had popped her good.

"No chance. Give me another round," she said. Taking the smooth red cartridge, she slid it into the magazine and closed the action. Kapow!

She fired six times before the sights were properly adjusted. It took two weeks for the bruise on her shoulder to disappear, but she felt ready. More than anything, she wanted to join her father on his annual deer hunt, and the prehunt preparation increased her anticipation.

She had always loved her father and the divorce a year before was shattering. They had been unusually close all her life. She could tell him things she couldn't tell her own mother ... like the time Jeff kissed her behind the school bus. His frank reply was so nonjudgmental for a parent. "Well, did you kiss him back, or did you just leave his lips hanging out there in mid-air?"

Now, she only saw him on weekends and, once a month, she also spent Friday and Saturday nights.

"Stupid judge. Stupid divorce."

She vowed she would never get a divorce.

An hour into the gun season, a 3-year-old doe decided to move another half-mile into the hills. Accompanied by her two fawns and her yearling daughter, the doe led the way through a spice-bush thicket that shielded their movement.

Unknown to the deer, two hunters were tracing their path with binoculars 200 yards away. When the deer were out of sight, the hunters lowered their glasses.

"See any bucks, Katie?"

"Looked like four does to me," she answered.

"I think I know where they're headed if you want to try for one of them. Probably going into the old logging area on the other side of the ridge. Lots of tree tops and brush piles in there. Impossible for us to follow without making noise, but I think we can get there before them."

"Yesterday you said we should be patient and stay in one place," she teased. "Can't practice what you preach, huh? How does it go? Do as I say, not as I do."

She grinned. She loved dishing Dad's words back at him.

"You talk too much. Take after your mother. How 'bout handing me that thermos?"

Three hours passed, and although they heard plenty of gunshots in the distance, the foursome was the only deer they saw all morning. Around noon, two shots echoed from just over the ridge where the does had gone. Shortly after, three deer ran over the crest headed for the spice bush. Then they paused, milled around for five minutes, then headed up the draw toward Katie and her dad.

The lead deer stopped less than 100 yards from the hunters, and the other two followed suit. They blended perfectly with the background. Were it not for an occasional flick of an ear, Katie was sure she wouldn't know they were still there.

The big doe didn't like where she was but liked moving around even less. She stood still, rotating her ears like tiny radar receivers, sometimes working them together, other times listening in two separate directions at the same time. She was aware of the noises and smells of the hunters who had shot earlier, and was now picking up another unfamiliar smell. But she couldn't locate the source. The swirling winds in the draw made her uneasy, so she found a log and eased down beside it where she could watch her back trail. The other

deer joined her, disappearing in the brown leaves.

Katie had never been so excited. Even the rides at Cedar Point were nothing like this. When the last doe lay down only 60 yards away, Katie thought her heart would explode. Her knees started to shake, and then her shoulders, until her father reached out and squeezed her left shoulder.

"Close your eyes and think of something else," he whispered.

"Sure," she thought, "that will help." She tried to think about Jeff, but he seemed too far away. He had laughed at her anyway when she told him she was taking a hunter education class so she could hunt with her dad. No, she needed something else.

She thought about the class and what the instructors said about marksmanship. Concentrate on your sights and squeeze the trigger. Follow through. She saw herself at the range with her dad and smiled at the thought of the target with the one hole in the X-ring. Her dad had stuck it on the refrigerator in his apartment like the drawings she used to make for him.

He used to save everything. The rock paper weights, clay ashtray and Father's Day cards had been stored in his desk drawers with all his other junk. His "Daddy Museum" he called it. She wondered where it all was now.

Katie opened her eyes when she realized the shaking had

stopped. Nothing had changed. The deer was still there, and her dad was right behind her. Time was suspended. The scene now had clarity, as if a fog had lifted to reveal important details. Gone, too, was the tunnel vision that accompanies excitement, and now Katie enjoyed the panorama around her. She was surprised at how green the woods were, given that it was late fall. Moss covered rocks and ferns, pale lichens covered surfaces like patchwork quilts, and ground pines were scattered up and down the slopes.

When all the deer faced uphill, ears forward, Katie knew they heard or saw something. Her dad squeezed her shoulder again, and whispered, "See him?"

And there he was, walking carefully down the same path the does used when they first appeared. The slanting rays of the afternoon sun illuminated his antlers, which rose and curved high above his ears.

Without thinking, Katie picked up her gun and propped it across her knees. She was afraid the buck would go the wrong way, and just as afraid he would come closer. Another load of adrenalin raced through her body, and now all Katie could see were antlers. She closed her eyes and tried to think of something else.

Her dad's words came back to her. "Don't shoot at the whole deer," he said. "Pick a spot on his shoulder and concentrate on it. It's that simple."

That was just like him, making things short and simple. He had helped her get a part in a school play the same way.

When she felt the hand on her shoulder again, the buck was standing in the middle of the does, looking straight toward her. He started a slow walk. When he passed behind a big white oak, Katie put her cheek to her gun stock.

At 40 yards, she took off the gun's safety, pinching it between two fingers so it wouldn't make a sound. At 35 yards, she took a deep breath and held it while positioning the front sight 6 inches below the hump of his shoulder.

Katie never heard the gun or felt the recoil as the buck fell and rolled once, then lay still. The hand was on her shoulder again, and her dad was talking to her.

"Reload and put the safety back on," he said, but she couldn't make her body move. With gentle hands, the man took the gun, and put the safety on. He helped her stand, and they stood together until the shaking stopped.

"Dad how can an old guy like you stand all this excitement?" she finally asked. "I thought I was gonna die."

He laughed and squeezed her shoulder. "You did good, Katie, you did real good."

Shot Placement for Whitetails

Making quick, certain kills should be the main goal of every gun- and bow-hunter. Keep these five facts in mind before taking a shot:

1. When shooting at deer with bow and arrow, ■ aim for the heart region.

If the deer "jumps the string" by dropping sharply before bounding away, the arrow will still hit the lungs.

2. The average white-tailed deer, weighing ■ about 150 pounds, carries about eight pints of blood in its circulatory system.

Massive hemorrhage is necessary to bring a deer down quickly.

3. A deer must lose at least 35 percent of its ■ blood, or 2.75 pints in a 150-pound animal, before falling. The better the hit, the quicker blood loss occurs.

4. Deer blood carries high levels of Vitamin K1 ■ and K2 in early autumn. Vitamin K is an anti-hemorrhagic agent, which greatly aids blood clotting.

5. Frightened whitetails produce high levels of ■ B-endorphin, which supports rapid wound healing.

Endorphins consist of morphine-like chemicals from the pituitary gland, allowing the animal to control pain.

6. Deer, particularly in northern areas, have ■ thick layers of tallow along the back and below the brisket. This can plug wounds, preventing a good blood trail.

For this reason, bow-hunters should avoid straight-down shots from tree stands.

7. A string tracking device attached to a ■ bow and arrow is sometimes useful in recovering game. However, the string does affect the arrow flight on long shots.

For these reasons, hunters must study white-tailed deer anatomy, and put their bullet or arrow where it can quickly destroy the deer's circulatory and/or respiratory system. The following five pages include shot-placement and anatomy drawings.

Head-On Shot: For Guns Only

This shot presents gun hunters with three vital targets. A shot in the chest will hit the heart or lungs. A bullet in the neck will usually break the neck or cause enough shock to drop the animal instantly. It could also destroy the esophagus and/or carotid artery or jugular vein.

The head-on shot is not good for bow-hunters. Unless the arrow hits the chest dead-center, which presents a very small target, it can easily deflect off bone.

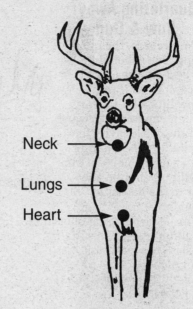

Neck

Lungs

Heart

Broadside Shot: Bow & Gun

Gun hunters can drop deer instantly with a broadside shot by putting a bullet through the shoulder blade. A well-constructed bullet will pass through the blade and hit the spine.

The broadside shot is also good for bow-hunters, but it doesn't leave much room for error as the quartering-away shot does. Arrows that pass through the vital organs produce quick, clean kills. Aim for the heart, knowing that a high shot will still hit the lungs. Archers must avoid the shoulder blade.

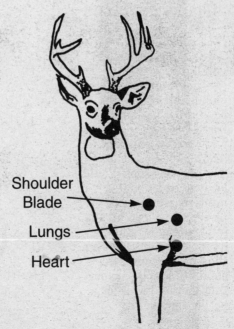

Shoulder Blade

Lungs

Heart

Quartering Away: Bow & Gun

For archers, the quartering-away shot offers the best chances for success. Even if the arrow hits a bit too far back, it can angle forward into the chest cavity for a quick kill. When taking this shot, the point of aim should be through the deer to the opposite shoulder.

This is also a great shot for gun-hunters. As with the bow, the gun-hunter's point of aim should be through the deer to the opposite shoulder.

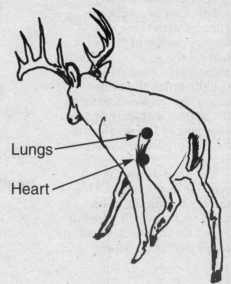

Lungs

Heart

Quartering Toward

As with the head-on shot, the quartering-toward shot is good for gun-hunters.

A shot high in the chest will usually break the base of the neck and travel through the lungs. A lower shot will hit the heart.

While this shot should be avoided by bow-hunters, a properly placed arrow can hit the lungs or heart, making for a clean kill. However, the target again is very small. If possible, avoid this shot and wait for a better opportunity.

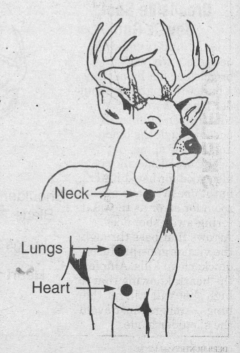

Neck

Lungs

Heart

SKELETON

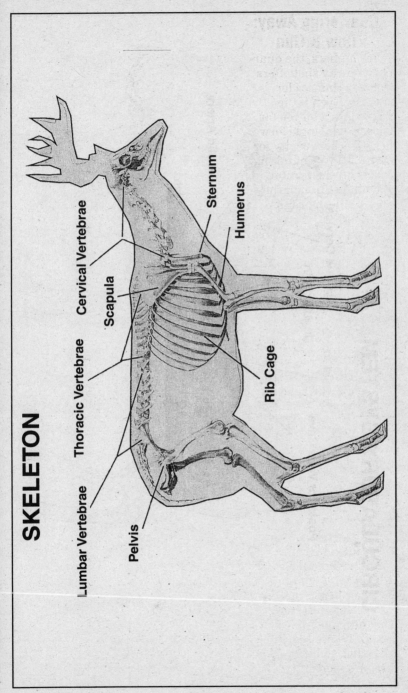

Cervical Vertebrae

Sternum

Humerus

Scapula

Thoracic Vertebrae

Rib Cage

Lumbar Vertebrae

Pelvis

CIRCULATORY SYSTEM

Carotid Artery

Aortic Arch

Exterior Pectoral

Oblique Cervical

Jugular Vein

Dorsal Aorta

Heart

Interior Pectoral

Posterior Vena Cava

ORGANS

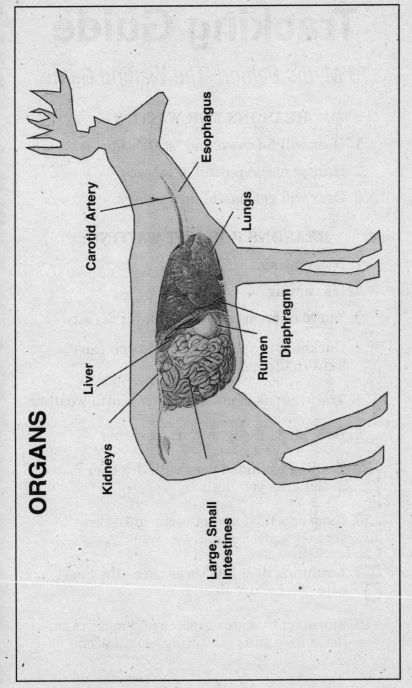

Esophagus

Carotid Artery

Lungs

Diaphragm

Rumen

Liver

Kidneys

Large, Small
Intestines

Tracking Guide

13 Myths Behind 'The Waiting Game'

REASONS FOR WAITING:

1. Deer will lie down and "stiffen up."

2. Hunter needs pipeful of tobacco.

3. Deer will get the "blind staggers."

REASONS FOR NOT WAITING:

1. It's snowing.

2. It's raining.

3. You're in an area of high hunter density.

4. Darkness is approaching and you can't hunt in the morning.

5. Tracking takes place freely in warm weather.

6. Deer bleed freely in warm weather.

7. Trailing wounded deer with dogs permitted in the area you hunt.

8. Rigor mortis does not occur until three to six hours after death.

9. A running deer has three times the heart rate of a bedded deer.

10. Movement creates greater and more rapid blood loss, thus inhibiting coagulation.

How Far Will a Deer Travel When Hit Through the Heart?

Every fall around the evening fires in the deer camps the old question has come up as to how it is possible for a deer to run from fifty to 200 yards after his heart had been perforated by a bullet. We all know he does this but to date no answer has really explained how. We usually wound up the evening in agreement on but two points: 1) The deer should drop when circulation ceases and the brain ... "suffocates." This should happen almost immediately after the heart is perforated, for, of course, it is taken for granted the heart stops instantly. 2) As we know deer have run 200 yards after a heart shot, this explanation cannot be true and there is something phony about it somewhere. So the question has never been logically answered as far as the deer hunters are concerned.

Then, on October 31, 1928, murderer John W. Deering was placed before a stone wall in Utah State Prison with an electro cardiograph attached to his person. He was outwardly calm. The prison doctor placed a target over his heart. Five picked riflemen fired at that target at short range and four bullets simultaneously pierced his heart. Yet Deering's heart did not stop when pierced by four bullets but continued to beat for 15.6 seconds thereafter. The cardiograph record also showed that a few moments before the shots were fired, through fear, Deering's heart beats, normally 72 per minute, were increased to 180 per minute.

Now I cannot say that the effect of a heart shot on a deer and a man are in any way similar. But let us see what would happen if we suppose this might have a bearing on the deer question.

If the deer is frightened before the shot, his heart beats would increase tremendously, also increasing circulation of blood to the brain and muscles. And how far would he run in the 15.6 seconds before his heart stopped? At Anticosti Island I timed a mature white-tailed deer over a measured course with a stopwatch. It was shot at but purposely missed, Its speed was 18 miles per hour.

The highest speed when another deer was fully extended and had to run, was about 30 miles per hour. At 18 miles per hour, the deer could travel 137 yards in 15.6 seconds. At 25 miles per hour the deer could travel about 152 yards. At 30 miles per hour the deer could travel about 229 yards.

Doesn't it sound to you a little bit as if John Deering may have solved the riddle and that the deer's heart does not stop when perforated?

— *William Monypeny Newsom*

Wounded Deer Behavior

A. Broken Foreleg

A deer with a broken foreleg will leave drag marks in the snow or dirt. A drag mark might not be evident at first. Another sign of a broken foreleg is the evidence of only three hoofprints in the tracks. (See figure on next page)

B. Broken Hind Leg

A deer with a broken hind leg will also leave drag marks in the snow or dirt. Tracks from a deer with this wound will only include three hoofprints: the two forelegs and one hind leg. (see figure on next page).

C. Bullet Through Lungs, Liver or Intestines

Deer shot through the intestines, liver or lungs often leave tracks that are bunched in twos. (see figure on next page).

Wounded Deer Behavior

D. Bullet Through Intestines or Liver

A cross jump track results from a bullet through the intestines or liver with the animal standing broadside to the shooter. (see figure below).

Tracking Patterns of Wounded Deer

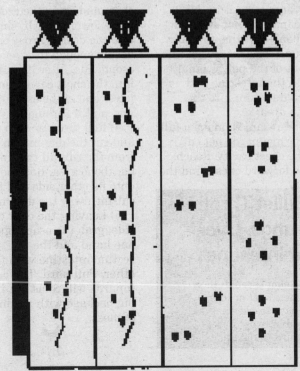

Field-Dressing Tips

Field dressing a deer doesn't have to be a tedious, messy chore. Do it the easy way. Follow these five simple steps the next time you field-dress a whitetail:

1) With the deer on its back, carefully open the deer's abdomen.

2) Place a small log under the rump to get it off the ground. Cut deeply around the rectum, being careful not to cut off or puncture the intestine. Pull to make sure the rectum is separated from tissue connecting it to the pelvic canal. Do not split the pelvic bone. Lift the animal's back quarters a bit, reach into the front of the pelvic canal, and pull the intestine and connected rectum into the stomach area.

3) If you want to make a full shoulder mount, do not cut open the chest cavity. Reach into the forward chest, find the esophagus, cut it off as far up as possible, and pull it down through the chest. If the buck won't be mounted, split the chest and sever the esophagus at its lower end. Or, simply cut into the deer's throat patch deeply enough to sever the esophagus. After it's cut, reach into the chest cavity, find the lower end of the esophagus and pull it through.

4) Roll the deer onto one side and cut the diaphragm away from the ribs all the way to the backbone area. Roll the deer onto its other side and finish cutting away the diaphragm.

5) Leaving the deer on its side, grab the esophagus with one hand and the rectum/intestine with the other. Pull hard. The deer's innards will come out in one big package with a minimum of mess.

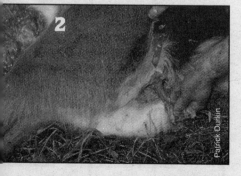

Skinning Made Easy

Skinning deer does not have to be a laborious chore that leaves hair all over the meat. Using a car, truck or come-along, you can winch off the hide in about five minutes of work.

1) With the deer hanging by its neck, slice the hide around the neck as close to the head as possible. (Don't cut into the meat. The neck muscles bear much force later as the hide is pulled off.)

2) Cut down the front of the neck to the opening made during field dressing.

3) Saw off the legs slightly above the knee joints.

4) Pull the neck hide down until about one foot of it is free. Take a golf-ball sized rock or 1.5-inch section of 2-by-2 and wrap it into the hide's end. Make a tight package and cinch it off with high-quality nylon rope of about 3/8-inch thickness. A double half-

hitch works well.

5) Tie the rope's other end to a car, truck or come-along hook. Back up the vehicle until the hide is pulled to the brisket and shoulders. It will bind slightly here. If necessary, have someone work the hide around the brisket. With tension on the rope, the hide will slide over fairly easily.

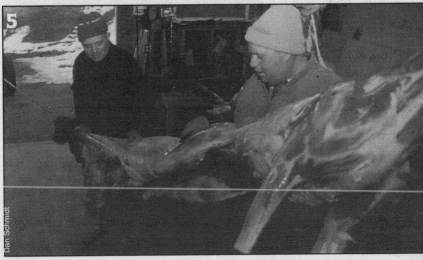

How to Cape a Trophy

Caping — the process of skinning out a trophy deer's shoulder and head — is best left to the taxidermist. In a remote setting, however, storage problems may require you to cape a deer if you want to preserve it as a full shoulder mount. Follow the illustration above when making your cuts.

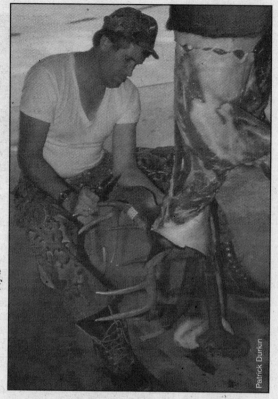

Patrick Durkin

1) With a short, sharp knife, slit the skin from the top of the withers, up the back of the neck to the midpoint between the ears. Now, going back to the withers, circle the body with another cut. This should leave plenty of hide for the taxidermist.

2) Peel the skin forward up to the ears and jaws, exposing the point where you want to cut through the neck. The easiest way to separate the head from the neck is to make an encircling cut through the neck to the atlas joint, the first vertebra under the skull. This is the only joint on the neck that has no interlocking bones.

3) Remember, when field dressing a trophy to be mounted, don't cut into the chest or neck area. If blood gets on the area to be mounted, wash it off with snow or water as soon as possible. Also, when taking the deer out of the woods, place it on a sled or rickshaw. All it takes is one sharply broken branch on a deadfall to damage the hide.

Pre-Tanning Tips

Your deerskin is a valuable resource. Properly cared for and tanned, deerskin is a soft material that can be made into a durable jacket or attractive pair of gloves. There is one catch: the way you skin and preserve the hide prior to the tanning process will affect the final appearance of the leather and its value.

By following a few simple steps, you can ensure your white-tailed deer hide will provide quality material to be made into quality garments.

Assuming the animal is in good condition, proper care during the skinning process is your first concern. Begin the skinning process with a sharp knife and then switch to using your hands. By using your hands to pry and pull the hide off the animal, you can avoid cutting holes into the hide. Knife cuts close to the surface of the hide can open up during the tanning process, ruining portions of the hide.

Another tip: Allow tallow to remain on the hide, but carefully remove all flesh.

Next, lay the hide flat, hair side down, and salt it. The average hide can be preserved with 3 to 5 pounds of canning or table salt. Spread the salt firmly onto the hide, taking care to cover it all the way to the edges. The salt draws mois-

Patrick Durkin

To avoid damaging a deer's hide, use your hands to pull it from the carcass.

ture out of the hide, impeding the growth of bacteria.

After the hide is salted, it should be spread flat and left in a cool, dry place for two or three days until a crust forms. If your deer is frozen when skinned, allow the hide to thaw before salting it. Your hide is ready for tanning when the salt forms a crust.

If you plan to mail the hide to a tannery, fold the sides of the hide toward the center and roll up, hair side out. The hide should be wrapped in paper because plastic causes the hide to "sweat," which breeds bacteria. Wrap extra paper around the package to absorb any additional fluid, place the contents in a cardboard box, and ship immediately.

— Contributed by W.B. Place, Box 160, Dept. DDH, Hartford, WI 53027.

Weights and Heart Girth

To calculate live or hog-dressed weight, first measure heart girth, the circumference of the body just behind the front legs. Then consult this chart to convert girth into a close estimate of weight.

Heart girth (inches)	Field-Dressed Weight (pounds)	Live weight (pounds)
26	46	69
27	52	72
28	58	75
29	64	83
30	70	90
31	76	98
32	82	106
33	88	113
34	94	121
35	101	128
36	107	136
37	113	144
38	119	151
39	125	159
40	131	166
41	137	174
42	143	182
43	149	190
44	155	197
45	161	205
46	167	212
47	173	220
48	180	227
49	187	235
50	194	242
51	201	250
52	208	257
53	215	265

The Duel

The adrenaline was wearing off, but Carl felt alert and more relaxed. Even the shaking had subsided. He felt in control. He would get this buck! All he needed was one small break.

■ *Mike Moutoux*

The threat of snow grew steadily as the afternoon wore on. When the wind picked up another notch and flurries started to fall, Carl started back to his pickup. Slinging his shotgun over his shoulder, he picked up his seat cushion, clipped it to his belt, and looked around one more time. His legs tingled as a reminder that he had been sitting too long. He stamped his feet to get the circulation going.

"No sense flogging a dead horse," he reasoned. "Might as well admit this isn't my year."

For five years, Carl had been coming here, hoping to tag his first buck. Now another season was ending without so much as seeing one. He was tired, hungry, cold and frustrated as he began climbing the low hill that sheltered the valley he had watched all afternoon.

His course intersected a well-used deer trail, which he planned to follow until he hit the logging road where his truck was parked. By the time he topped the hill, the snow was falling harder, sticking to the ground and the shoulders of his coat. The weatherman had predicted 2 to 4 inches by morning.

He found the trail and stopped to look around. The path angled down the opposite side of the hill and crossed a small creek at the bottom before petering out on the opposite side. He would be at the truck in another 20 minutes.

The snow was melting on his scope, so Carl dug around in his pockets for the rubber scope covers. A feeling of finality swept over him as he stretched the black rubber over the eye piece.

At the creek, Carl opened the action on his Ithaca and caught the unfired shell in his right hand. With the gun in his left hand and the rifled slug in his right, he navigated a set of stepping stones across a shallow riffle. As he started up the other side, he lost his balance, and fell squarely on his rump. The impact jarred the slug out of his hand and his lungs made a loud whooshing noise.

A Buck Appears

Carl had just gotten his knees under him when he heard a twig snap nearby. A deer had evidently been bedded just ahead and was spooked by his fall. Carl froze and looked for the source of the noise. There! A deer took one step and looked toward Carl. It was a big buck, and not more than 30 yards away!

At that moment, adrenaline jolted into Carl's bloodstream. His heart rate jumped, his breathing sped up and his arteries dilated. He began shaking.

He tried to control it by taking stock of his situation: The deer evidently couldn't see or smell him, or it would be long gone.

As Carl watched, the buck continued to stare in his direction. He feared the animal would see the gun shaking in his hand. He was close enough to see the buck lick its nose, and then it seemed to look away.

"He has no idea what he heard," Carl thought. He tightened his grip on the gun. Slowly, he began to raise the shotgun when he remembered the scope cover. Resting the barrel on his left knee, Carl reached for the cover's tab when the buck looked his way again. The deer's ears rotated in various directions, searching for a sound that would betray an intruder's presence.

A Perfect Chance

When the buck turned his head away again, Carl popped the cover off his scope, letting it fall silently into the snow at his feet. At this range, Carl knew he couldn't miss. The gun came up quickly and Carl leaned into the stock. As he did, the gun's forearm slid forward and locked with a loud click. The buck's head snapped back. Every muscle was tensed for a quick escape, but his caution — honed by three years and several close escapes — kept him rooted in place until he knew what was out there.

Carl quickly figured out his problem. For safety reasons, he had left the action open when he crossed the creek. His fall had partially closed it. In his excitement, he had forgotten the gun's chamber was empty. Two slugs were still in the magazine, but he would have to cycle the pump-action to reload. The noise would surely spook the buck.

Carl decided to wait until the buck relaxed before he chanced reloading. He figured he had another 45 minutes of legal shooting time left. He would wait as long as it took for a second chance.

Ten minutes had passed, and neither Carl nor the buck seemed to have an advantage. The adrenaline was wearing off, but Carl felt alert and more relaxed. Even the shaking had subsided. He felt in control. He would get this buck! All he needed was one small break.

The standoff continued. Five minutes later, Carl was developing another problem. His right leg was cramping. He shifted his weight slowly to his left foot while keeping his eyes on the buck. Then, he carefully twisted his right foot into a more comfortable position and recentered his weight.

The buck didn't seem to notice, but he was steadily growing more restless. He stamped his hoof once, and then again. Nothing. He backed up a step and stood with just his head peering around a tree, watching and listening.

The snow swirled in great clouds, cutting visibility to mere yards. Carl shifted again, thankful for the opportunity, but worrying that the cold was finding dozens of places to assault his skin. The snow let up, and the buck was still staring at him from around the same tree. A thin layer of snow now covered his back. When the buck turned again, Carl got a good look at his antlers. It occurred to him that he had never tried to count the points before. Starting on the left beam, he counted the high brow tine and four others, including the tip of the main beam. On the

right, the brow tine seemed to be missing or broken off, but four other tines were visible.

Suddenly, a tickle developed at the back of Carl's throat. He turned all his concentration toward stifling it. The tickle soon became a burn. He tried to swallow it back, but it was futile. His eyes watered, and his chest hurt from holding back. He would have to let it out.

The buck was looking straight at him as he coughed into his collar. The animal never blinked. The wind was blowing in the hunter's favor, and the buck could neither smell nor hear much with all the noise.

The Spell Breaks

Soon after, now 20 minutes into the encounter, the buck seemed to relax. His ears dropped, and some of the tension left his muscles. He looked left, right and to the rear. He snorted. The wind ruffled the hair along his back. He turned around, faced into the wind, and began walking away.

Carl knew he must chamber a round and shoot. When the buck passed behind a tree, Carl pushed the forearm release and pulled it back, listening for the next shell to pop into the receiver. As he slid the forearm forward, the buck snapped his head back. Carl could see two-thirds of the buck's head and nothing more.

"Come on boy, one more step," he pleaded silently. "Just one little step." The cross-hairs settled where he expected the buck's shoulder to appear. It was getting hard to see in the low light, and water spots from the melting snowflakes covered the lens.

Again the snow swirled, closing a white curtain between them. The buck, sensing his opportunity, walked 20 yards and stopped again behind another tree for one last look.

Carl, realizing his own opportunity, quickly walked forward and found a tree to lean against. The snow let up again. The buck was gone. "Darn it," he muttered to himself. "Where did he go?"

He slowly raised the gun while scanning the nearby woods. Antlers revealed the buck standing about 50 yards away, his entire body now visible.

Carl took a deep breath and silently pushed the safety off. He tried to get the proper sight picture, but lost the cross-hairs against the buck's dark body.

"Too dark," he thought. "What time is it?" Sneaking a look at his watch, he saw it was already five minutes after legal shooting time. He set his jaw, took another breath, and raised the cross-hairs until he could see daylight between them and the deer's shoulders. He lowered the cross-hairs to a lethal level and smiled.

Securing the Memory

When Carl got home, the lights were on, and he could see the TV's blue light glowing in the living room. He pulled into the garage, went around to the back of the truck, and opened the tailgate before going inside.

"Hey, everybody, I'm home," he called cheerfully.

His wife was the first to greet him. She noticed the tiny crinkles at the corner of his eyes and a slight smile on his lips.

"Did you get one?" she asked. "You're late."

"Sort of," he grinned. The rest of his crew crowded into the kitchen. Carl told them of his duel with the biggest buck he had ever seen, and how he had outfoxed him in the end. He told them how he raised the gun and yelled, "pow!" to the old buck's astonishment. Then, in a shower of snow and pounding hoofs, the deer had exploded away into the dark.

"So, the buck beat you after all, huh, Dad?" asked his oldest.

"Well, I figure I beat him, but the clock beat me," Carl answered. "I reckon it was sort of a tie."

Carl went back out to the truck to get his gear. The smile he had been wearing since leaving the woods was still on his face.

Tactical Tips
& Tricks

The March 1996 edition of *Deer & Deer Hunting* included the first installment of the magazine's "Tactical Tips & Tricks" column. The column is an outlet in which *Deer & Deer Hunting* readers can share their time-proven deer hunting secrets. The response has been overwhelming. Hundreds of readers have submitted their tips, tricks, tactics and suggestions.

The next several pages include some of the best tips and tricks that were printed in the past year. They will help you:

✓ Learn an easier way to drag a deer from the woods.

✓ Find out how a piece of rubber can be used to pull arrows easily from a foam target.

✓ Discover how steam can save the fletchings on your arrows.

✓ Improve bow-string waxing with a simple procedure.

✓ Make a drop-proof thumb release.

✓ Use a feather to keep track of wind and thermal currents.

... and much more!

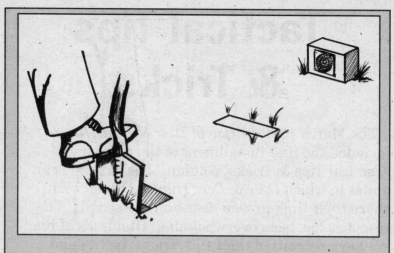

How Far Away is that Target?

Set up archery yardage markers in your back yard to determine your exact range. Use a shovel to dig rectangular holes at several shooting distances. Fill the holes with clay or sand. These markers will stay free of weeds and will be easy to spot when it's time to practice.

— *Charles Baechtle*
Lake Katrine, N.Y.

Pull Arrows Easily from Foam Targets

I found that a piece of inner-tube rubber works great for removing arrows quickly and easily from foam archery targets.

To make your own arrow puller, simply take an 8-inch section of inner-tube rubber and slice it in half. You can keep the puller handy by punching a hole in one end and tying a thin rope or cord to it.

Make some for your friends: One bicycle tire inner tube makes eight to 10 pullers.

— *Scott Pousson*
Lake Charles, La.

Built-in Bow Rest Reduces Fatigue

I sew a small, loose, open-topped pocket onto my hunting pants slightly above the kneecap for use while bow-hunting. This pocket comes in handy when a deer is slow in approaching.

While waiting for my shot, I slip the lower wheel of the bow into the pocket. This allows me to rest my bow arm so it's not tired when the time comes to draw and shoot.
— *Thomas Brink*
Plymouth, Wis.

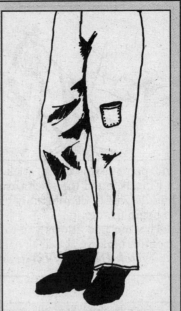

Use Cotton Ball as Weather Silencer

Moleskin often does not stick to arrow rests in cold temperatures. So, to keep my flipper-style arrow rest quiet, I use a cotton ball. I tear the cotton ball in half and slide it onto the flipper arm, ensuring there is just enough cotton cushion above the flipper to eliminate arrow noise, but not so much as to affect the arrow's release and flight.
— *Charles Perry*
Beulah, Mich.

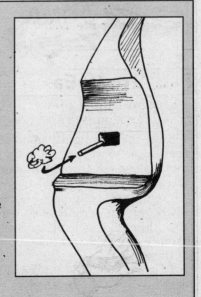

Get a Handle on Dragging

An inexpensive, simple way to drag a deer out of the woods is to use a small sapling or piece of brush as a "snout handle."

First, cut a handle that is 6 to 8 inches long. Then, sharpen one end of the stick.

Finally, push the stick through the deer's nostrils. The handle will fit comfortably between your fingers, allowing you to begin dragging.

This method allows you to lift the deer's weight off the ground, making the drag easier for one person.

— *Rick Hodgson, Beaver Dam, Wis.*

Hoof-to-Mouth Method

About 10 years ago, I stumbled upon a new way to drag deer out of the woods that makes the work steady and less clumsy than conventional methods.

The only materials needed are a rope and stick.

Snug the legs tightly up to the deer's head by cinching them close to the bottom of its jaw. To do this, I use my knife and make a slit through its jaw just beside the tongue, and lace the rope through the opening and back to the legs.

Next, I put a slip knot loop over one hoof and then a half-hitch over the second hoof. After securing a knot, I pull the rope through the mouth to bring the legs up near the head. Finally, I tie a short stick — about 6 inches long — to the end of the rope.

This method makes it possible to keep the front end of the deer up in the air, which gives you more control as you drag.

— *William Dickson, Pittsville, Wis.*

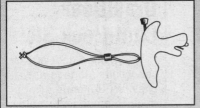

Make a Drop-Proof Thumb Release

Like many bow-hunters, I find the thumb release works best to improve my shooting. However, I had trouble keeping it in the tree with me.

Using a piece of shoe lacing and an eye-hook from an old fishing lure, I created a wrist sling for my release. The handle of my release was soft enough to allow the eye-hook to thread itself. However, a metal release could be drilled to accept a small eye-hook. By cutting the lacing to fit my wrist, I can let go of the release and relax my hand while waiting on the stand. When a deer approaches, I just ease the release back into my hand, and I'm ready to shoot.

To make a more customized fit, add a short piece of snug-fitting plastic tubing or a flattened piece of copper tubing to the lace. The tubing allows you to tighten the loop to better fit your wrist.

— *William J. Robinson, Millville, N.J.*

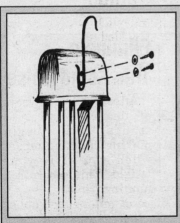

Make a Handy Quiver Hook

When in a tree stand, I don't like to hunt with my bow-quiver attached to my bow. Until recently, I found it difficult to keep the quiver handy and steady once I detached it from my bow.

I solved this problem by taking a 6-inch piece of No. 12 electrical wire and bending each end into a hook. I make one hook wide so it can hang on a rope, branch or screw-in hook. I make the other hook very narrow so I can attach it to the hood of my bow-quiver with two self-tapping panhead screws. For an extra firm grip between the wire and quiver, slip a small washer under the head of each screw.

— *Steve Barnum, Hastings, Mich.*

Drag Deer Cant-Hook Style

Dragging a deer out of the woods alone is not easy. While using a cant hook to move logs one day, it dawned on me to try the same thing on a deer. It worked very well!

The process is simple: Find a pole that's 2 inches in diameter and 60 inches in length, or longer. Next, tie a rope 18 inches from the bottom of the pole and attach the other end around the deer's head or antlers.

Use the pole as a lever to move the deer. The process is a little slower than usual, but it's steady, and the pushing action doesn't wear you out.

If you have a partner, you can tie the rope in the middle of the pole, place it across your chests, and pull like a team of oxen.

— *William Trag, Sharon, Conn.*

Eliminate Tree Stand Noise

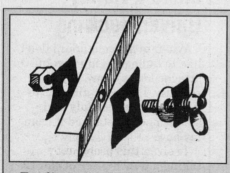

After a couple of years of usage, some tree stands will begin making creaking noises when you shift your weight. This can ruin a hunting trip.

To eliminate this noise, find a piece of inner-tube rubber and cut several 1-inch squares. Take the squares and use a center-hole punch to make holes in the rubber pieces. Next, use the rubber pieces as "washers" between metal nuts, bolts and the frame of the tree stand.

The rubber cushions the metal pieces, preventing them from rubbing together and making noise.

— *Steven K. Hunt, Aiken, S.C.*

Keep Hunting License Handy

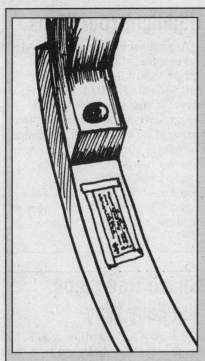

To ensure that I always have my bow-hunting license with me in the field, I place it in a plastic sandwich bag and tape the bag to the lower portion of the handle of my compound bow.

The plastic bag keeps the license dry, and it's easy to remove when needed.

Keeping my license with my bow gives me one less thing to worry about when gathering my gear for a hunting trip.

— Bob Weber,
Mattoon, Ill.

Use Wax to Add Life to Your Bowstring

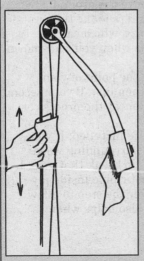

Proper waxing will add life to your bow-string. Coating the surface with wax is not sufficient, however. The wax must be worked into the string's strands to achieve maximum protection.

To do the job properly, apply wax liberally to the string's surface. Next, wrap a piece of wax paper or thick plastic around the string, and rub vigorously up and down the length of the string. The friction will melt the wax enough to apply evenly on the string.

— Charles Baechtle,
Lake Katrine, N.Y.

Highlight Your Steps

Anyone who has ever stepped out of a tree stand after dark knows that it is sometimes difficult to locate the first step. Most screw-in tree steps are dark in color and are nearly invisible after dark when viewed from above.

To correct that problem, and prevent a possible fall, I paint a white stripe across the top of all my tree steps. The steps now stand out clearly when I look down on them, but the white paint is not easily seen when viewed from below.

If you're worried about the paint smell, be sure to paint the steps well in advance of deer season. This will allow the odor of fresh paint to wear off before the steps are used.

— *Jerry Goddard, Verona, Wis.*

Space Tree Steps the Easy Way

An easy way to allow a safe, proper distance between tree steps is to use your arm and hand as a guide.

Here's how: Install the first step about 12 inches to 14 inches above the ground. (Too many hunters make this first step a doozy, which can be dangerous when you come down in the dark.)

Next, place your elbow on the step. At the point of your extended fingertips, mark the spot and then install your second step about 7 inches to the right or left. Repeat the process as you go up.

Here's another tip for after the steps are installed: If you leave your steps in the tree for long, the surrounding wood sometimes puts them in a vise-like grip. To break that grip, I pack a 10-inch long, 1-inch diameter plastic pipe inside my fanny pack. This lightweight pipe fits over the step to allow extra torque for easy removal. The pipe also helps when installing steps.

— *Erwin Fleury, Mount View, N.Y.*

Extra Steps Mean Safety

When installing portable tree steps to reach your tree stand, don't stop short of the platform. Install two extra steps slightly above the stand.

Here's why: For one, when you reach your stand, you can use the steps above to pull yourself aboard. Then, when you depart, you'll have steady handholds when stepping down from the stand. Such safety considerations are especially important when it's cold or dark.

In addition, while you're hunting from the tree stand, you can use the extra steps to hang your day pack, binoculars or bow-quiver. The steps allow you to keep this equipment within easy reach.

Finally, when using your safety belt, secure it to the tree above the steps. This ensures the strap will slide no farther than the steps if you fall.

— *Thomas S. Brink, Plymouth, Wis.*

Mark Tree Step Holes

I move my tree stand frequently during deer season to take advantage of changing deer movements. If I plan to use the tree again that season, I mark the holes for my tree steps as I remove them. I like to reuse the holes because tree steps can be installed more quickly and quietly in existing holes.

How do I mark the holes? I simply insert twigs or small branches into them. Although any twig will work, I prefer to use evergreen twigs on hardwood trees and hardwood twigs on evergreen trees. Because these twigs stick out from the trunk, they're easy for me to spot when I return to the site. Even so, I've found that few other hunters seem to notice my stand locations.

— *Benjamin Bolte, Nekoosa, Wis.*

Trick Funnels Deer to Your Tree Stand

When hunting grown-over fence lines, you can funnel deer to your tree stand by blocking off natural runways.

To do this, pile branches, logs or rocks at low areas where deer typically cross. This barrier will cause deer to find an alternative route. Next, create an opening in the fence line near your tree stand.

— *Thomas S. Brink, Plymouth, Wis.*

Editor's note: *This tip should never be used without first obtaining the landowner's permission.*

Find Arrows at Night the Easy Way

In addition to using bright-colored fletchings and nocks, I use luminescent paint on my arrows. This helps me find arrows quickly when blood-trailing at night.

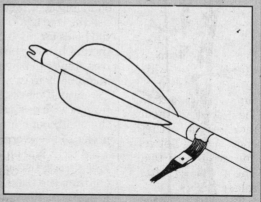

For best results, paint a 1-inch ring around the arrow just below the nock or feathers. Let the paint dry, and coat the ring with clear nail polish. The luminescent paint shows up brightly at night when shined with a flashlight.

— *Robert Magnan, Fanwood, N.J.*

Extra Glue Keeps Fletchings Intact

Many bow-hunters face problems when factory-applied fletchings peel away from arrow shafts. This becomes frustrat-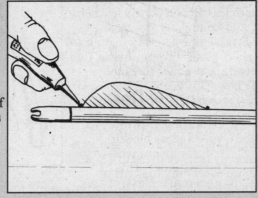ing if you have to reattach fletchings after just a few practice sessions.

To keep my fletchings intact, I add a small dot of glue on both ends of each fletching. This helps keep the fletchings from pulling away from the arrow shaft when pulling them out or through a target. The extra glue does not alter the arrow's flight.

— *Beau D'Arcy, Plainfield, Ill.*

Add Movement to Your Decoys

You can add excitement to your pre- and post-rut hunting by using decoys. Luring a buck within bow-range is thrilling, but difficult.

One way to enhance a decoy is to add movement to the presentation. I do this by attaching a turkey feather atop the decoy's rump to simulate tail movement. Tie a string to the feather, and tack it to the decoy, leaving enough room between the string  and the feather to allow the feather to twitch from side to side. The movement often fools deer into thinking the decoy is a live, relaxed deer.

This trick also works to create ear movement. Use smaller, light-colored feathers tacked to one or both ears to simulate ear twitching.

— *Steve Gilsdorf, Little Chute, Wis.*

Keep Track of Air Currents

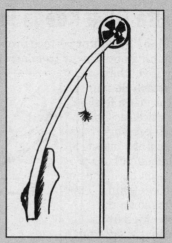

To keep track of the wind and thermal currents, I strategically place thread and downy feathers in and around my stand site.

First, I glue a downy feather to a short piece of white thread, and then tape it under the top limb of my bow. This keeps me aware of the air currents immediately around me.

Second, I cut several 10-inch lengths of white thread and glue a downy feather to each. Then, before ascending to my tree stand, I walk the area around my stand and hang the thread/feathers about 3 feet off the ground in several locations. This allows me to keep an eye on the air currents around my stand's perimeter.

— Randy Coffey, Mahomet, Ill.

Recycle Unused Ironing Board

I recycled an old ironing board and now use it as a portable shooting bench.

The ironing board works well when shooting at places that don't have permanent shooting rests. Add a shoulder strap, and you have a light, portable and inexpensive shooting rest.

— Ken Diener, Kimberly, Wis.

User Rollers for Heavy Tree Stands

Ladder tree stands can be heavy, making it difficult to place them against a tree. To make things easier, temporarily install rollers at the top of the ladder stand and roll the stand up the tree.

These rollers are sold in woodworking catalogs as out-feed rollers for table saws. They have push-pins so you can remove them once the stand is in place.

Be especially careful how you mount the rollers. If you damage the stand, you could weaken it, which might cause an accident. Also, if you mount rollers to a commercially made stand, you might void its warranty.

— *Rick Menard, Troy, N.H.*

Knives for the

A quality fixed-blade can make field-dress tasks easy. This hun prepares to field dre Northern Forest buc a Gerber Bolt-Action Point.

eer Woods

For most hunters, one knife will do an adequate job for everything from field dressing to skinning. It takes several knives, however, if you plan on hunting more than just a few days in fall.

■ *Text and Photos by Dan Schmidt*

Tony and I gawked at the big Northern Forest buck that lay at our feet. Its swollen neck and broad chest reminded us of the powerful linebackers we watched play football every Sunday. We weren't sure what to do next so we waited as Dad hurried toward us through a patch of prickly ash.

"Wow, nice buck!" Dad said before he had even exited the thicket. "Well, let's get to work."

Without hesitating, Dad unsheathed his knife, wiped it twice across his pant leg, and knelt between the buck's back legs. Tony knew what to do; he grabbed the buck's chest and held the deer steady as Dad worked the knife.

I could tell Dad had performed this task many times. After carefully slitting open the buck's abdomen, he maneuvered the blade deeply around its rectum. He then returned to the abdomen and slit it open to the bottom of the buck's rib cage.

He continued his work by placing both hands inside the deer while telling us how important it was to be careful when using a wet or bloody knife. And just like that he was done.

"OK, Tony," he said. "Turn him over." Like one big package, the buck's intestines rolled onto the fresh snow.

I was just a clumsy 16-year-old, but I couldn't wait until my hands could perform such precise work with a simple piece of steel.

Tools of Tradition

It took a few years for me to get a chance to field dress a deer by myself. However, by that time I had already accumulated two quality knives — a straight-blade hunter Tony gave me for Christmas, and a Buck 110 folding knife Dad gave me for my birthday.

Most hunters I know were introduced to knives in the same fashion: Their first blades were new models of what their dads, brothers or uncles used.

A typical "first knife" is a fixed-blade with upswept tip, claw finger guard and nickel pommel. Although few mentors stress it, a quality leather sheath is an important companion for a knife. The sheath keeps the knife clean and dry, but also protects young hunters from accidentally cutting themselves if they slip and fall.

Some hunters prefer to start the younger members of their group with folding knives. Besides some obvious size and safety advantages, folding knives can also teach responsibility. Like guns, folding knives require extensive cleaning after heavy use. Any young hunter who puts away a dirty folding knife quickly learns to take better care of all of his hunting gear.

Knives of Today

For most hunters, one knife will do an adequate job for everything from field dressing to skinning. It takes several knives, however, if you plan on hunting more than just a few days in fall. Although I don't carry all of them at one time, I've discovered it takes no less than six knives to get me through one hunting season: a

What Makes a Good Hunting Knife?

If your budget allows you to purchase just one hunting knife, look for a knife that has three or more of the following qualities:
✓ Drop-point blade that is less than 5 inches long.
✓ Checkered handle that is made of hard rubber, Kraton plastic, or non-polished hardwood.
✓ Finger grooves on the handle or a protruding blade guard to prevent your hand from slipping across the blade.
✓ Blood grooves on the top of the blade for thumb support and control.
✓ Sheath that is made of thick, well-sewn leather or nylon, or a molded plastic sheath.

quality serrated folder, small pocket knife, utility knife, belt hunter, and boning and skinning knives. That's just me — I feel naked without the world's first tool by my side.

How many knives do you need? Probably just two or three. You can perform most of your cutting and chopping chores by picking out a few knives from the following categories:

Serrated Folders

Several companies now offer excellent serrated folding knives. These razor-sharp knives are the most useful blades a hunter can own. The serrated blades outperform all other knives when it comes to slicing rope, vines, nylon material and cloth. The knives also act as mini-saws in your tree stand if you need to prune a few small branches.

I've found the best serrated folders include a pocket clip or belt sheath and a thumb hole or push pin on the blade for easy one-hand opening.

Spyderco's Clip-It and Goddard knives are not only light and handy — a pocket-clip design keeps the knives within easy reach — they are also extremely sharp. Other knives falling into this category are Gerber's Gator Serrater and E-Z Out, Beretta's Airlight, Schrade's Cliphanger and Outdoor Edge's FieldLight. I've used these knives to cut through everything from a deer's rib cage to thick nylon rope. In all cases, the blades made numerous cuts before showing any signs of losing their edge.

Another good choice is Remington's Grizzly, a double-lockback with a partially-serrated blade and a small gut hook/bone saw blade.

Belt Hunters

The knives deer hunters carry on their belts probably can be attributed more to family tradition than anything else. Many hunters prefer a medium-sized folder such as the Buck 110, while others opt for a quality fixed-blade like the Camillus/Western WL66. And, the recent surge in popularity of gut-hook knives has added a third style to that mix.

In light of the success of its

Knife Maintenance

A quality hunting knife does not come cheaply. To ensure your knife provides many years of razor-sharp performance, follow these guidelines:

Do:

✓ Clean the knife thoroughly after using it. This is especially important for folding knives. Before placing the knife back in its sheath, wipe the blade with a drop or two of gun oil.

✓ Sharpen the blade after heavy usage. Remember, sharpening a knife only returns its edge to what it was before it was used. A blade cannot become sharper than its original shape. A few swipes across a stone or down a steel sharpener will do the trick. Over-sharpening will cause the blade to round off and could permanently damage your knife.

Do Not:

✓ Use your knife for any chore that involves prying, pounding, twisting or lifting. Certain knives can perform these tasks, but will certainly lose their ability to properly field-dress a whitetail.

✓ Put your knife away dirty. Blood and dirt will ruin a knife if not removed immediately from the blade and/or other working parts of the knife.

---

popular folders, Buck has not stopped designing quality belt knives. New models include the Protege, a rubber-handled version of the famous 110, and the Mentor, a fixed-blade knife that features a contoured rubber handle.

Several knives featuring gut hooks are hot sellers this year. Gut hooks allow you to open a deer with zipper-like precision. They also come in handy when cutting off a deer's windpipe, or getting a cut started during the skinning process.

The industry standard in gut-hook knives is the Buck Crosslock, a two-bladed folding knife. I field-tested one of these knives recently on Quebec's Anticosti Island.

While still-hunting a bog, I crept within 110 yards of a feeding buck and killed him with a well-placed sabot slug. Although the buck dropped in his tracks, I quickly realized field-dressing him would not be easy. The water in the bog was about 5 inches deep.

That's where the Crosslock came in handy. The knife's design allowed me to use one hand to open and close the gutting and straight blades, leaving my other hand to steady the carcass and roll out the intestines. A potentially sloppy field-dressing job was made easy with that knife.

Another quality gut-hook knife is Schrade's Blade Runner. This fixed-blade gut hook features a Safe-T-Grip handle. The handle provides a firm grip even when hands become covered with blood. The gut hook on this knife is big enough to prevent it from becoming clogged with hair.

Another quality belt hunter is the Western Dakota Hunter, a 10-inch knife that features a 5-1/2-inch hollow ground blade.

Skinners

Quality skinning knives have one thing in common: They are

Tools such as this mini ax from Camillus are small enough to clip to your belt and come in handy when pruning trees, and cutting shooting lanes near your tree stand.

built for rugged use. Most of today's top skinners include 440 stainless steel blades and tough non-slip handles.

Hunters who are looking for a durable skinning knife should check out the Katz Black Kat 100, Schrade Outfitter, Camillus High Country and the Kellam Rugged Tommi.

The Black Kat 100 features XT 80 stainless steel, which is known for its ability for holding and retaining an edge. This knife is built solidly and includes a contoured Kraton handle. The handle provides a controlled grip, putting less strain on the wrist while skinning. The same can be said of Outdoor Edge's Whitetail Skinner, a knife that is held with a closed fist, allowing you to work hard-to-reach places.

Although it carries a higher price tag, Kellam's Rugged Tommi is an outstanding skinner. This knife features a hardwood handle and a hand-forged blade. I skinned four whitetails with this knife before resharpening it. Other excellent skinners are Gerber's Bolt Action and Colt's Serengeti.

Combination Sets

Knife companies realize hunters need more than one knife to do one job. With that in mind, several companies offer combination sets that include two or more knives in one sheath.

The Kershaw Alaskan Blade Trader combines the usefulness of all three belt-style knives in one package. Like its name indicates, the Blade Trader allows you to remove the knife's blade and exchange it for another style. Stored in a leather sheath, the knife includes a drop-point straight blade, giant gut hook/skinner and a 6-inch saw blade. These blades are secured tightly by a unique locking mechanism, yet can be removed quickly when performing jobs that require different blade styles.

Knives of Alaska offers the Brown Bear Combo, which includes a mini cleaver and skinning/caping knife. Both knives fit neatly in a leather sheath and are built with heavy-duty use in mind. The tip of the skinner/caping knife offers precise cutting action and is an excellent tool for removing skin and flesh from deer skulls. The cleaver is durable and is a dandy choice for tasks such as chopping kindling, clearing short shooting lanes and removing bark from drag poles.

One of the best all-purpose tools is the Leatherman Super Tool. Like the original Leatherman, the Super Tool features a pliers, knife blades, screwdriver heads, picks and file. However, the Super Tool features a locking mechanism that prevents the tools from moving when in use.

The Weekender from Swiss Army Brands is another quality all-purpose tool, featuring a scissors, file, screwdriver tip, tweezers and knife blade.

The Western Mighty Axe Combo consists of a gut-hook/straight-blade knife and a mini ax. The ax is 11¾ inches long with a 3-inch stainless steel blade. Both tools fit in a black nylon belt sheath.

Conclusion

It isn't hard to find a quality knife that will perform a variety of hunting-related tasks. Most factory-made knives are

Deer Hunting Knife Manufacturers

Bear MGC
1 O'Connell SW, Dept. DDH
Jacksonville, AL 36265

Benchmark
Box 2089, Dept. DDH
Gastonia, NC 28053-2089

Beretta USA
72 Loveton, Dept. DDH
Sparks, MD 21152

Blackjack Knives
1307 W. Wabash, Dept. DDH
Effingham, IL 62401

Boker USA
1550 Balsam St., Dept. DDH
Lakewood, CO 80215

Browning
Rt. 1, Dept. DDH
Morgan, UT 84050

Buck Knives
Box 1267, Dept. DDH
El Cajon, CA 92022

Camillus (Western)
54 Main St., Dept. DDH
Camillus, NY 13031

Case
Owens Way, Dept. DDH
Bradford, PA 16701

Cold Steel
2128 D-Knoll, Dept. DDH
Ventura, CA 93003

Gerber
14200 SW 72nd
Dept. DDH
Portland, OR 97281-3088

Katz
Box 730, Dept. DDH
Chandler, AZ 85224-0730

Kellam
1770 Motor Parkway 2A
Dept. DDH
Hauppauge, NY 11788

Kershaw
25300 SW Parkway
Dept. DDH
Wilsonville, OR 97070

Knives of Alaska
Box 675, Dept. DDH
Cordova, AK 99574

Leatherman Tool Group
12106 NE Ainsorth Circle
Dept. DDH
Portland, OR 97220

Remington
Delle Donne Corporate Center
1011 Centre Road, Dept. DDH
Wilmington, DE 19805-1270

SOG Specialty Knives
Box 1024, Dept. DDH
Edmonds, WA 98020

Schrade
7 Schrade, Dept. DDH
Ellenville, NY 12428

Spyderco
Box 800, Dept. DDH
Golden, CO 80402

Swiss Army Brands
One Research Drive, Dept. DDH
Shelton, CT 06484-0874

Timberline
Box 750, Dept. DDH
Mancos, CO 81328

Winchester
c/o Blue Grassy Cutlery
304 W. 2nd St., Dept. DDH
Manchester, OH 45144

built with one thing in mind: performance.

Whether the next knife you purchase is for necessity or simply an upgrade, give some thought to buying two blades — one for you and one for a young hunter.

This way you'll create a tradition of your own.

Learn to Estimate Distances

The best archery equipment is only as good as the person who uses it. To be successful, a bow-hunter needs to be a woodsman and a good shooter. Above all, the bow-hunter must be a master in yardage estimation.

You can judge distances in the deer woods more accurately by practicing in your back yard. To get started, follow these six steps:

✓ Begin by choosing a distance that you can spot easily. The most common reference distance used by bow-hunters is 20 yards.

✓ Use this distance as your starting point for shorter or farther shots.

✓ Using only the 20-yard reference, estimate the distance of the shot.

✓ Fine-tune your estimation. Count toward the target in 10-yard increments. For example, if the target is 15 yards away, glance at your 20-yard reference point, estimate the half-way point, then count toward the target in 1-yard increments.

✓ Compare the fine-tuned yardage estimation with your first estimation. Split the difference if you're within 3 yards. For example: Using the 20 yards as a reference, you estimate the target to be 25 yards away. However, when fine-tuning the estimation, you count 29 yards.

Splitting the 4-yard difference in half, you estimate the target to be 27 yards away. Start over if the figures are off by more than 3 yards.

✓ Use the same method for farther shots.

The more you practice this method, the less time it takes to complete the process. Seasoned bow-hunters use this method to estimate the distances of trees, logs, rocks or other objects near shooting lanes.

No matter what method you use, never take a shot until you are satisfied with your yardage estimation. A lack of confidence is one of the biggest reasons why bow-hunters miss.

— Contributed by Bear Archery, 4600 SW 41st Blvd., Dept. DDH, Gainesville, FL 32608-4999.

Tips from 'The Old Bowhunter'

1. Make your landowner contacts early and get permission.

2. If possible, select several stand locations.

3. Ask questions of the landowner, a farmer, mailman, or anyone who travels through the area each day. Where, when, and how often does he see deer?

4. Visit your hunting territory as often as possible, both early morning and late afternoon.

5. Don't start patterning deer earlier than late August or early September. Deer often change their feeding and traveling habitats in early fall.

6. Look for deer sign on well-used trails, feeding areas and beds.

7. Check the barbed wire at fence crossings for hair.

8. Look for special feeding areas.

9. Keep a record of what you see and when you see it. Note number of deer seen by you and by others.

10. Make a map of the area and plot deer sightings, signs, stand locations and feeding areas.

11. Finally, use all your scouting data to select the spots for your stands.

12. Be sure to select several morning and evening stand locations.

13. Plot the route to each stand so you can follow it in the dark.

14. Unless you want company, don't blaze a trail or give away your stand locations.

15. Know the prevailing wind directions and locate more than one spot for a stand in case the wind changes.

— Contributed by the National Bowhunter Education Foundation, 249-B E. 29th St., No. 503, Loveland, CO 80538. Dedicated to the memory of W.H. "Bill" Wadsworth, "The Old Bowhunter."

Become a Better Bow-Hunter

The first step to becoming a better bow-hunter is honing your shooting skills and gaining the confidence that you can place an arrow with pinpoint accuracy at a given distance.

Rather than plunking shot after shot into a straw bale, systemize your practice routines. This will not only improve your accuracy, but it will make you more disciplined when a deer walks into shooting range when you're in your tree stand or ground blind. Here are 14 ways to further improve your archery skills:

✓ Place your archery target in a wooded area when possible.

✓ Practice with the same size arrows and broadheads that you intend to hunt with.

✓ Always use an *unmarked* outline of a deer as your target. If you want to see if your shots are in the vital area, lightly sketch that area on the target, but make the outline light enough so you cannot focus on it while shooting.

✓ Shoot for a specific spot on the deer, never shoot "at" a deer.

✓ Once you can hit the target at 30 yards and less, make it a rule not to take more than one practice shot from each spot. It is the first shot that counts. You probably won't get a second chance.

✓ Shoot from behind trees and shrubs, down on one knee and both knees, with bow canted left and right, and standing on your tiptoes to shoot over a limb.

✓ When practicing, wear the clothes and equipment you'll be hunting in.

✓ Practice shooting from a tree stand. Take shots in every direction and angle possible to simulate realistic hunting situations.

✓ Practice year-round, if you can, by bow-fishing, varmint hunting and stump shooting.

✓ Set up an action archery course using plastic jugs and rubber blunts. This is easily done in a limited space and gives you a variety of shooting opportunities.

✓ If you use a sight, zero it in at a given distance (20 yards is common). When you get good, you can figure out how much lower or higher you can hold the sight to shoot at 12 yards or at 30 yards.

— *Contributed by the National Bowhunter Education Foundation, 249B E. 29th St., Box 503, Dept. DDH, Loveland, CO 80538.*

10 Strategies for Concealment

Innovations in camouflage clothing allow deer hunters to literally blend in with any surrounding or terrain. White-tailed deer rely on their keen eyesight to avoid danger. Hunters, however, can escape detection by wearing a quality camouflage outfit and by following these 10 tips:

1. Match your camouflage pattern to the background of the area that you will be hunting. For maximum break-up, consider wearing different patterns on your jacket and pants.

2. Always use camouflage on your hands and face. Many hunters dress in full camouflage and fail to cover these important areas.

3. Cover anything that is shiny, such as your watch, buttons, snaps and zippers.

4. Purchase pants that are 2 inches to 3 inches longer than needed. This will keep light-colored socks and boots from standing out.

5. Wear boots with dark soles. A hunter's boots are sometimes the first things a deer will see if the hunter is sitting at ground level.

6. Avoid direct sunlight. If possible, face west in the morning and east in the afternoon.

7. Think about your intentions when you pick a spot. Your outline should blend in with the surroundings from at least 40 yards out.

8. Set up on edges and avoid hunting in the middle of thick cover. Hunting in thick cover hampers your vision.

9. Keep your outline as low as possible, but avoid setting up at a deer's eye level.

10. Use face paint to touch up glare areas around your eyes, even if you're wearing a face net.

— *Contributed by Haas Outdoors (Mossy Oak Camouflage), Box 757, Dept. DDH, West Point, MS 39773.*

How to Select Camouflage

With so many patterns to choose from, it isn't difficult to find camouflage clothing that perfectly meets your needs. However, maintaining hunting apparel isn't easy. Without proper care camouflage patterns can fade quickly.

Follow these tips for selecting and maintaining your hunting outfits:

Selecting

✓ *Buy name brands.*

You'll build your camo wardrobe over time, so buy from a company that has a reputation for quality and longevity.

✓ *Read product reviews.*

Most hunting magazines print product reviews. These reviews highlight product features and innovations.

✓ *Match your camo with the terrain.*

Before choosing a pattern, think carefully about the terrain and seasons you hunt. Match camo accordingly. You might choose to have a wardrobe for each situation.

✓ *Details make the garment.*

Pay attention to details. Look for extra pockets, comfortable linings, quiet cloth and form-fitted hoods.

✓ *Purchase larger sizes.*

Remember, you'll wear extra clothing in cold temperatures. If you dress in layers, you'll need bigger camo garments.

✓ *Make sure it's quiet.*

Select a material that doesn't make noise when scratched. Make sure the zippers are covered and operate quietly.

Maintaining

✓ *Wash new garments.*

Always wash garments in unscented soap in cold water. A tablespoon of vinegar should be added to help set the dye.

✓ *Keep garments scent free.*

Store clean garments in an air-proof bag to keep them scent free. Sprinkle baking soda in odor areas — armpits, crotch and footwear — and keep clothes in the bag until you're in the field.

✓ *Dry your clothes on a cool dryer setting, or hang them outside to dry.*

Heat will break down inks and make your camo clothing fade. Properly cared for, camo clothing will last up to five years. Clothing not cared for can break down in one year.

— Contributed by Skyline Camouflage, 184 Ellicott Road, Dept. DDH, West Falls,

Determining Correct Arrow Length

From Easton

Your correct arrow length is determined by drawing back an extra-long arrow and having someone mark the arrow as shown below.

Correct Arrow Length for hunting arrows with broadheads shot from bows with cut-out sight windows (including overdraw). Also for target/field arrows shot from any bow.

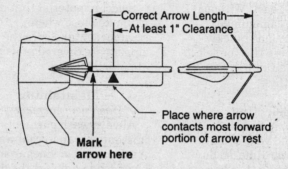

Correct Arrow Length for hunting arrows with broadheads shot from bows without cut-out sight windows.

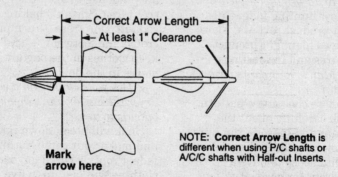

NOTE: **Correct Arrow Length** is different when using P/C shafts or A/C/C shafts with Half-out Inserts.

Correct Arrow Length is measured from the bottom of the nock groove to the end of the shaft.

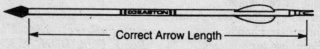

Guide to Beman Carbon Shafts

The five charts on this page will help you choose the correct carbon arrows for your bow if you choose to purchase Beman shafts.

To use these charts, you must first determine your correct shaft length. This is usually 1 inch longer than your draw length. Draw length is the distance between the nocking point on the string and the front of the bow at full draw.

— Contributed by Beman USA, 513 N. Neil Armstrong Road, Box 22850, Dept. DDH, Salt Lake City, UT 84116.

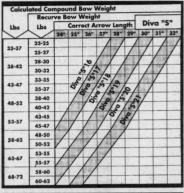

Calculated Compound Bow Weight — Recurve Bow Weight — Diva "S"

Lbs	Lbs	Correct Arrow Length (24"–32")
33-37	23-25 / 25-27	Diva "S" 16
38-42	28-30 / 30-32	Diva "S" 17
43-47	33-35 / 35-37	Diva "S" 18
48-52	38-40 / 40-42	Diva "S" 19
53-57	43-45 / 45-47	Diva "S" 20
58-62	48-50 / 50-52	Diva "S" 21
63-67	53-55 / 55-57	
68-72	58-60 / 60-62	

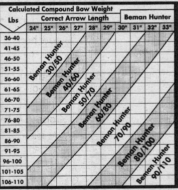

Calculated Compound Bow Weight — Beman Hunter

Lbs	Correct Arrow Length (24"–33")
36-40	Beman Hunter 30/50
41-45	Beman Hunter 40/60
46-50	Beman Hunter 50/70
51-55	Beman Hunter 60/80
56-60	Beman Hunter 70/90
61-65	Beman Hunter 80/100
66-70	Beman Hunter 90/110
71-75	
76-80	
81-85	
86-90	
91-95	
96-100	
101-105	
106-110	

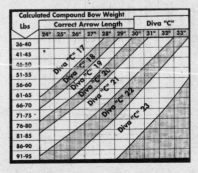

Calculated Compound Bow Weight — Recurve Bow Weight — Club

Lbs	Lbs	Correct Arrow Length (22"–29")
25-34	15-19 / 20-24	Club 26
35-44	25-29 / 30-34	Club 27
45-54	35-39 / 40-44	Club 28
55-64	45-49 / 50-54	Club 29
65-74	55-59 / 60-64	Club 30

Calculated Compound Bow Weight — Diva "C"

Lbs	Correct Arrow Length (24"–33")
36-40	Diva "C" 17
41-45	Diva "C" 18
46-50	Diva "C" 19
51-55	Diva "C" 20
56-60	Diva "C" 21
61-65	Diva "C" 22
66-70	Diva "C" 23
71-75	
76-80	
81-85	
86-90	
91-95	

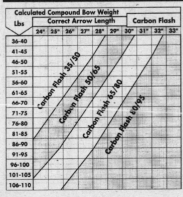

Calculated Compound Bow Weight — Carbon Flash

Lbs	Correct Arrow Length (24"–33")
36-40	Carbon Flash 35/50
41-45	Carbon Flash 50/65
46-50	Carbon Flash 45/80
51-55	Carbon Flash 60/95
56-60	
61-65	
66-70	
71-75	
76-80	
81-85	
86-90	
91-95	
96-100	
101-105	
106-110	

EASTON. Aluminum Arrow Shafts

EASTON ALUMINUM ARROW SHAFT SPECIFICATIONS AND SIZES

SHAFT MODEL	ALLOY	STRENGTH[†] psi	NOCK TAPER/UNI	NOCK TYPE	WEIGHT TOLERANCE	STRAIGHT-NESS[§]	HARD ANODIZED[‡] COLOR/PATTERN	ULTRALITE	SUPERLITE	LITE	STANDARD
XT7 Eclipse III	7178-T9	105,000	UNI or Super UNI System[*]	ACE, Super Nock or Conventional	±3/4%	±.001" (.002" T.I.R.)	Black				2317 2216 / 2316 2410
E75 Gold	7075-T9	98,000	Full Diameter Taper	Conventional	±1%	±.003" (.006" T.I.R.)	Gold	1413		1415 1516 1616 / 1716 1816 1916	
XX75 Autumn Orange	7075-T9	98,000	Reduced Diameter Taper[*]	Conventional	±1%	±.002" (.004" T.I.R.)	Autumn Orange		1713 1813 1913 2013 / 2113 2114 2213 / 2314 2413 2514	2016 / 2115 2215 2216	2016 / 2117 2219 / 2317 2216
Easton Classic[*] PermaGraphic[*]	7075-T9	95,000	Full Diameter Taper	Conventional	±1%	±.002" (.004" T.I.R.)	Cedar-grain PermaGraphic		2213 2413	1916 2016	2016 2117 2219
XX78[*] Super Slam[*] PermaGraphic[*]	7178-T9	100,000	Super UNI System[*]	Super Nock or Conventional	±1%	±.0015" (.003" T.I.R.)	3-Tone PermaGraphic Brown, Tan & Black Camo	2212 2312	2114 2314 2213 2514	2016 2115 2215 2316	2016 2117 2219 / 2317 2217
XX75 Camo Hunter[*] PermaGraphic[*]	7075-T9	95,000	Super UNI System[*]	Super Nock or Conventional	±1%	±.002" (.004" T.I.R.)	4-Tone PermaGraphic Green, Brown, Tan & Black Camo		2013 / 2113 2114 2213 / 2314 2413 2514	2016 2115 2215 2316	
XX75 Camo Hunter	7075-T9	98,000	Reduced Diameter Taper[*]	Conventional	±1%	±.002" (.004" T.I.R.)	4-Tone Black, Brown, Dk. & Lt. Green Camo		1912 2013 / 2113 2114 2213 / 2314 2413 2514	1816 1916 2016 / 2115 2215 2316	2016 / 2117 2219 / 2317 2410
GameGetter II	7075-T9	98,000	Full Diameter Taper	Conventional	±1¼%	±.003 (.006" T.I.R.)	3-Tone Black, Tan & Brown Camo			1816 2016 / 2115 2215 2315	2016 2117 2219
GameGetter	7075-T9	98,000	Full Diameter Taper	Conventional	±1¼%	±.003" (.006" T.I.R.)	Dark Green			2016 2216	2016 2117 2219
Eagle Target	5086	58,000	Full Diameter Taper	Conventional	±4%	±.006" (.012" T.I.R.)	Red			1516 1716 1916 / 1616 1816	
Eagle Hunter	5086	58,000	Full Diameter Taper	Conventional	±5%	±.010" (.020" T.I.R.)	Light Green			2016	2016 2117 2219

* Shaft sizes in lighter-face type have a full diameter nock taper.
† Typical Ultimate Tensile Strength at Final Draw before anodize. Due to variances in alloy, material or manufacturing processes, tensile strength value may vary ± 3%.
‡ All shafts have a hard anodized finish.
§ Straightness tolerance (T.I.R.=Total Indicator Reading as shaft is rotated 360°)

* UNI=Universal Nock Installation System.
Shaft sizes in italics use the UNI or Super UNI System.

®/°Registered Trademark/Trademark of Jas. D. Easton, Inc.
Super Slam Registered Trademark of Chuck Adams

Rev. 9/94

Arrow Shaft Sizes and Weight Groups

SHAFT MODEL	SHAFT WEIGHT CATEGORY				
	UltraLite A/C/E	UltraLite Aluminum SuperLite A/C/C SuperLite P/C	SuperLite Aluminum	Lite Aluminum	Standard Aluminum
Models Used for Competition and Recreational Archery					
A/C/E Aluminum/Carbon/Extreme	1000 780 620 470 920 720 570 430 850 670 520 400 370				
X7 Eclipse		1511 1711 1912 2312 1512 1712 2012 2512 1611 1811 2112 1612 1812 2212	1514 1714 1914 2114 15+14 17+14 19+14 2214 1614 1814 2014 16+14 18+14 20+14	1516 1716 1916 1616 1816	
E75 Gold			1413	1416 1716 1916 1516 1816 2016 1616 2115	
Eagle Target				1516 1716 1916 1616 1816	
Models Used for Competition, Recreational Archery and Bowhunting					
A/C/C Aluminum/Carbon/Competiton		2-00 2L-04 3-04 3-39 3L-00 2-04 3L-18 3-49 3-00 3X-04 3-18 3-60 3L-04 3-28 3-71			
P/C Pure/Carbon		4.5 5.0 5.5 6.1 4.7 5.2 5.7 6.3 4.9 5.4 5.9 6.5			
P/C Specter		4.5 5.0 5.5 6.1 4.7 .5.2 5.7 6.3 4.9 5.4 5.9 6.5			
XX75 Autumn Orange			1713 1913 2113 2314 1813 2013 2114 2413 2213 2514	1816 2115 2315 1916 2215 2016 2216	2018 2117 2317 2219 2419
Easton Classic PermaGraphic			2213 2413	1916 2216 2315 2016	2018 2117 2317 2219
Models Used for Bowhunting					
XX78 Super Slam		2212 2312 2512	2114 2314 2213 2413 2514	2016 2115 2315 2215 2216	2018 2117 2317 2219
XX75 Camo Hunter — 4-color PermaGraphic w/Super UNI Bushing			2013 2113 2314 2114 2413 2213 2514		
XX75 Camo Hunter — 4-color Standard Camo w/swage			1913 2113 2314 2013 2114 2413 2213 2514	1816 2115 2315 1916 2215	2018 2117 2317 2219 2419
GameGetter II				1816 2115 2315 1916 2215 2016 2216	2018 2117 2219
GameGetter				2016 2216	2018 2117 2219
Eagle Hunter					2018 2117 2219

— Contributed by Easton Aluminum,
5040 Harold Gatty Drive, Dept. DDH,
Salt Lake City, UT 84116.

Fletching Guide

Q: What size feathers should I use for my hunting arrows?

A: For hunting arrows tipped with broadheads, three 5-inch feathers or four 4-inch feathers work well. Lightweight carbon arrows can be fletched with three 4-inch feathers. Larger feathers might be required due to individual differences in equipment and shooting style. Good flight can also be achieved with smaller feathers.

Practice with different styles before choosing one.

It's important to remember that broadheads need more guidance than field points. Picking the correct fletching setup will ensure your arrows fly "dead straight" with no yawing or fishtailing. An arrow that fishtails will fly erratically and lose much of its penetration power.

Q: How can I tell if my feathers are right or left wing?

A: Look at the nock end of an arrow (as though it is about to be shot), and rotate it so that one fletching is on top of the shaft. If the "catch lip" is to the left of the web, it is a right wing feather. If the catch lip is to the right of the web, it is a left wing feather (see diagram).

Q: I'm right-handed. Should I use right- or left-wing feathers?

A: You can shoot either wing successfully. An arrow does not rotate noticeably until it's well clear of the bow.

Left-wing feathers should be used to rotate the arrow counter clockwise. Right-wing feathers should be used to rotate the arrow clockwise (as viewed by the shooter).

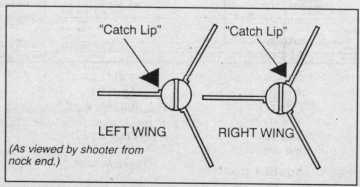

"Catch Lip"   "Catch Lip"

LEFT WING   RIGHT WING

(As viewed by shooter from nock end.)

FEATHER SPLICING

Cut quill only here ⟶

Cut quill only here ⟶

Butt quills together in clamp and fletch

(Smooth webs together after glue has set and the clamp has been removed.)

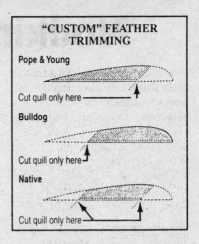

"CUSTOM" FEATHER TRIMMING

Pope & Young

Cut quill only here ⟶

Bulldog

Cut quill only here ⟶

Native

Cut quill only here ⟶

Q: Should I use straight, offset or helical fletching clamps?

A: Most hunters prefer offset or helical fletching on their arrows.

Offset and helical fletching causes arrows to rotate in flight just like the rifling in a gun barrel causes a bullet to rotate. This is important to proper arrow flight because the rotation stabilizes the arrow.

Helical fletching offers more stability than a simple offset and is often a hunter's first choice for arrows tipped with broadheads.

Q: How much fletching offset should I use?

A: If the forward end of a 5-inch feather is offset $\frac{1}{16}$ inch from its rear, this equals about ¾ of one degree. This works well for most offset or helical fletched arrows.

Q: How should I prepare the shaft for feather fletching?

A: Begin by wiping the fletching area of the shaft with alcohol, then lightly scuff the area with 600-grit sandpaper or fine steel wool. Wipe the shaft with alcohol a second time and then wait a few minutes before fletching.

Q: How can I waterproof my feathers?

A: Several powders are on the market that do excellent jobs of waterproofing feathers. These powders add virtually no weight to an arrow, and do not stiffen the feather web.

If you are caught in the rain without any waterproofing powder, cover your feathers with a small plastic bag until you are ready to shoot.

—Contributed by Trueflight Mfg., Box 1000, Dept. DDH, Manitowish Waters, WI 54545.

Nocking Tips

Serious bow-hunters know little things — like arrow nocks — make the difference between success and failure. Though often overlooked, nocks play a major role in arrow accuracy.

This guide to Bohning nocks will help you choose the right style of nocks for your arrows.

 Signature Nock: A tuneable insert nock made of a high-impact plastic material. It provides correct nock/arrow alignment in a streamlined design. The nock throat is designed to help the arrow remain on the bowstring during draw or let down. This press-fit nock requires no adhesive. An installation tool is available for precise nock alignment.

Throat diameter is .111 inch.

 "T" Nock: An all-purpose nock that incorporates a tighter fit and a slightly deeper throat. Safety nodes are built into the inside rear of the nock throat to keep the arrow on the bowstring during let down. Available sizes $^{11}\!/_{32}$T, 8.5mmT ($^{21}\!/_{64}$ inch), $^{5}\!/_{16}$T, $^{9}\!/_{32}$T, and $^{1}\!/_{4}$T.

Throat diameter is .115 inch.

 Legend II Nock: Designed for shooters who use short compounds and/or releases.

Available sizes $^{11}\!/_{32}$ inch, $^{5}\!/_{16}$ inch, $^{9}\!/_{32}$ inch, and $^{1}\!/_{4}$ inch.

Throat diameter is .115 inch.

 Classic Nock: A soft-snap speed nock that features quiet operation and fast release. Available sizes: $^{11}\!/_{32}$ inch, 8.5mm ($^{21}\!/_{64}$ inch), $^{5}\!/_{16}$ inch, $^{9}\!/_{32}$ inch, and $^{1}\!/_{4}$ inch.

Throat diameter is .118 inch.

 Apex CA Nock: A lightweight nock designed for the radical bowstring angles of short compound bows and carbon arrows. Apex-CA Nocks are available for AFC, Beman, Windsport, and Easton PC shafts.

Throat diameter is .118 inch.

Note: Apex nocks should be glued on carbon shafts.

— *Contributed by The Bohning Company, 6361 N. Seven Mile Road, Dept. DDH, Lake City, MI 49651.*

Nock Size Chart

Nock Size	Fits Shaft Sizes
¼ inch	**X7:** 1600, 1700, 1800 and 1900; **XX775:** 1600, 1700, 1800; **Eagle:** 1500, 1600, 1700; **AFC Exacta:** 1580 through 2540; **AFC Stealth:** 1800 through 2540; **AFC Max-5:** 1580 through 2540; **Deman Diva:** "S" 19, 20, 21, 22.
9⁄32 inch	**X7:** 2000 sizes; **XX75:** 1900, 2000; **Gamegetter:** 1800, 1900; **Eagle:** 1800, 1900; **Beman Hunter:** 30/50 through 80/100.
5⁄16 inch	**X7:** 2100; **XX75:** 2100 and 2200; **Gamegetter:** 2000; **Bear Magnum:** 8.4/2114, 8.5/2117, 8.6, 8.7; **Eagle:** 21.
8.5 Nocks	**XX75:** 2100, 2200, 2300; **Gamegetter:** 2100, 2200, 2300; **Bear Magnum:** 8.4/2114, 8.5/2117, 8.6, 8.7; **Eagle:** 21.
11⁄32 inch	**XX75:** 2300, 2400, 2500; **Gamegetter:** 2400.

Editor's note: *Keep in mind that several sizes of nocks might fit the same shaft size. This chart includes the most common nock sizes.*

Bohning Apex CA Nock Selection Guide

Nock Size	Easton Shafts	Beman Shafts	AFC Shafts	Windsport Shafts
1-L	—	—	2540	254
2-L	—	16⁄64	—	—
3-L	6.3mm	—	—	—
4-L	6.1mm	—	2400	240
5-M	5.9mm	—	—	—
6-M	—	15⁄64	—	—
7-M	—	—	2300	230
8-M	5.7mm	—	—	—
9-M	—	—	2200	220
10-M	5.5mm	14⁄64	—	—
11-S	5.4mm	—	2100	210
12-S	—	—	1960	196
13-S	—	13⁄64	—	—
14G	*For use with shafts with inside diameter of .266 inch.*			

Bow-Tuning Tips

Paper tuning is a helpful method that helps determine problems with bows and arrows. To paper-test your arrows, place a sheet of paper in a frame, and position the frame vertically in front of a backstop. Next, stand about four feet away from the frame and shoot two or three arrows through different areas of the paper.

The paper tears can be examined to determine incorrect arrow flight. Before paper tuning, make sure you are using the correct arrows for your bow. Using an arrow shaft that is too stiff or too weak might prevent paper tuning from being effective. Refer to the arrow charts in this book, or visit an archery shop for information on shaft sizes.

The best arrow performance coincides with a tear that shows the fletching hitting ¼ inch to ¾ inch higher than the point between 11 and 1 o'clock. Start with the nocking point set ¹⁄₁₆ inch above the top of an arrow that is squared to the bowstring. It's also important that the arrow is set to insure the fletching does not make contact.

The following instructions are for a right-handed archer. Left-handed archers should use the reverse solutions. High and low tear solutions are identical for right- and left-handed archers.

1. Left Tear

(This indicates a weak-spined arrow)

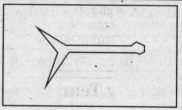

Solutions

a) Decrease the draw weight. Back out both limb bolts a quarter turn at a time. Adjust limbs equally to avoid changing the tiller and nock point. To avoid injury and bow damage, be careful not to back the limb bolts out too far.

b) Decrease the point weight. A lighter point will have some effect on increasing shaft stiffness. Too light of a point, however, might result in unstable arrow flight.

c) If these solutions don't reduce the length of the tear, change to a stiffer shaft.

d) Small tears can sometimes be improved by moving the arrow rest away from the riser or by increasing the tension on the cushion plunger or "berger button" if one is used.

2. Right Tear

(Indicates an arrow that is too stiff)

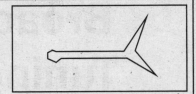

Solutions

a) Increase the draw weight. Tighten both limb bolts a quarter turn at a time. Adjust both limbs equally to avoid changing the tiller and nock point.

b) Increase the point weight. A heavier point will have some effect on decreasing shaft stiffness. However, arrow speed might be reduced.

c) If these solutions don't reduce the length of the tear, change to a weaker shaft.

d) Small tears can sometimes be improved by moving the arrow rest away from the riser or by increasing the tension on the cushion plunger or "berger button" if one is used.

3. High Tear

Solutions

a) Move the nocking point down in small increments.
b) If using a launcher or shoot-through rest, move the arrow support arm up. Increasing spring tension can also help.

c) Check for fletching interference and adjust rest position as needed.

4. Low Tear

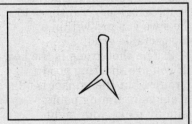

Solutions

a) Move the nocking point up in small increments.
b) If using a launcher or shoot-through rest, move the arrow support arm down. Increasing spring tension can also help.
c) Check for fletching interference and adjust rest position as needed.

— Contributed by New Archery Products, 7500 Industrial Drive, Dept. DDH, Forest Park, IL 60130

Broadhead Tuning Tips

Broadheads should be checked for flight after shafts have been paper tuned. It's not uncommon for the impact point of a broadhead to be different than a field point. Follow these steps to tune your broadheads:

1. Set up a broadhead target 20 to 30 yards away. Using the same arrow (with field point) that you used for paper tuning, shoot at the target. This will give you a reference point. If the shot is off, make the necessary adjustments to your sights.

2. Remove the field point and install a broadhead to the shaft. Use the same aiming point, and shoot again. If the broadhead hits close to where the field point did, shoot the same arrow several times to be sure you are within a respectable group size.

3. The shot group is the key. If you are shooting good groups, but the impact is off from your aiming point, simply make your sight adjustments.

Solutions to Problems

Small adjustments often help correct problems if your broadheads don't group well after tuning.

The following tips will only work if your arrows are properly spined or slightly over-spined. If your arrows are underspined, broadheads become extremely difficult, if not impossible, to tune.

1. Move the nock down if the broadhead hits below the field point.

2. Move the nock up if the broadhead hits above the field point.

3. Move the rest right or soften the cushion button spring tension if the broadhead hits left of the field point.

4. Move the rest left or stiffen the cushion button spring tension if the broadhead hits right of the field point.

If you experience problems, ask your local archery pro shop to check:

✓ Shaft spine/tip weight
✓ Tiller
✓ Center shot
✓ Wheel timing
✓ Shaft straightness and broadhead alignment/wobble.

— Contributed by New Archery Products, 7500 Industrial Drive, Dept. DDH, Forest Park, IL 60130

How to Make Your Rifle More Accurate

The process of "sighting in" or "zeroing" consists of making the rifle and its sight agree on where the bullets strike. With proper procedures, sighting in a rifle is neither mysterious nor difficult.

To sight in your rifle properly, follow these steps:

✓ The rifle and its sight should be in good condition and properly assembled. Check action screws and scope mounts. Bore sighting, or the use of a collimator, is not a substitute for actually sighting in by shooting on a range.

✓ Select ammunition for its intended purpose. Be sure to start with enough ammunition to complete the sighting-in process.

✓ Pick a safe area to shoot with an adequate backstop to stop your bullets. Wear shooting glasses and hearing protection.

✓ Shoot from a solid rest, such as a bench rest and sand bags. Shoot at close range to get "on paper," but verify the final zero at expected hunting ranges.

✓ From the solid rest, carefully squeeze off three aimed shots. The center of this group of bullet holes is the rifle's point of impact. Adjusting the sight moves this point of impact to your desired zero. Move open rear sights in the same direction you want the group to move. Adjust scopes following directions on the dials. Continue this process until the group is where you want it.

Do not adjust sights on the basis of single shots. An odd shot can lead to sight adjustment errors and ultimately wastes ammunition.

✓ Different brands and bullet weights may change the point of impact and necessitate re-sighting. If your rifle gets bumped or dropped, be sure to reverify your zero so you can bag your game with one shot.

— *Contributed by Federal Cartridge Co., 900 Ehlen Drive, Dept. DDH, Anoka, MN 55303.*

Maximum Range		
Load	**Velocity**	**Distance**
12 gauge 1 oz. slug	1,550 feet per second	1,260 feet / 420 yards
22 long rifle	1,255 feet per second	4,870 feet / 1 mile
.30-30 Winchester 150-grain	2,370 feet per second	9,030 feet / 1.7 miles
.270 Winchester 130-grain	3,050 feet per second	14,380 feet / 2.7 miles
7mm Remington 165-grain	2,940 feet per second	19,790 feet / 3.8 miles

TRAJECTORY

LINE OF SIGHT ------
BULLET PATH —————

| 0 YARDS | 50 YARDS | 100 YARDS +2.1" | 200 YARDS 0 | 250 YARDS -3.7" |

Bullet Trajectory Determined by Velocity, Bullet Design

Trajectory is the arc of the bullet from the firearm's muzzle.

Bullets appear to rise because the barrel is angled up. The bullet's path crosses the line of sight twice — going up near the muzzle and going down through the down-range zero.

The mid-range trajectory is the bullet's highest point above the line of sight. It usually occurs half way between the muzzle and the zero range.

Velocity and bullet design determine trajectory. Low-velocity cartridges with round-nosed bullets, if sighted for long ranges, will have a very high mid-range trajectory — possibly high enough to cause a miss on close-range targets.

For big game hunting, a trajectory height of 3 to 4 inches is considered acceptable. For small game, about 2 inches is maximum. Consult a ballistic table for velocity, trajectory and appropriate down-range zero for your specific cartridge/bullet.

— Contributed by Federal Cartridge Co., 900 Ehlen Drive, Dept. DDH, Anoka, MN 55303.

How to Mount a Riflescope

Although the process takes time and requires attention to details, mounting a riflescope properly can mean the difference between success and failure in the deer woods.

Use this guide when mounting a scope to your favorite deer rifle.

Tools required

✓ Hex wrench set (English)
✓ Gunsmith screwdrivers
✓ Scope-mounting adhesive
✓ Gun oil
✓ Long cotton swabs
✓ Soft cotton cloth
✓ Acetone, ether, or other cleaning/degreasing agent
✓ Riflescope bore-sighting device and arbors
✓ Scope alignment rods
✓ Shims
✓ Rubber hammer
✓ Rifle vise
✓ Short steel ruler
✓ Lapping kit
✓ Reticle leveler

Instructions

1. Place gun's safety in "on" position. Unload firearm and remove bolt, cylinder, clip, etc. Make sure the chamber is empty.

2. Remove old bases or rings. If the gun is new, you might have to remove the factory screws from the receiver. These screws protect the scope's mounting holes until needed.

3. Degrease the base screws and the receiver's mounting holes.

4. Temporarily install the bases. Shimming might be required under part of the base if the top of the receiver is not parallel to the axis of the bore. Mismatches might require a different set of bases and/or the help of a gunsmith.

5. Install the scope alignment rods into the rings and place on the firearm. If there is a misalignment, some shimming might be required. Very small adjustments can be made later by tapping the base with a rubber hammer.

6. Remove the rings when the rods indicate the system is aligned. Apply a light coating of gun oil to the underside of the base and to the top of the receiver.

Also install the base and screws, using adhesive. Be sure the adhesive does not drip into the action. Use cotton swabs to check clean spillage.

7. Re-install the rings with the alignment rods. Again, if there is a small alignment problem, tapping with the rubber hammer might correct it. If there's gross misalign-

ment, shimming might be required.

8. Once you are satisfied the rings and the base are aligned, install the riflescope in the rings. Degrease the inner surface of the rings and the area of contact on the scope.

Inspect the fit of the rings to the riflescope. Some inexpensive rings are not perfectly round, making for a poor fit between the ring and the scope's body tube.

If you're using Weaver-style rings, install them loosely on the scope, then attach them to the base. For Redfield-style rings, attach the twist-lock front ring by using a metal or wooden dowel that's 1 inch in diameter.

Do not use the riflescope to twist the ring in place.

When the scope is mounted on the gun, make sure there is at least ⅛ inch clearance between the bell of the scope and the gun. Also, make sure the action isn't touching the scope during cycling or power change.

9. Set up the bore-sighting system on the firearm. Adjust the ring screws so the scope can rotate but not wobble. Be careful not to scratch the scope body. Adjust the distance the scope is from the eye to prevent injury during recoil — about 3 inches.

10. Turn the scope to high power and adjust the windage and elevation controls so the image of the bore-sighting grid and the scope reticle do not

move with each other as the scope is rotated. This step can also be performed by placing the scope in a cardboard V-block and sighting it in at a distant object.

11. Gently rotate the scope in the rings so the horizontal portion of the reticle is level when the gun is held in the shooting position. To aid this adjustment, use a bubble level or reticle leveler. Next, tighten all rings and base screws. Use adhesive on the screws, and let set over night.

12. Adjust the windage and elevation controls to place the center of the reticle on the center of the bore-sighting grid. Shimming might be required to bring it in alignment with the bore. If so, consider using a scope-mount system with windage control.

13. With everything secure, the riflescope is now ready for the range. The shooter should pick a common distance — 25, 50 or 100 yards — and adjust accordingly. Remember, ammunition, outside temperature, temperature of the barrel, and cleanliness of the barrel all affect a gun's accuracy.

14. Always make sure the scope's rings and the bases are tight. This will prevent movement during recoil.

— Contributed by Bushnell Sport Optics, 9200 Cody St., Dept. DDH, Shawnee Mission, KS 66214.

Average Normal Temperatures and Precipitation

City	September T	P	October T	P	November T	P	December T	P
Albany, N.Y.	61	3.0	50	2.8	40	3.2	27	2.9
Asheville, N.C.	66	3.9	56	3.6	48	3.6	40	3.5
Atlanta, Ga.	73	3.4	62	3.1	53	3.9	45	4.3
Birmingham, Ala.	73	3.9	63	2.8	53	4.3	45	5.1
Bismarck, N.D.	57	1.5	46	0.9	29	0.5	14	0.5
Caribou, Maine	54	3.5	43	3.1	31	3.6	15	3.2
Columbus, Ohio	66	3.0	54	2.2	43	3.2	32	2.9
Dallas, Texas	77	3.4	67	3.5	56	2.3	47	1.8
Denver, Colo.	62	1.2	51	1.0	39	0.9	31	0.6
Des Moines, Iowa	65	3.5	54	2.6	39	1.8	24	1.3
Duluth, Minn.	54	3.8	44	2.5	28	1.8	13	1.2
Fairbanks, Alaska	46	1.0	25	0.9	3	0.8	-7	0.9
Galveston Texas	80	5.9	73	2.8	64	3.4	56	3.5
Grand Junct., Colo.	67	0.7	55	0.9	40	0.6	28	0.6
Helena, Mont.	55	1.2	45	0.6	32	0.5	21	0.6
Indianapolis, Ind.	67	2.9	55	2.6	43	3.2	31	3.3
Jackson, Miss.	76	3.6	65	3.3	56	4.8	48	5.9
Juneau, Alaska	49	6.4	42	7.7	33	5.2	27	4.7
Kansas City, Mo.	68	4.9	57	3.3	43	1.9	30	1.6
Lexington, Ky.	68	3.2	57	2.6	46	3.4	36	4.0
Little Rock, Ark.	74	7.4	63	6.3	52	5.2	43	4.3
Louisville, Ky.	70	3.2	58	2.7	47	3.7	37	3.6
Marquette, Mich.	54	4.1	44	3.6	30	2.9	17	2.6
Memphis, Tenn.	74	3.5	63	3.0	53	5.1	44	5.7
Milwaukee, Wis.	62	3.4	50	2.4	38	2.5	24	2.3
Minneapolis, Minn.	61	2.7	49	2.2	33	1.6	18	1.1
New Orleans, La.	78	5.5	69	3.1	61	4.4	55	5.8
Norfolk, Va.	72	3.9	61	3.2	53	2.9	44	3.2
Okla. City, Ok.	73	3.4	62	2.7	49	1.5	40	1.2
Omaha, Nebr.	65	3.7	53	2.3	39	1.5	25	1.0
Philadelphia, Pa.	68	3.4	56	2.6	46	3.3	35	3.4
Phoenix, Ariz.	86	0.9	75	0.7	62	0.7	54	1.0
Portland, Maine	59	3.1	49	3.9	39	5.2	27	4.6
Portland, Ore.	63	1.8	55	2.7	46	5.3	40	6.1
Rapid City, S.D.	60	1.2	49	1.1	35	0.6	24	0.5
Salt Lk. City, Utah	65	1.3	53	1.4	41	1.3	30	1.4
San Antonio, Texas	79	3.4	70	3.2	60	2.6	52	1.5
Seattle, Wash.	61	1.9	54	3.3	46	5.7	42	6.0
Syracuse, N.Y.	62	3.8	51	3.2	41	3.7	28	3.2

T = Temperature   **P = Precipitation**

Deer and the Wind

Generally speaking, deer activity decreases as wind speed increases. Calm and light winds produce more deer sightings while moderate and gusty winds reduce them. The dividing line seems to be somewhere around 15 mph.

However, some researchers and hunters have documented an increase in buck activity during calm winds.

Deer tend to group up and become excitable in high winds. During cold months, high winds cause deer to seek shelter on the lee slopes of hills and in dense coniferous woodlands. Conifer stands reduce wind speed by up to 50 to 75 percent.

Research proves that even though deer will move in all directions in relation to the wind, they'll move directly into the wind whenever possible. Deer trails closely match the prevailing wind direction and traditional wind changes. Wind fits two basic patterns:

Pattern A — Occurs during stable, high-pressure weather systems with clear or partly cloudy skies. This pattern brings little or no wind at sunrise and sunset, and maximum wind speeds in mid to late afternoon.

Pattern B — Occurs during changing weather conditions. This pattern brings constant wind speeds throughout the day with frequent gusts reflecting atmospheric turbulence.

Thermal winds — Thermal currents move uphill as the air temperature increases in the morning. Thermals move downhill as air cools toward evening.

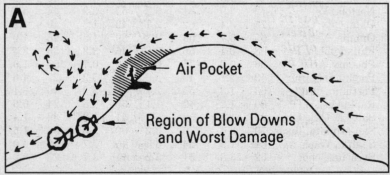

A

Air Pocket

Region of Blow Downs
and Worst Damage

Gale winds force deer to pick sheltered bedding sites in the air pockets on the lee side of ridges about one-third of the way down from the crest.

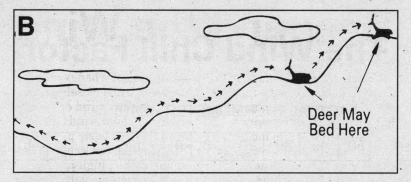

B

Deer May
Bed Here

Whitetails prefer to bed on slightly higher ground when the terrain permits. Consequently, when they move down-slope toward their feeding area in the afternoon, they experience ideal wind coverage on their trails with the thermal air currents still moving upslope.

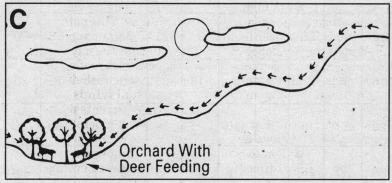

C

Orchard With
Deer Feeding

When returning to their bedding areas in the morning, whitetails take advantage of ideal wind coverage with the downwind thermal air currents still holding from the higher elevations to the lower ground.

Tips for Judging Wind Speeds

✓ Calm, less than 1 mph: Smoke rises vertically, leaves on tree remain motionless.

✓ 1 to 3 mph: Smoke drifts, but wind vanes stay motionless.

✓ 7 to 10 mph: Flags extend and leaves are in constant motion.

✓ 11 to 16 mph: Small branches move, dust blows and loose paper flies.

✓ 17 to 21 mph: Noticeable motion in tall tree tops; small trees sway.

✓ 22 to 27 mph: Large branches in motion, whistling in wire.

The Wind Chill Factor

ACTUAL THERMOMETER READING (F°)

50	40	30	20	10	0	-10	-20	-30	-40

EQUIVALENT TEMPERATURE (F°)

Calm	50	40	30	20	10	0	-10	-20	-30	-40
5	48	37	27	16	6	-5	-15	-26	-36	-47
10	40	28	16	4	-9	-21	-33	-46	-58	-70
15	36	22	9	-5	-18	-36	-45	-58	-72	-85
20	32	18	4	-10	-25	-39	-53	-67	-82	-96
25	30	16	0	-15	-29	-44	-59	-74	-88	-104
30	28	13	-2	-18	-33	-44	-63	-79	-94	-109
35	27	11	-4	-20	-35	-49	-67	-82	-98	-113
40	26	10	-6	-21	-37	-53	-69	-85	-100	-116

Over 40 MPH (little added effect)	Little Danger (for properly clothed)	Increasing Danger	Great Danger

White-Tailed Deer Harvest Records

The following harvest figures were obtained from Department of Wildlife officials.

Though the numbers were updated as much as possible before press time, harvest totals for the 1995 season were not available for some states.

Some states in the West combine mule deer and whitetails in their harvest statistics. In many of these cases we used the best estimates of deer biologists to determine what percentage of the kill were whitetails.

In addition, be aware that all states do not use the same procedures to calculate deer harvest figures. Still, the information listed here shows harvest trends in each state.

Alabama

Year	Firearm	Bow	Total	Year	Firearm	Bow	Total
1963-64			31,123	1979-80			140,685
1964-65			59,230	1980-81			130,532
1965-66			37,819	1981-82			202,449
1966-67			47,842	1982-83			141,281
1967-68			68,406	1983-84			192,231
1968-69			63,674	1984-85			237,378
1969-70			74,239	1985-86			280,436
1970-71			63,502	1986-87	288,487	17,653	306,140
1971-72			80,184	1987-88	309,517	15,683	325,200
1972-73			82,555	1988-89	257,734	18,854	276,588
1973-74			121,953	1990-91	263,100	31,300	294,400
1974-75			120,727	1991-92	269,500	25,500	295,000
1975-76			125,625	1992-93	261,500	31,600	293,100
1976-77			144,155	1993-94	305,300	45,200	350,500
1977-78			147,113	1994-95	290,600	40,400	331,000
1978-79			152,733				

Arizona

Year	Firearm	Bow	Total	Year	Firearm	Bow	Total
1958	5,096		5,096	1977	2,319		2,319
1959	5,421		5,421	1978	2,287		2,287
1960	4,982		4,982	1979	3,264		3,264
1961	4,734		4,734	1980	3,523		3,523
1962	4,194		4,194	1981	3,504		3,504
1963	4,343		4,343	1982	4,002	60	4,062
1964	4,339		4,339	1983	4,221	71	4,292
1965	3,612		3,612	1984	7,116	65	7,181
1966	2,993		2,993	1985	6,902	138	7,040
1967	2,662		2,662	1986	5,934	94	6,028
1968	2,927		2,927	1987	4,895	115	5,010
1969	2,202		2,202	1988	4,600	108	4,708
1970	2,232		2,232	1989	4,387	189	4,576
1971	1,535		1,535	1990	4,449	100	4,549
1972	1,673		1,673	1991	5,375	129	5,504
1973	2,097		2,097	1992	5,737	95	5,832
1974	3,248		3,248	1993	5,556	152	5,772
1975	2,870		2,870	1994	5,363	1,315	6,678
1976	2,662		2,662				

Arkansas

Year	Firearm	Bow	Total	Year	Firearm	Bow	Total
1938	203		203	1967	21,751		21,751
1939	540		540	1968	20,063		20,063
1940	408		408	1969	24,018	1,678	25,696
1941	433		433	1970	24,784	1,233	26,017
1942	1,000		1,000	1971	23,375	1,345	24,720
1943	1,723		1,723	1972	31,415	672	32,087
1944	1,606		1,606	1973	32,292	1,502	33,794
1945	1,687		1,687	1974	32,168	1,595	33,763
1946	1,661		1,661	1975	32,210	1,112	33,322
1947	2,016		2,016	1976	27,249	540	27,789
1948	2,779		2,779	1977	27,862	1,247	29,109
1949	3,075		3,075	1978	41,018	2,434	43,452
1950	4,122		4,122	1979	32,841	3,233	36,074
1951	4,600		4,600	1980	41,693	3,509	45,202
1952	6,090		6,090	1981	41,567	3,024	44,591
1953	6,245		6,245	1982	35,051	7,822	42,873
1954	7,343		7,343	1983	42,709	17,539	60,248
1955	6,856		6,856	1984	53,679	12,360	66,039
1956	8,249		8,249	1985	48,027	12,049	60,076
1957	9,438		9,438	1986	67,941	11,939	79,880
1958	9,993		9,993	1987	89,422	16,970	106,392
1959	12,280		12,280	1988	94,193	16,014	110,207
1960	15,000		15,000	1989	97,031	16,048	113,079
1961	19,359		19,359	1990	70,498	20,412	90,910
1962	27,772		27,772	1991			110,896
1963	25,148		25,148	1992			110,401
1964	16,637		16,637	1993	106,119	15,944	122,063
1965	17,138		17,138	1994	104,061	16,433	120,494
1966	20,028		20,028	*Bow totals include crossbow kills.			

Colorado

Colorado does not distinguish between white-tailed deer and mule deer in its harvest statistics. Biologists there estimate that approximately 1,000 whitetails have been taken during each of the past five years. Most of these animals come from the river bottoms of the eastern plains of Colorado.

Connecticut

Year	Firearm	Bow	Total	Year	Firearm	Bow	Total
1975	475	75	550	1986	4,575	819	5,394
1976	530	100	630	1987	5,618	854	6,472
1977	780	125	905	1988	6,843	799	7,642
1978	805	125	930	1989	7,837	926	8,763
1979	870	140	1,010	1990			9,896
1980	2,189	376	2,565	1991			11,311
1981	2,463	393	2,856	1992			12,486
1982	2,233	391	2,624	1993			10,360
1983	3,152	639	3,791	1994			10,438
1984	3,742	596	4,338	1995	10,140	2,606	12,746
1985	3,817	722	4,539				

Delaware

Year	Firearm	Bow	Total	Year	Firearm	Bow	Total
1976-77	1,475	19	1,494	1986-87	2,772	78	2,850
1977-78	1,630	22	1,652	1987-88	3,420	121	3,541
1978-79	1,679	20	1,699	1988-89	3,844	154	3,998
1979-80	1,783	20	1,803	1989-90	4,292	212	4,504
1980-81	1,737	17	1,754	1990-91	4,814	252	5,066
1981-82	2,080	31	2,111	1991-92	4,970	362	5,332
1982-83	2,046	48	2,094	1992-93	6,721	524	7,245
1983-84	2,210	21	2,231	1993-94	6,917	548	7,465
1984-85	2,473	41	2,514	1994-95	7,151	673	7,824
1985-86	2,383	58	2,439				

Florida

Year	Firearm	Bow	Total	Year	Firearm	Bow	Total
1971			48,900	1983			77,146
1972			58,500	1984			73,895
1973			57,122	1985			80,947
1974			54,102	1986			89,212
1975			54,380	1987			105,917
1976			60,805	1988			107,240
1977			85,744	1989			85,753
1978			NA	1990			79,170
1979			54,765	1991			81,255
1980			72,039	1992			81,942
1981			66,489	1993			104,178
1982			64,557	1994			84,408

Georgia

Year	Firearm	Bow	Total	Year	Firearm	Bow	Total
1980-81			135,500	1987-88			280,536
1981-82			134,000	1988-89			300,624
1982-83			144,000	1989-90			293,167
1983-84			164,000	1990-91			351,652
1984-85			177,000	1991-92	265,352	15,708	281,060
1985-86			189,600	1992-93	284,412	21,841	306,253
1986-87			226,000	1993-94	309,522	37,331	346,853

Idaho

Year	Firearm	Bow	Total	Year	Firearm	Bow	Total
1980			45,988	1991	16,721	364	17,085
1981			50,580	1992			23,633
1982			48,670	1993	23,251	303	23,554
1983			50,600	1994	29,760	595	30,355
1984			42,600				
1985			48,950				
1986			59,800				
1987			66,400				
1988			82,200				
1989			95,200				
1990			72,100				

NOTE — The figures before 1991 include white-tailed deer and mule deer because Idaho has not traditionally distinguished between the two in its harvest totals.

Illinois

Year	Firearm	Bow	Total	Year	Firearm	Bow	Total
1957	1,709		1,709	1976	15,308	1,600	16,908
1958	2,493		2,493	1977	16,231	2,810	19,041
1959	2,604		2,604	1979	20,058	1,074	21,132
1960	2,438		2,438	1980	20,825	1,463	22,288
1961	4,313		4,313	1981	20,800	1,766	22,566
1962	6,289		6,289	1982	22,657	2,205	24,862
1963	6,785		6,785	1983	26,112	2,554	28,666
1964	9,975		9,975	1984	29,212	3,023	32,235
1965	7,651		7,651	1985	31,769	3,746	35,515
1966	7,357		7,357	1986	36,056	4,357	40,413
1967	6,588		6,588	1987	42,932	6,646	49,578
1968	8,202		8,202	1988	47,786	7,820	55,606
1969	8,345		8,345	1989	56,143	10,000	66,143
1970	8,889	590	9,479	1990			81,000
1971	10,359	566	10,925	1991	83,191	18,099	101,290
1972	10,100	552	10,652	1992	84,537	19,564	104,101
1973	12,902	960	13,862	1993	92,276	23,215	115,491
1974	12,853	1,425	14,278	1994	97,723	25,607	123,330
1975	15,614	1,608	17,222	1995	105,106	NA	NA

Indiana

Year	Firearm	Bow	Total	Year	Firearm	Bow	Total
1951			1,590	1974			9,461
1952			1,112	1975			8,758
1953			83	1976			11,344
1954			68	1977			12,476
1955			149	1978			9,896
1956			198	1979			13,718
1957			NA	1980			19,780
1958			592	1981	12,600	5,527	18,127
1959			800	1982	16,267	4,651	20,918
1960			1,523	1983	21,244	3,988	25,232
1961			2,293	1984	21,944	5,640	27,584
1962			3,212	1985	25,768	6,371	32,139
1963			4,634	1986	33,837	9,621	43,458
1964			6,001	1987	38,937	12,841	51,778
1965			4,155	1988	46567	13,667	60,234
1966			5,775	1989	62,901	16,417	79,318
1967			6,560	1990	70,928	17,775	88,703
1968			6,659	1991	77,102	21,581	98,683
1969			7,323	1992	73,396	21,918	95,314
1970			5,175	1993	77,226	23,988	101,214
1971			5,099	1994	89,037	23,379	112,416
1972			NA	1995	92,496	25,233	117,729
1973			8,244				

Did You Know?

A white-tailed deer, if it lives for just 15 seconds after being shot through the heart, could travel more than 220 yards. Research indicates wounded white-tails can run as fast as 30 mph.

Iowa

Year	Firearm	Bow	Total	Year	Firearm	Bow	Total
1953	4,007	1	4,008	1974	15,817	2,173	17,990
1954	2,413	10	2,423	1975	18,948	2,219	21,167
1955	3,006	58	3,064	1976	14,257	2,350	16,607
1956	2,561	117	2,678	1977	12,788	2,400	15,188
1957	2,667	138	2,805	1978	15,168	2,957	18,125
1958	2,729	162	2,891	1979	16,149	3,305	19,454
1959	2,476	255	2,731	1980	18,857	3,803	22,660
1960	3,992	277	4,269	1981	21,578	4,368	25,946
1961	4,997	367	5,364	1982	21,741	4,720	26,461
1962	5,299	404	5,703	1983	30,375	5,244	35,619
1963	6,612	538	7,151	1984	33,756	5,599	39,355
1964	9,024	670	9,694	1985	38,414	5,805	44,219
1965	7,910	710	8,620	1986	52,807	9,895	62,702
1966	10,742	579	11,321	1987	66,036	9,722	75,758
1967	10,392	791	11,183	1988	83,184	9,897	93,756
1968	12,941	830	13,771	1989	87,300	11,857	99,712
1969	10,731	851	11,582	1990	87,856	10,146	98,002
1970	12,743	1,037	13,780	1991	74,828	8,807	83,635
1971	10,459	1,232	11,691	1992	68,227	8,814	77,684
1972	10,485	1,328	11,813	1993	67,139	9,291	76,430
1973	12,208	1,822	14,030	1994	75,191	12,040	87,231

Kansas

Year	Firearm	Bow	Total	Year	Firearm	Bow	Total
1965	1,340	164	1,504	1980	7,296	3,007	10,303
1966	2,139	376	2,515	1981	9,413	2,939	12,352
1967	1,542	434	1,976	1982	11,446	3,441	14,887
1968	1,648	614	2,262	1983	13,640	3,918	17,558
1969	1,668	583	2,251	1984	19,446	4,167	23,613
1970	2,418	793	3,211	1985	21,296	4,230	25,526
1971	2,569	578	3,147	1986	24,123	4,358	28,481
1972	2,318	664	2,982	1987	31,664	4,329	35,993
1973	3,220	892	4,112	1988	35,236	5,118	40,354
1974	4,347	1,130	5,477	1989	34,000	5,550	39,550
1975	4,352	1,136	5,488	1990	40,800	5,000	45,800
1976	3,955	1,114	5,069	1991	34,770	4,500	39,270
1977	3,766	1,174	4,940	1992	26,400	4,500	30,900
1978	4,942	1,738	6,680	1993			
1979	5,810	2,259	8,069	1994			

Kentucky

Year	Firearm	Bow	Total	Year	Firearm	Bow	Total
1976	3,476		3,476	1986	34,657	4,863	39,520
1977	5,682		5,682	1987	54,372	6,000	60,372
1978	6,012	421	6,433	1988	57,553	6,707	64,260
1979	7,442	620	8,062	1989	62,667	7,482	70,149
1980	7,988	1,714	9,702	1990	66,151	7,767	73,918
1981	13,134	1,849	14,983	1991	84,918	8,016	92,934
1982	15,804	2,165	17,969	1992	73,664	8,274	81,938
1983	16,027	2,705	18,732	1993	64,598	8,680	73,278
1984	20,344	2,668	23,012	1994	93,444	12,672	106,116
1985	26,024	4,051	30,075				

Louisiana

Year	Firearm	Bow	Total	Year	Firearm	Bow	Total
1960-61	16,500		16,500	1978-79	85,000		85,000
1961-62	NA		NA	1979-80	90,000	5,000	95,000
1962-63	NA		NA	1980-81	105,500	5,000	110,500
1963-64	24,000		24,000	1981-82	115,000	5,500	120,500
1964-65	23,000		23,000	1982-83	132,000	5,500	137,500
1965-66	26,000		26,000	1983-84	131,000	6,000	137,000
1966-67	32,500		32,500	1984-85	128,000	6,500	134,500
1967-68	36,000		36,000	1985-86	139,000	7,500	146,500
1968-69	50,000		50,000	1986-87	149,000	8,750	157,750
1969-70	53,000		53,000	1987-88	164,000	9,500	173,500
1970-71	53,500		53,500	1988-89	161,000	10,500	171,500
1971-72	61,000		61,000	1989-90	162,000	11,000	173,000
1972-73	65,000		65,000	1990-91	176,200	18,200	194,300
1973-74	74,500		74,500	1991-92	186,400	17,700	204,100
1974-75	82,000		82,000	1992-93	192,300	22,600	214,900
1975-76	77,000		77,000	1993-94	193,000	20,100	213,100
1976-77	84,500		84,500	1994-95	193,700	24,000	217,700
1977-78	82,500		82,500				

Maine

Year	Firearm	Bow	Total	Year	Firearm	Bow	Total
1919	5,784		5,784	1957	40,125	17	40,142
1920	5,829		5,829	1958	39,375	18	39,393
1921	8,861		8,861	1959	41,720	15	41,735
1922	7,628		7,628	1960	37,752	22	37,774
1925	8,379		8,379	1961	32,740	7	32,747
1927	8,112		8,112	1962	38,795	12	38,807
1928	9,051		9,051	1963	29,816	23	29,839
1929	11,708		11,708	1964	35,286	19	35,305
1930	13,098		13,098	1965	37,266	16	37,282
1931	14,694		14,694	1966	32,142	18	32,160
1932	15,465		15,465	1967	34,693	14	34,707
1933	18,935		18,935	1968	41,064	16	41,080
1934	13,284		13,284	1969	30,388	21	30,409
1935	19,726		19,726	1970	31,738	12	31,750
1936	19,134		19,134	1971	18,873	30	18,903
1937	19,197		19,197	1972	28,664	34	28,698
1938	19,363		19,363	1973	24,681	39	24,720
1939	19,187		19,187	1974	34,602	65	34,667
1940	22,201		22,201	1975	34,625	50	34,675
1941	19,881		19,881	1976	29,918	47	29,965
1942	22,591		22,591	1977	31,354	76	31,430
1943	24,408		24,408	1978	28,905	97	29,002
1944	21,708		21,708	1979	26,720	101	26,821
1945	24,904		24,904	1980	37,148	107	37,255
1946	31,728		31,728	1981	32,027	140	32,167
1947	30,349		30,349	1982	28,709	125	28,834
1948	35,364		35,364	1983	23,699	100	23,799
1949	35,051		35,051	1984	19,225	133	19,358
1950	39,216		39,216	1985	21,242	182	21,424
1951	41,730		41,730	1986	19,290	302	19,592
1952	35,171		35,171	1987	23,435	294	23,729
1953	38,609		38,609	1988	27,754	302	28,056
1954	37,379		37,379	1989	29,844	416	30,260
1955	35,591		35,591	1990	25,658	319	25,977
1956	40,290		40,290	1991	26,236	500	26,736

Maine White-tailed Deer Harvest Records, Continued

Year	Firearm	Bow	Total	Year	Firearm	Bow	Total
1992	28,126	694	28,820	1994	23,967	716	24,683
1993	26,608	682	27,402	1995			

Maryland

Year	Firearm	Bow	Total	Year	Firearm	Bow	Total
1983	16,239	2,181	18,420	1990	37,712	8,605	46,317
1984	17,324	2,501	19,825	1991	36,169	10,454	46,623
1985	17,241	2,549	19,790	1992	39,858	11,240	51,098
1986	22,411	3,404	25,815	1993	39,429	11,251	51,234
1987	24,846	4,216	29,062	1994	39,547	11,324	50,871
1988	27,625	5,983	33,608	1995	49,237	12,397	61,634
1989	38,305	7,988	46,293				

Massachusetts

Year	Firearm	Bow	Total	Year	Firearm	Bow	Total
1989	5,818	890	6,708	1993	6,514	1,387	8,345
1990	5,829	1,061	6,890	1994	7,545	1,587	9,132
1991	8,085	1,378	9,463	1995	9,442	1,901	11,343
1992	8,470	1,570	10,040				

Michigan

Year	Firearm	Bow	Total	Year	Firearm	Bow	Total
1878			21,000	1941	73,430	24	73,454
1879			80,000	1942	62,190	22	62,212
1880			70,000	1943	51,610	37	51,647
1881			80,000	1944	51,730	37	51,767
1899			12,000	1945	85,080	68	85,148
1900			12,000	1946	90,510	170	90,680
1911			12,000	1947	82,360	390	82,750
1916			8,000	1948	64,540	580	65,120
1919			20,000	1949	77,750	780	78,530
1920			25,000	1950	84,410	1,340	85,750
1921			11,520	1951	82,240	1,320	83,560
1922			11,700	1952	162,630	1,840	164,470
1923			13,270	1953	97,650	1,820	99,470
1924			15,190	1954	67,740	1,820	69,560
1925			18,120	1955	74,160	2,310	76,470
1926			20,200	1956	74,050	2,430	76,480
1927			22,810	1957	77,300	1,760	79,060
1928			24,810	1958	100,010	2,570	102,580
1929			28,710	1959	115,400	1,840	117,240
1930			32,150	1960	75,490	1,230	76,720
1931			23,500	1961	58,090	1,980	60,070
1932			20,500	1962	95,917	1,643	97,560
1933			25,500	1963	124,217	2,143	126,360
1934			27,000	1964	141,466	2,814	144,280
1935			30,000	1965	112,347	2,173	114,520
1936			42,000	1966	94,327	1,933	96,260
1937	39,760	4	39,764	1967	104,170	2,650	106,820
1938	44,390	8	44,398	1968	101,669	2,681	104,350
1939	44,770	6	44,776	1969	106,698	2,582	109,280
1940	51,380	10	51,390	1970	68,843	3,187	72,030

Michigan White-tailed Deer Harvest Records, Continued

Year	Firearm	Bow	Total	Year	Firearm	Bow	Total
1971	62,076	3,354	65,430	1986	219,260	57,960	277,220
1972	55,796	3,694	59,490	1987	265,860	72,820	338,680
1973	66,359	4,631	70,990	1988	311,770	72,020	383,790
1974	92,111	7,969	100,080	1989	355,410	97,080	452,490
1975	106,800	8,790	115,590	1990	338,890	93,800	432,690
1976	107,625	10,365	117,990	1991	318,460	115,880	434,340
1977	137,110	21,250	158,360	1992	274,650	99,990	374,640
1978	145,710	25,140	170,850	1993	232,820	98,160	330,980
1979	119,790	25,640	145,430	1994	251,420	112,490	363,910
1980	137,380	28,110	165,490				
1981	175,090	33,320	208,410				
1982	163,520	38,420	201,940				
1983	127,770	30,640	158,410				
1984	131,280	32,630	163,910				
1985	197,370	42,050	239,420				

NOTE: Firearm harvest totals prior to 1975 did not include muzzleloader harvest. Also, harvest totals since 1978 do not include deer taken with camp deer permits. In addition, prior to 1961, camp deer harvests were not separated by firearm and bow.

Minnesota

Year	Firearm	Bow	Total	Year	Firearm	Bow	Total
1918	9,000		9,000	1957	67,000	392	67,392
1919	18,300		18,300	1958	75,000	403	75,403
1920	18,600		18,600	1959	104,000	390	104,390
1921	13,600		13,600	1960	95,000	445	95,445
1922	11,200		11,200	1961	107,000	490	107,490
1923	closed			1962	96,000	519	96,519
1924	15,600		15,600	1963	113,000	713	113,713
1925	closed			1964	122,000	780	122,780
1926	28,000		28,000	1965	127,000	871	127,871
1927	closed			1966	115,000	604	115,604
1928	27,300		27,300	1967	107,000	598	107,598
1929	closed			1968	103,000	819	103,819
1930	27,800		27,800	1969	68,000	776	68,776
1931	closed			1970	50,000	453	50,453
1932	42,300		42,300	1971	closed	1,279	1,279
1933	26,200		26,200	1972	73,400	1,601	75,001
1934	39,100		39,100	1973	67,100	1,935	69,035
1935	closed			1974	65,000	2,176	67,176
1936	50,100		50,100	1975	63,600	2,265	65,865
1937	33,600		33,600	1976	36,200	1,167	37,367
1938	44,500		44,500	1977	58,100	2,609	60,709
1939	closed			1978	57,800	2,608	60,408
1940	56,000		56,000	1979	55,400	2,578	57,978
1941	closed			1980	77,100	3,641	80,741
1942	77,000		77,000	1981	108,100	5,535	113,635
1943	67,700		67,700	1982	107,000	5,566	112,566
1944	62,800		62,800	1983	NA	5,977	NA
1945	67,100		67,100	1984	132,000	6,390	138,390
1946	93,400		93,400	1985	138,000	7,575	145,575
1947	74,400		74,400	1986	129,800	7,610	137,410
1948	61,600		61,600	1987	135,000	7,535	142,535
1949	49,900		49,900	1988	138,900	8,262	147,162
1950	closed			1989	129,600	9,307	138,907
1951	72,700	43	72,743	1990	166,600	11,106	177,706
1952	57,300	34	57,334	1991	206,300	12,964	219,264
1953	61,000	66	61,066	1992	230,064	13,004	243,068
1954	56,000	182	56,182	1993	188,109	13,722	202,928
1955	79,000	214	79,214	1994	180,008	13,818	193,826
1956	69,000	325	69,325	1995	200,638	14,180	214,818

Mississippi

Year	Firearm	Bow	Total	Year	Firearm	Bow	Total
1971-72	580	39	619	1983-84	176,400	19,747	196,147
1972-73	816	53	869	1984-85	209,574	17,815	227,389
1973-74	919	57	976	1985-86	216,959	18,120	235,079
1974-75	NA	NA	NA	1986-87	237,075	19,209	256,284
1975-76	NA	NA	NA	1987-88	240,337	24,662	264,999
1976-77	2,529	975	3,504	1988-89	236,012	28,744	264,756
1977-78	NA	NA	NA	1989-90	236,012	28,744	262,386
1978-79	NA	NA	NA	1990-91	218,347	29,982	249,572
1979-80	NA	NA	NA	1991-92	243,175	33,940	277,714
1980-81	184,163	17,437	201,600	1992-93	260,093	40,886	300,980
1981-82	196,856	14,860	211,716	1993-94	229,425	32,971	262,409
1982-83	227,432	16,222	243,654	1994-95	262,342	47,345	309,687

Missouri

Year	Firearm	Bow	Total	Year	Firearm	Bow	Total
1944	583		583	1970	28,400	828	29,228
1945	882		882	1971	31,722	962	32,684
1946	743		743	1972	30,084	1,130	31,214
1947	1,387		1,387	1973	33,438	1,285	34,723
1948	1,432		1,432	1974	29,262	1,437	30,699
1949	1,353		1,353	1975	51,823	1,850	53,673
1950	1,623	1	1,624	1976	40,683	1,973	42,656
1951	5,519		5,519	1977	36,562	2,199	38,761
1952	7,466	2	7,468	1978	40,261	2,781	43,042
1953	7,864	5	7,869	1979	53,164	3,327	56,491
1954	7,648	22	7,670	1980	49,426	3,661	53,087
1955	7,988	37	8,025	1981	50,183	3,495	53,678
1956	7,864	33	7,897	1982	55,852	4,191	60,043
1957	9,986	58	10,044	1983	57,801	4,626	62,427
1958	13,610	71	13,681	1984	71,569	5,134	76,703
1959	16,306	90	16,396	1985	80,792	5,621	86,413
1960	17,418	263	17,681	1986	102,879	5,832	108,711
1961	15,967	116	16,083	1987	132,500	8,077	140,577
1962	16,516	231	16,747	1988	139,726	10,183	149,909
1963	17,304	268	17,572	1989	157,506	10,970	168,476
1964	20,619	316	20,935	1990	161,857	11,118	172,975
1965	18,785	371	19,156	1991	149,112	14,096	164,384
1966	27,965	458	28,423	1992	150,873	15,029	166,929
1967	22,802	380	23,182	1993	156,704	14,696	172,120
1968	22,090	559	22,649	1994	164,624	17,136	181,760
1969	23,265	619	23,884				

Montana

Year	Firearm	Bow	Total	Year	Firearm	Bow	Total
1984			56,760	1990			49,419
1985			43,019	1991			56,789
1986			44,733	1992	58,565	2,067	60,632
1987			40,675	1993	60,369	2,038	62,407
1988			43,971	1994	67,577	1,857	69,434
1989			44,261				

Nebraska

Year	Firearm	Bow	Total	Year	Firearm	Bow	Total
1945	2		2	1972	5,635	624	6,259
1949	0		0	1973	7,090	865	7,955
1950	7		7	1974	7,894	1,032	8,926
1951	2		2	1975	8,404	1,155	9,559
1952	7		7	1976	7,595	831	8,426
1953	353		353	1977	5,921	769	6,690
1954	219		219	1978	6,164	958	7,122
1955	189		189	1979	7,899	1,151	9,050
1956	344	8	352	1980	9,939	1,639	11,578
1957	258	21	279	1981	11,364	2,025	13,389
1958	340	103	443	1982	12,957	2,049	15,006
1959	975	111	1,086	1983	15,980	2,781	18,761
1960	1,355	108	1,463	1984	19,679	2,471	22,150
1961	1,443	198	1,641	1985	20,930	2,593	23,523
1962	3,280	194	3,474	1986	22,859	2,291	25,150
1963	3,710	246	3,956	1987	24,266	2,812	27,078
1964	5,138	326	5,464	1988	24,938	2,951	27,889
1965	6,853	338	7,191	1989	24,359	2,847	27,206
1966	6,920	375	7,295	1990	21,973	2,716	24,689
1967	4,773	546	5,319	1991	20,820	2,931	23,751
1968	5,067	399	5,466	1992	20,125	3,141	23,266
1969	5,440	524	5,964	1993	23,377	3,282	26,683
1970	6,460	654	7,114	1994	26,050	3,830	29,880
1971	6,343	662	7,005	1995			

New Hampshire

Year	Firearm	Bow	Total	Year	Firearm	Bow	Total
1922	1,896		1,896	1950	10,051		10,051
1923	1,402		1,402	1951	11,462		11,462
1924	1,537		1,537	1952	6,932		6,932
1925	1,493		1,493	1953	9,517		9,517
1926	1,665		1,665	1954	9,328		9,328
1927	1,481		1,481	1955	10,275		10,275
1928	1,474		1,474	1956	10,917		10,917
1929	1,598		1,598	1957	9,901		9,901
1930	1,735		1,735	1958	10,221		10,221
1931	1,498		1,498	1959	8,435		8,435
1932	1,687		1,687	1960	7,560	9	7,569
1933	2,064		2,064	1961	7,763	12	7,775
1934	1,526		1,526	1962	7,917	5	7,922
1935	1,845		1,845	1963	8,626	2	8,628
1936	2,751		2,751	1964	7,559	9	7,568
1937	3,216		3,216	1965	9,676	3	9,679
1938	3,363		3,363	1966	9,105	16	9,121
1939	3,820		3,820	1967	14,153	33	14,186
1940	5,699		5,699	1968	12,712	36	12,748
1941	3,897		3,897	1969	8,778	13	8,791
1942	4,844		4,844	1970	7,214	17	7,231
1943	5,029		5,029	1971	7,263	12	7,275
1944	5,029		5,029	1972	6,923	20	6,943
1945	6,449		6,449	1973	5,440	22	5,462
1946	6,356		6,356	1974	6,875	20	6,895
1947	10,172		10,172	1975	8,308	24	8,332
1948	6,767		6,767	1976	9,076	14	9,090
1949	9,852		9,852	1977	6,877	62	6,939

New Hampshire White-tailed Deer Harvest Records, Continued

Year	Firearm	Bow	Total	Year	Firearm	Bow	Total
1978	5,545	57	5,602	1987	5,864	257	6,121
1979	4,939	42	4,981	1988	5,900	225	6,125
1980	5,353	31	5,384	1989	6,749	489	7,238
1981	6,028	125	6,153	1990	6,466	482	7,872
1982	4,577	97	4,674	1991	8,060	732	8,792
1983	3,156	124	3,280	1992	9,013	1,202	10,215
1984	4,169	120	4,289	1993	9,012	877	9,889
1985	5,523	148	5,671	1994	7,478	901	8,379
1986	6,557	263	6,820	1995	9,627	1,580	11,207

New Jersey

Year	Firearm	Bow	Total	Year	Firearm	Bow	Total
1909	86		86	1953	4,824	287	5,111
1910	127		127	1954	4,767	319	5,086
1911	141		141	1955	6,114	368	6,482
1912	109		109	1956	6,070	690	6,760
1913	149		149	1957	6,643	1,104	7,747
1914	149		149	1958	6,115	1,252	7,367
1915	180		180	1959	9,612	1,230	10,842
1916	481		481	1960	6,072	1,298	7,370
1917	255		255	1961	11,325	1,081	12,406
1918	327		327	1962	7,219	978	8,197
1919	353		353	1963	7,868	952	8,820
1920	522		522	1964	6,933	1,116	8,049
1921	834		834	1965	5,136	1,109	6,245
1922	771		771	1966	8,517	1,329	9,846
1923	890		890	1967	8,467	1,456	9,923
1924	1,216		1,216	1968	7,100	1,501	8,601
1925	1,063		1,063	1969	7,121	1,356	8,477
1926	1,249		1,249	1970	6,866	1,387	8,253
1927	1,790		1,790	1971	6,111	1,434	7,545
1928	1,415		1,415	1972	9,557	1,464	11,021
1929	1,331		1,331	1973	9,629	1,689	11,318
1930	1,484		1,484	1974	11,429	1,717	13,146
1931	1,702		1,702	1975	10,675	2,013	12,688
1932	1,575		1,575	1976	10,908	2,110	13,018
1933	1,875		1,875	1977	11,828	2,591	14,419
1934	2,466		2,466	1978	13,177	2,641	15,818
1935	2,387		2,387	1979	13,843	2,263	16,106
1936	2,034		2,034	1980	16,030	5,161	21,191
1937	2,173		2,173	1981	16,291	5,846	22,137
1938	2,339		2,339	1982	16,817	6,928	23,745
1939	2,336		2,336	1983	16,403	6,902	23,305
1940	2,622		2,622	1984	17,920	7,699	25,619
1941	2,182		2,182	1985	21,480	7,971	29,451
1942	2,532		2,532	1986	23,590	10,187	33,777
1943	2,458		2,458	1987	27,415	11,813	39,228
1944	2,633		2,633	1988	33,140	12,760	45,900
1945	2,704		2,704	1989	34,812	13,714	48,526
1946	3,043		3,043	1990	34,372	13,850	48,222
1947	3,938		3,938	1991	29,936	15,480	45,416
1948	3,249		3,249	1992	31,257	16,418	47,675
1949	3,618	9	3,627	1993	32,936	17,006	49,942
1950	3,796	12	3,808	1994	32,602	18,840	51,442
1951	5,005	14	5,019	1995	39,176	20,593	59,769
1952	4,514	141	4,655				

New York

Year	Firearm	Bow	Total	Year	Firearm	Bow	Total
1941	18,566		18,566	1969	86,888	1,241	88,129
1942	19,217		19,217	1970	63,865	1,148	65,013
1943	31,510		31,510	1971	47,039	1,243	48,282
1944	38,808		38,808	1972	54,041	1,596	55,637
1945	15,136		15,136	1973	73,191	2,002	75,193
1946	22,296		22,296	1974	100,097	3,206	103,303
1947	24,194		24,194	1975	99,835	3,288	103,123
1948	54,896	8	54,906	1976	86,421	3,794	90,215
1949	27,584	13	27,597	1977	79,035	4,169	83,204
1950	38,924	47	38,971	1978	81,749	3,810	85,559
1951	31,049	75	31,124	1979	90,691	3,368	94,059
1952	59,986	341	60,327	1980	131,606	4,649	136,255
1953	29,273	529	29,802	1981	161,593	3,792	165,385
1954	37,879	670	38,549	1982	178,825	6,175	185,000
1955	58,593	939	59,532	1983	161,640	5,466	167,106
1956	71,208	1,107	72,315	1984	124,244	5,400	129,644
1957	71,478	1,199	72,677	1985	142,802	9,705	152,507
1958	65,439	1,030	66,469	1986	168,366	9,705	178,071
1959	41,345	961	42,306	1987	192,867	11,325	204,192
1960	44,913	842	45,755	1988	181,186	11,644	192,830
1961	57,723	731	58,454	1989	167,558	12,770	180,328
1962	62,042	739	62,781	1990	175,544	14,664	190,208
1963	63,244	623	63,867	1991	192,812	19,008	211,820
1964	60,174	582	60,756	1992	212,988	18,947	231,935
1965	66,577	843	67,420	1993	200,240	20,048	220,288
1966	73,092	1,065	74,157	1994	146,255	19,428	165,683
1967	77,834	821	78,655	1995	166,430	21,854	188,284
1968	90,758	1,407	92,165				

North Carolina

Year	Firearm	Bow	Total	Year	Firearm	Bow	Total
1949			14,616	1982	35,840	2,092	37,932
1951			17,739	1983	45,316	2,543	47,859
1952			15,572	1984	47,565	2,355	49,920
1953			18,598	1985	52,315	2,759	55,074
1954			20,084	1986	59,767	2,924	62,691
1955			20,114	1987	74,767	3,498	78,265
1962			28,808	1988	79,694	3,405	83,099
1964			39,793	1989	85,030	4,660	89,690
1967			38,688	1990	98,978	5,978	104,956
1970			38,405	1991	98,121	6,655	104,776
1972			47,469	1992	109,911	8,727	118,638
1974			53,079	1993	125,130	9,322	134,452
1976	22,645	539	23,184	1994	116,462	8,235	124,697
1977	28,182	679	28,861	1995	115,443	8,003	123,446
1978	29,193	781	29,974				
1979	29,246	841	30,087				
1980	27,792	1,142	28,934				
1981	33,644	1,400	35,044				

* — Harvest figures prior to 1976 are from mail survey estimates. Figures since then are the known minimum harvests reported to wildlife cooperator agents.

Did You Know?
New York's deer harvest has increased 190 percent since 1970. New York hunters took 188,284 deer in '95.

North Dakota

Year	Firearm	Bow	Total	Year	Firearm	Bow	Total
1941			2,665	1973			27,780
1943			2,765	1974			23,445
1950			13,933	1975			20,666
1952			27,024	1976			19,969
1954			22,705	1977			17,201
1955			17,123	1978			17,120
1956			21,790	1979			18,118
1957			19,714	1980			24,179
1958			9,828	1981			27,006
1959			23,812	1982			31,210
1960			25,262	1983			35,709
1961			26,324	1984			41,582
1962			23,429	1985			43,074
1963			9,929	1986			60,122
1964			24,311	1987			47,157
1965			25,837	1988			41,190
1966			26,469	1989			46,739
1967			26,524	1990			41,372
1968			10,761	1991			46,632
1969			18,367	1992			51,903
1970			22,882	1993			62,252
1971			28,673	1994			59,592
1972			25,424	1995			

Ohio

Year	Firearm	Bow	Total	Year	Firearm	Bow	Total
1952			450	1975			14,972
1953			4,000	1976			23,431
1954			closed	1977			22,319
1955			4,200	1978			22,967
1956			3,911	1979			34,874
1957			4,784	1980			40,499
1958			4,415	1981			47,634
1959			2,960	1982			52,885
1960			2,584	1983			59,812
1961			closed	1984			66,860
1962			2,114	1985			64,263
1963			2,074	1986			67,626
1964			1,326	1987			79,355
1965			406	1988			100,674
1966			1,073	1989			91,236
1967			1,437	1990	80,109	12,087	92,196
1968			1,396	1991	94,342	17,109	111,451
1969			2,105	1992	97,676	19,577	117,253
1970			2,387	1993	104,540	23,160	138,752
1971			3,831	1994	141,137	29,390	170,527
1972			5,074				
1973			7,594				
1974			10,747				

NOTE: Totals for Ohio prior to '94 do not include deer taken during the primitive weapons hunt; '94 bow kill includes 16,283 deer killed with crossbows.

Did You Know?
Deer droppings might be the best scouting tool a hunter can find.

Oklahoma

Year	Firearm	Bow	Total	Year	Firearm	Bow	Total
1964	3,368	140	3,508	1980	12,800	1,497	14,297
1965	4,090	213	4,303	1981	11,446	1,964	13,410
1966	4,925	275	5,200	1982	17,006	2,249	19,255
1967	4,976	259	5,235	1983	19,222	2,698	21,920
1968	5,490	260	5,750	1984	20,041	2,568	23,609
1969	6,069	304	6,373	1985	16,664	3,523	20,187
1970	6,895	331	7,226	1986	25,096	3,320	28,416
1971	6,587	465	7,052	1987	29,239	4,115	33,354
1972	7,714	508	8,222	1988	34,436	4,414	38,850
1973	7,140	427	7,567	1989	33,752	4,589	38,341
1974	7,821	489	8,310	1990	38,545	5,525	44,070
1975	9,028	649	9,677	1991	40,197	7,079	47,286
1976	10,544	1,004	11,548	1992	42,620	7,792	50,412
1977	10,192	680	10,872	1993	49,978	7,853	57,831
1978	13,080	1,028	14,108	1994	51,145	9,054	60,199
1979	13,023	1,185	14,208	1995	56,770	9,116	65,886

Oregon

Year	Firearm	Bow	Total
1992	422	NA	422
1993	594	NA	594
1994	707	NA	707

NOTE: The 1992 season was the first time Oregon Department of Wildlife officials distinguished between mule deer and white-tailed deer in its harvest totals.

Pennsylvania

Year	Firearm	Bow	Total	Year	Firearm	Bow	Total
1949	130,723		130,723	1973	123,239	3,652	126,891
1950	54,817		54,817	1974	121,743	3,909	125,652
1951	72,534		72,534	1975	133,134	5,061	138,195
1952	64,969	24	64,993	1976	118,385	3,648	122,033
1953	53,552	84	53,636	1977	141,400	4,678	146,078
1954	40,870	55	40,925	1978	116,188	5,053	121,241
1955	86,036	119	86,155	1979	110,562	4,232	114,794
1956	41,697	224	41,921	1980	129,703	5,774	135,477
1957	103,758	1,358	105,116	1981	142,592	5,938	148,530
1958	110,567	1,358	111,925	1982	130,958	7,264	138,222
1959	88,845	1,327	90,172	1983	130,071	6,222	136,293
1960	67,489	1,174	68,663	1984	133,606	6,574	140,180
1961	54,515	1,517	56,032	1985	154,060	7,368	161,428
1962	71,603	1,310	72,913	1986	148,562	8,570	157,132
1963	83,028	1,388	84,416	1987	164,055	8,901	172,956
1964	89,534	1,600	91,134	1988	185,565	9,834	195,399
1965	97,669	2,119	99,788	1989	184,856	10,951	195,807
1966	116,416	2,337	118,753	1990	396,529	19,032	415,561
1967	141,164	3,251	144,415	1991	365,267	22,748	388,015
1968	139,127	2,747	141,874	1992	335,439	25,785	361,224
1969	113,515	3,169	116,684	1993	359,224	49,409	408,557
1970	96,688	2,998	99,686	1994	345,184	49,897	395,081
1971	101,458	2,769	104,227	1995	375,961	54,622	430,583
1972	104,270	2,945	107,215				

Rhode Island

Year	Firearm	Bow	Total	Year	Firearm	Bow	Total
1972	93	57	150	1984	139	109	248
1973	46	56	102	1985	144	112	256
1974	62	48	110	1986	299	126	425
1975	57	54	111	1987	252	179	431
1976	61	50	111	1988	323	125	448
1977	95	62	157	1989	466	169	635
1978	91	78	169	1990	701	238	943
1979	103	93	196	1991	857	291	1,148
1980	145	72	217	1992	1,052	417	1,474
1981	155	88	243	1993	945	378	1,323
1982	112	104	216	1994	1,157	252	1,409
1983	123	99	222	1995	1,542	246	1,788

South Carolina

Year	Firearm	Bow	Total	Year	Firearm	Bow	Total
1972			18,894	1984			60,182
1973			23,703	1985			62,699
1974			26,727	1986			69,289
1975			29,133	1987			86,208
1976			33,749	1988			98,182
1977			36,363	1989			107,081
1978			39,721	1990			125,171
1979			43,569	1991			130,848
1980			44,698	1992			126,839
1981			56,410	1993			142,795
1982			54,321	1994			138,964
1983			57,927				

South Dakota

Year	Firearm	Bow	Total	Year	Firearm	Bow	Total
1985	43,989	2,738	46,727	1991	39,915	2,686	42,601
1986	40,798	1,953	42,751	1992	41,959	2,964	44,923
1987	32,018	2,456	34,474	1993	45,431	2,963	48,394
1988	33,265	2,327	35,592	1994	47,142	2,325	49,467
1989	42,947	3,081	46,028	1995	39,868	2,625	42,493
1990	38,902	2,986	41,888				

Tennessee

Year	Firearm	Bow	Total	Year	Firearm	Bow	Total
1970	8,258	372	8,630	1980	27,196	3,457	30,653
1971	6,202	365	6,567	1981	28,885	3,407	32,292
1972	7,354	499	7,853	1982	35,726	4,644	40,370
1973	10,937	474	11,411	1983	42,528	6,347	48,875
1974	12,624	685	13,309	1984	49,493	5,883	55,376
1975	13,897	993	14,890	1985	53,118	7,278	60,396
1976	16,374	1,739	18,113	1986	69,044	8,578	77,622
1977	19,527	1,770	21,297	1987	86,777	12,040	98,817
1978	22,819	2,465	25,284	1988	81,469	10,796	92,265
1979	25,970	2,570	28,540	1989	95,475	13,287	108,762

Tennessee White-tailed Deer Harvest Records, Continued

Year	Firearm	Bow	Total	Year	Firearm	Bow	Total
1990	97,172	16,061	113,233	1993	118,946	19,596	138,542
1991	105,832	15,764	121,596	1994	111,598	20,832	132,430
1992	106,168	19,728	125,896	1995	124,179	20,953	145,132

Texas

Year	Firearm	Bow	Total	Year	Firearm	Bow	Total
1980	253,993	6,390	260,383	1988	458,576	16,392	474,968
1981	292,525	7,527	300,052	1989	460,896	16,595	477,491
1982	328,678	8,943	337,621	1990	413,910	15,622	429,532
1983	309,409	8,935	318,344	1991	459,083	14,964	474,047
1984	361,811	11,451	373,262	1992	453,361	15,532	468,893
1985	370,732	12,767	383,499	1993			452,509
1986	431,002	14,117	445,119	1994			421,423
1987	489,368	15,585	504,953				

Vermont

Year	Firearm	Bow	Total	Year	Firearm	Bow	Total
1897	103		103	1933	2,397		2,397
1898	134		134	1934	1,633		1,633
1899	90		90	1935	2,039		2,039
1900	123		123	1936	1,997		1,997
1901	211		211	1937	2,446		2,446
1902	403		403	1938	2,433		2,433
1903	753		753	1939	2,589		2,589
1904	541		541	1940	3,400		3,400
1905	497		497	1941	3,111		3,111
1906	634		634	1942	3,280		3,280
1907	991		991	1943	2,871		2,871
1908	2,208		2,208	1944	3,657		3,657
1909	4,597		4,597	1945	3,510		3,510
1910	3,609		3,609	1946	4,523		4,523
1911	2,644		2,644	1947	5,635		5,635
1912	1,692		1,692	1948	4,298		4,298
1913	1,802		1,802	1949	5,983		5,983
1914	2,041		2,041	1950	6,106		6,106
1915	6,042		6,042	1951	6,940		6,940
1916	1,630		1,630	1952	6,554		6,554
1917	992		992	1953	7,475	7	7,482
1918	825		825	1954	8,402	8	84,10
1919	4,092		4,092	1955	9,936	42	9,978
1920	4,477		4,477	1956	9,645	62	9,707
1921	1,507		1,507	1957	11,293	142	11,435
1922	787		787	1958	10,510	150	10,660
1923	686		686	1959	11,268	232	11,500
1924	1,537		1,537	1960	11,164	261	11,425
1925	952		952	1961	15,526	297	15,823
1926	882		882	1962	15,898	277	16,175
1927	869		869	1963	10,024	176	10,200
1928	1,063		1,063	1964	14,502	352	14,854
1929	1,438		1,438	1965	16,029	544	16,573
1930	1,481		1,481	1966	20,616	704	21,320
1931	1,758		1,758	1967	21,942	934	22,876
1932	1,992		1,992	1968	12,934	1,432	14,366

Vermont White-tailed Deer Harvest Records, Continued

Year	Firearm	Bow	Total	Year	Firearm	Bow	Total
1969	20,753	1,547	22,300	1983	6,092	538	6,630
1970	17,592	1,197	18,789	1984	12,418	630	13,048
1971	7,760	604	8,364	1985	13,150	727	13,877
1972	8,980	1,073	10,053	1986	11,943	810	12,753
1973	8,560	1,040	9,600	1987	8,046	958	9,004
1974	11,254	1,580	12,834	1988	6,451	627	7,078
1975	9,939	1,606	11,545	1989	8,030	1,202	9,232
1976	10,278	1,200	11,478	1990	7,930	1,053	8,983
1977	10,029	2,094	12,123	1991	9,993	1,591	11,584
1978	7,087	1,688	8,775	1992	11,215	3,245	14,460
1979	14,936	1,587	16,523	1993	10,043	2,999	13,333
1980	24,675	1,257	25,932	1994	9,177	3,276	12,903
1981	19,077	1,169	20,246	1995			18,116
1982	9,148	798	9,946				

Virginia

Year	Firearm	Bow	Total	Year	Firearm	Bow	Total
1935			1,158	1966			25,920
1936			1,475	1967			24,934
1937			1,526	1968			28,041
1938			1,391	1969			34,150
1939			1,365	1970			38,138
1940			1,691	1971			42,369
1941			1,901	1972			48,775
1942			1,448	1973			60,789
1943			2,282	1974			61,989
1944			3,433	1975			63,443
1945			4,545	1976			63,671
1946			6,543	1977			67,059
1947			4,019	1978			72,545
1948			5,162	1979			69,940
1949			6,910	1980			75,208
1950			5,699	1981			78,388
1951			7,230	1982			88,540
1952			10,874	1983			85,739
1953			11,797	1984			84,432
1954			14,079	1985			101,425
1955			14,227	1986			121,801
1956			20,855	1987			119,309
1957			22,473	1988			114,562
1958			26,841	1989			135,094
1959			28,969	1990			160,411
1960			36,145	1991			179,344
1961			32,875	1992			200,446
1962			38,838	1993	185,222	15,900	201,122
1963			38,391	1994	190,673	18,700	209,373
1964			31,179	1995	202,277	16,199	218,476
1965			27,983				

Did You Know?

A deer must lose 35 percent of its blood (or 2.75 pints in a 150-pound animal), before falling. The average deer carries about 8 pints of blood in its circulatory system.

Washington

Year	Firearm	Bow	Total
1992	10,593	1,007	.11,600
1993	7,430	882	8,312
1994	9,709	1,153	10,860
1995			

NOTE: Washington does not differentiate between black-tailed deer, mule deer and white-tailed deer in its harvest totals. The total deer kill in 1994 was 46,618 and it is estimated that 23 percent of those animals were white-tailed deer.

West Virginia

Year	Firearm	Bow	Total	Year	Firearm	Bow	Total
1933	379		379	1967	18,318	163	18,481
1934	309		309	1968	10,364	187	10,551
1936	242		242	1969	13,620	470	14,090
1937	456		456	1970	13,399	589	13,988
1938	896		896	1971	15,905	714	16,619
1939	897		897	1972	20,960	1,443	22,403
1940	1,116		1,116	1973	24,179	1,684	25,863
1941	1,064		1,064	1974	27,821	2,119	29,940
1942	1,575		1,575	1975	32,368	2,968	35,336
1943	1,827		1,827	1976	38,712	2,323	41,035
1947	5,473	2	5,475	1977	37,987	2,531	40,518
1948	4,958	5	4,963	1978	40,096	4,350	44,446
1949	6,466	6	6,472	1979	49,625	5,461	55,086
1950	6,549	10	6,559	1980	47,022	7,144	54,166
1951	21,851	22	21,873	1981	65,505	9,003	74,508
1952	17,140	16	17,156	1982	74,642	13,454	88,096
1953	19,844	13	19,857	1983	78,605	11,235	89,840
1954	16,703	29	16,732	1984	94,132	12,578	106,710
1955	13,081	67	13,148	1985	71,183	13,416	84,599
1956	18,158	87	18,245	1986	101,404	17,207	118,611
1957	6,187	19	6,206	1987	109,367	19,742	129,109
1958	18,436	117	18,553	1988	112,155	16,537	128,692
1959	19,588	90	19,678	1989	129,350	16,217	145,567
1960	15,850	80	15,930	1990	148,233	21,715	169,948
1961	4,930	113	5,043	1991	149,536	27,448	176,984
1962	5,627	152	5,779	1992	177,265	28,659	205,924
1963	7,609	119	7,728	1993	142,589	26,425	169,014
1964	8,474	183	8,657	1994	120,954	24,448	145,402
1965	19,686	226	19,912	1995	172,718	26,878	199,596
1966	21,249	199	21,448				

Wisconsin

Year	Firearm	Bow	Total	Year	Firearm	Bow	Total
1897	2,500		2,500	1909	5,550		5,550
1898	2,750		2,750	1910	5,750		5,750
1899	3,000		3,000	1911	9,750		9,750
1900	3,500		3,500	1912	8,500		8,500
1901	4,000		4,000	1913	9,750		9,750
1902	4,000		4,000	1914	9,850		9,850
1903	4,250		4,250	1915	5,000		5,000
1904	4,500		4,500	1916	7,000		7,000
1905	4,250		4,250	1917	18,000		18,000
1906	4,500		4,500	1918	17,000		17,000
1907	4,750		4,750	1919	25,152		25,152
1908	5,000		5,000	1920	20,025		20,025

Wisconsin White-tailed Deer Harvest Records, Continued

Year	Firearm	Bow	Total	Year	Firearm	Bow	Total
1921	14,845		14,845	1962	45,835	na	na
1922	9,255		9,255	1963	65,020	na	na
1923	9,000		9,000	1964	93,445	3,164	96,609
1924	7,000		7,000	1965	98,774	4,995	103,769
1926	12,000		12,000	1966	110,062	5,986	116,048
1928	17,000		17,000	1967	128,527	7,592	136,119
1930	23,000		23,000	1968	119,986	6,934	126,920
1932	36,000		36,000	1969	98,008	5,987	103,995
1934	21,251	1	21,252	1970	72,844	6,520	79,364
1936	29,676	1	26,677	1971	70,835	6,522	77,357
1937	14,835	0	14,835	1972	74,827	7,087	81,914
1938	32,855	1	32,856	1973	82,105	8,456	90,561
1939	25,730	6	25,736	1974	100,405	12,514	112,919
1940	33,138	5	33,142	1975	117,378	13,588	130,966
1941	40,403	18	40,421	1976	122,509	13,636	136,145
1942	45,188	15	45,203	1977	131,910	16,790	148,700
1943	128,296	76	128,372	1978	150,845	18,113	168,958
1944	28,537	78	28,615	1979	125,570	16,018	141,588
1945	37,527	160	37,687	1980	139,624	20,954	160,578
1946	55,276	256	55,532	1981	166,673	29,083	195,756
1947	53,520	368	53,888	1982	182,715	30,850	213,565
1948	41,954	279	42,233	1983	197,600	32,876	230,476
1949	159,112	551	159,663	1984	255,240	38,891	294,131
1950	167,911	383	168,294	1985	274,302	40,744	315,046
1951	129,475	188	129,663	1986	259,240	40,490	299,730
1952	27,504	126	27,630	1987	250,530	42,651	293,181
1953	19,823	355	20,178	1988	263,424	42,393	305,817
1954	24,698	743	25,441	1989	310,192	46,394	356,586
1955	35,060	na	na	1990	350,040	49,291	399,331
1956	35,562	na	na	1991	352,328	67,005	419,333
1957	68,138	na	na	1992	288,906	60,479	349,385
1958	95,234	na	na	1993	217,584	53,008	270,592
1959	105,596	na	na	1994	307,629	66,254	373,883
1960	61,005	na	na	1995	397,942	69,158	467,100
1961	38,772	na	na				

Wyoming

Year	Firearm	Bow	Total	Year	Firearm	Bow	Total
1968	13,891		13,891	1982	7,608		7,608
1969	12,863		12,863	1983	8,498		8,498
1970	9,878		9,878	1984	9,888		9,888
1971	7,806		7,806	1985	9,267		9,267
1972	4,306		4,306	1986	7,983	254	8,237
1973	9,174		9,174	1987	5,628	192	5,820
1974	12,832		12,832	1988	7,005	174	7,179
1975	14,001		14,001	1989	8,903	197	9,100
1976	11,298		11,298	1990	9,535	147	9,632
1977	11,049		11,049	1991	10,240	139	10,379
1978	7,796		7,796	1992	14,533	216	14,749
1979	7,452		7,452	1993	12,623	1,322	13,945
1980	7,014		7,014	1994	8,249	228	8,477
1981	7,286		7,286				

Did You Know? Texas boasts a deer herd of 3.5 million.

STATE DEER HUNTING REGULATIONS

In Alphabetical Order By State

State	Minimum Hunting Age	Is General Hunter Education Mandatory?	Is Bow-Hunting Education Mandatory?	Is A Separate Bow-Hunting Education Class Offered?	Is Bow-Hunting From Tree Stand Allowed?
Alabama	None	Yes	No	No	Yes
Arizona	10	No	No	No	Yes
Arkansas	None	Yes	No	No	Yes
California	12	Yes	No	No	Yes
Colorado	14	Yes	No	Yes	Yes
Connecticut	12	Yes	Yes	Yes	Yes
Delaware	None	Yes	No	Yes	Yes
Florida	None	Yes	Yes	Yes	Yes
Georgia	None	Yes	No	No	Yes
Idaho	12	Yes	Yes	Yes	Yes
Illinois	None	Yes	No	No	Yes
Indiana	None	Yes	No	No	Yes
Iowa	None	Yes	No	Yes	Yes
Kansas	14	Yes	No	No	Yes
Kentucky	None	Yes	No	No	Yes
Louisiana	None	Yes	No	Yes	Yes
Maine	10	Yes	Yes	Yes	Yes
Maryland	None	Yes	No	No	Yes
Massachusetts	12	No	No	Yes	Yes
Michigan	12	Yes	No	No	Yes
Minnesota	12	Yes	No	Yes	Yes
Mississippi	None	Yes	No	No	Yes
Missouri	11	Yes	No	No	Yes
Montana	12	Yes	Yes	Yes	Yes
Nebraska	14	Yes	Yes	Yes	Yes
Nevada	12	Yes	No	No	Yes
New Hampshire	None	Yes	No	Yes	Yes
New Jersey	10	Yes	Yes	Yes	Yes
New Mexico	12	Yes	No	Yes	Yes
New York	14	Yes	Yes	Yes	Yes
North Carolina	None	Yes	No	No	Yes
North Dakota	14	Yes	Yes	Yes	Yes
Ohio	None	Yes	No	No	Yes
Oklahoma	None	Yes	No	No	Yes
Oregon	12	Yes	No	No	Yes
Pennsylvania	12	Yes	No	No	Yes
Rhode Island	12	Yes	Yes	Yes	Yes
South Carolina	None	Yes	No	No	Yes
South Dakota	12	Yes	Yes	Yes	Yes
Tennessee	None	Yes	No	Yes	Yes
Texas	None	Yes	No	No	Yes
Utah	14	Yes	No	No	Yes
Vermont	None	Yes	No	No	Yes
Virginia	None	Yes	No	No	Yes
Washington	None	Yes	No	No	Yes
West Virginia	None	Yes	No	No	Yes
Wisconsin	12	Yes	No	Yes	Yes
Wyoming	14	Yes	No	No	Yes

STATE DEER HUNTING REGULATIONS

In Alphabetical Order By State

State	Is Gun Hunting From Tree Stand Allowed?	Is Blaze Orange Required?	May Food Bait Be Used?	May You Hunt Over Salt Or Minerals?	May Dogs Be Used To Trail Wounded Deer?	May Dogs Be Used To Hunt Deer?
Alabama	Yes	Yes	No	Yes	Yes	Yes
Arizona	Yes	No	No	Yes	No	No
Arkansas	Yes	Yes	Yes	Yes	Yes	Yes
California	Yes	No	No	No	Yes	Yes
Colorado	Yes	Yes	No	No	No	No
Connecticut	Yes	Yes	No	No	No	No
Delaware	Yes	Yes	No	No	No	No
Florida	Yes	Yes	Yes	Yes	Yes	Yes
Georgia	Yes	Yes	No	No	Yes	Yes
Idaho	Yes	No	No	No	No	No
Illinois	Yes	Yes	No	No	No	No
Indiana	Yes	Yes	No	No	No	No
Iowa	Yes	Yes	No	No	No	No
Kansas	Yes	Yes	Yes	Yes	No	No
Kentucky	Yes	Yes	Yes	Yes	No	No
Louisiana	Yes	Yes	Yes	Yes	Yes	Yes
Maine	Yes	Yes	No	No	No	No
Maryland	Yes	Yes	Yes	Yes	No	No
Massachusetts	Yes	Yes	No	No	No	No
Michigan	No	Yes	Yes	Yes	No	No
Minnesota	Yes	Yes	No	Yes	No	No
Mississippi	Yes	Yes	No	No	Yes	Yes
Missouri	Yes	Yes	No	Yes	No	No
Montana	Yes	Yes	No	No	No	No
Nebraska	Yes	Yes	Yes	Yes	Yes	Yes
Nevada	Yes	No	No	No	No	No
New Hampshire	Yes	No	Yes	No	No	No
New Jersey	Yes	Yes	Yes	Yes	No	No
New Mexico	No	No	No	No	No	No
New York	Yes	No	No	No	Yes	No
North Carolina	Yes	Yes	Yes	Yes	Yes	Yes
North Dakota	Yes	Yes	Yes	Yes	No	No
Ohio	Yes	Yes	Yes	Yes	No	No
Oklahoma	Yes	Yes	Yes	Yes	No	No
Oregon	Yes	No	Yes	Yes	No	No
Pennsylvania	Yes	Yes	No	No	No	No
Rhode Island	Yes	Yes	No	No	No	No
South Carolina	Yes	Yes	Yes	Yes	Yes	Yes
South Dakota	Yes	Yes	No	No	Yes	No
Tennessee	Yes	Yes	No	Yes	No	No
Texas	Yes	No	Yes	Yes	Yes	No
Utah	Yes	Yes	Yes	Yes	No	No
Vermont	Yes	No	Yes	No	No	No
Virginia	Yes	Yes	No	No	Yes	Yes
Washington	Yes	Yes	Yes	Yes	No	No
West Virginia	Yes	Yes	Yes	Yes	No	No
Wisconsin	Yes	Yes	Yes	Yes	No	No
Wyoming	Yes	Yes	Yes	Yes	No	No

Deer Hunting Statistics

Descending Numerical Order By State

State [1]	Estimated Deer Population [2]
Texas [8]	3,525,000
Mississippi	1,750,000
Alabama	1,500,000
Michigan	1,500,000
Pennsylvania	1,178,368
Minnesota	1,000,000
Wisconsin	1,000,000
Georgia	950,000
Montana [8]	910,000
New York	900,000
North Carolina	900,000
Virginia	900,000
Louisiana	875,000
Florida	819,420
West Virginia	800,000
Tennessee	780,000
California [7,8]	760,700
Missouri	760,281
South Carolina	750,000
Arkansas	700,000
Oregon [7,8,9]	686,600
Colorado [7,8]	600,000
Wyoming [7,8]	460,000
Kentucky	400,000
Washington [7,8,9]	398,000
Ohio	350,000
South Dakota [8]	340,000
Oklahoma [8]	322,500
Kansas [8]	320,000
Iowa	300,000
Indiana	290,000
Maine	275,000
New Mexico	260,000
Utah [7,8]	250,000
Arizona [7,8,10]	243,000
North Dakota [8]	230,000
Nebraska [8]	210,000
Maryland	200,000
New Jersey	150,000
Nevada [7,8]	149,000
Vermont	105,000
Massachusetts	70,000
New Hampshire	67,662
Connecticut	65,000
Delaware	20,000
Rhode Island	5,500
Idaho [7,8]	Unknown
Illinois	Unknown
TOTAL	**29,026,031**

State	Total Deer Population [3]
Texas	476,000
Pennsylvania	408,557
Michigan	374,640
Georgia	345,100
Mississippi	301,000
Alabama	295,000
Wisconsin	270,592
New York	220,288
Louisiana	214,900
Minnesota	202,000
Virginia	201,122
North Carolina	177,000
Missouri	172,141
West Virginia	169,014
Montana	153,928
South Carolina	142,302
Tennessee	138,615
Ohio	135,000
Illinois	113,000
Arkansas	110,401
Indiana	101,250
Kentucky	95,300
Florida	81,942
Iowa	78,000
Wyoming	70,450
North Dakota	70,293
Oregon	70,000
South Dakota	66,800
Colorado	61,500
Idaho	61,200
Oklahoma	58,125
Washington	55,297
Maryland	51,209
New Jersey	49,942
California	45,000
Nebraska	37,277
Kansas	36,600
Utah	30,733
Maine	27,402
Arizona	18,565
New Mexico	17,597
Vermont	13,333
Connecticut	10,360
New Hampshire	9,889
Massachusetts	8,200
Delaware	7,424
Nevada	6,276
Rhode Island	1,322
TOTAL	**5,861,886**

State	Resident Deer Hunters [4]	Non-Res. Deer Hunters [5]	Season Bag Limit [6]
Pennsylvania	1,407,822	29,000	1/day
Michigan	1,248,770	4,351	2
Wisconsin	857,756	Unknown	3
New York	803,000	2,055	2
Texas	666,000	71,500	1
Ohio	649,000	3,350	11
Missouri	541,488	2,241	2
Minnesota	516,000	3,813	2/day
West Virginia	508,868	23,212	5
North Carolina	456,000	21,109	1
Georgia	445,000	Combined	1
Virginia	400,452	5,725	10
Tennessee	366,902	1,200	3
California	337,661	Just Started	4
Indiana	302,900	5,639	2
Mississippi	297,000	2,807	6
Alabama	290,000	32,635	1
Kentucky	271,600	26,283	6
Oregon	259,655	1,928	2
Oklahoma	246,664	28,153	4
Louisiana	244,097	9,658	1
Florida	229,612	28,610	8
Illinois	227,325	11,934	4
Washington	199,330	23,000	4
Maryland	199,000	2,369	2
Iowa	184,353	10,520	1
New Jersey	178,801	16,664	2
Idaho	177,600	4,796	20+
Maine	177,250	6,433	1
South Carolina	172,500	35,900	6
Montana	160,000	24,554	5
Utah	135,407	1,338	6
Vermont	125,821	6,000	3
Colorado	117,300	1,211	5
New Hampshire	105,284	3,394	1
North Dakota	101,737	104,182	8
Massachusetts	100,000	650	8
Arizona	82,708	34,500	10
Wyoming	80,383	4,100	32
South Dakota	75,000	15,684	20+
Nebraska	72,963	14,000	6
Kansas	70,179	11,910	1
New Mexico	69,041	24,263	3
Nevada	48,154	20,233	3
Connecticut	43,000	1,307	1
Delaware	31,527	71,490	7
Rhode Island	16,058	32,141	1
Arkansas	Unknown	52,786	9
TOTAL	**14,296,786**	**838,628**	

Leading Deer Hunting States

Licensed Resident Deer Hunters (1993-94)

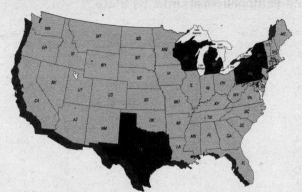

Pennsylvania
1,407,822

Michigan
1,248,770

Wisconsin
857,756

New York
803,000

Texas
666,000

Leading White-tailed Deer States

Estimated Whitetail Populations

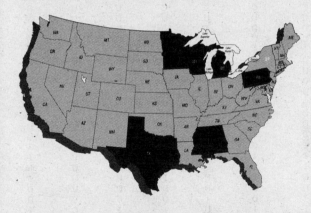

Texas
3,525,000

Mississippi
1,750,000

Alabama
1,500,000

Michigan
1,500,000

Wisconsin
1,300,000

Pennsylvania
1,178,368

Minnesota
1,000,000

1. *Several western states that have more than one species of deer usually allow hunters to buy one license that will allow them to hunt multiple deer species within that state.*
2. *Deer population numbers listed here are the best estimates of state Game & Fish Departments.*
3. *Deer harvest is the actual registered harvest recorded, or the best estimates by the respective state Game & Fish Departments based on a combination of license sales and hunter surveys.*
4. *Resident Deer Hunter numbers are based on actual license sales, or best estimates by the respective state Game & Fish Departments based on a combination of license sales and hunter surveys. **Note:** Numbers based on license sales are not "weapon specific" and may count a hunter more than once.*
5. *Non-resident hunter numbers are unknown in some states. Some states provide this data "combined" with the resident hunter numbers.*
   Note: *Numbers based on license sales are not "weapon specific" and may count a hunter more than once.*
6. *Season bag limit is defined here as the general statewide bag limit, or that which is available for the majority of hunters within that state for the year.*
7. *There is a limited number of white-tailed deer, if any, in the state.*
8. *Mule deer are present and included in the estimated deer population figures and/or the deer harvest figures.*
9. *Black-tailed deer are present and included in the estimated deer population figures and/or the deer harvest figures.*
10. *Coues deer are present and included in the estimated deer population figures and/or the deer harvest figures.*

DEER HUNTING TRENDS

In Alphabetical Order By State

State	Deer Vehicle Collisions	Deer Crop Damage	Number Of Youth Hunters	Total Number Of Hunters	Number Of Male Hunters	Number Of Female Hunters	Hunting With Rifles
Alabama	U	I	D	D	D	D	D
Arizona	C	I	U	I	I	I	I
Arkansas	U	C	U	U	U	U	C
California	U	U	U	D	U	U	C
Colorado	U	D	U	C	U	U	C
Connecticut	C	C	C	C	C	C	C
Delaware	I	I	U	I	I	I	NA
Florida	U	C	U	D	U	U	U
Georgia	I	C	U	C	C	I	C
Idaho	U	D	I	I	I	U	I
Illinois	I	U	U	I	U	U	U
Indiana	D	U	U	I	I	I	NA
Iowa	C	C	C	C	U	U	NA
Kansas	C	C	U	C	U	U	C
Kentucky	D	C	D	C	C	C	C
Louisiana	U	D	U	U	U	U	C
Maine	C	U	D	D	U	U	C
Maryland	C	C	D	C	U	U	C
Massachusetts	U	U	U	U	U	U	NA
Michigan	D	D	I	D	D	D	D
Minnesota	U	U	U	C	U	U	U
Mississippi	I	D	U	C	U	U	C
Missouri	D	I	U	I	U	U	C
Montana	U	D	U	C	U	U	U
Nebraska	C	D	U	C	U	U	C
Nevada	U	D	U	D	U	U	D
New Hampshire	D	C	C	C	U	U	C
New Jersey	C	C	D	D	U	U	NA
New Mexico	U	U	U	D	U	U	D
New York	D	C	I	D	U	U	U
North Carolina	C	C	C	C	C	C	U
North Dakota	I	I	I	I	U	U	I
Ohio	I	I	U	I	U	U	NA
Oklahoma	C	I	U	I	U	U	I
Oregon	U	U	D	D	U	U	D
Pennsylvania	I	D	I	D	U	U	D
Rhode Island	I	I	U	I	I	C	I
South Carolina	I	C	C	I	U	U	I
South Dakota	U	I	I	I	I	U	I
Tennessee	U	I	U	C	U	U	C
Texas	U	U	U	I	I	I	U
Utah	D	D	C	D	D	D	D
Vermont	I	I	U	D	U	U	D
Virginia	D	U	I	C	U	U	D
Washington	I	U	D	D	D	C	D
West Virginia	D	D	I	I	I	I	I
Wisconsin	C	C	U	C	U	U	C
Wyoming	D	U	I	D	D	D	D

C = CONSTANT   I = INCREASED   D = DECREASED   U = UNKNOWN   NA = NOT ALLOWED

DEER HUNTING TRENDS

In Alphabetical Order By State

State	Hunting With Shotguns	Hunting With Handguns	Hunting With Muzzle-loaders	Hunting With Bows	Coyote Pressure On Deer Herd	Anti-Hunting Pressure	Problems With Poaching
Alabama	D	D	D	I	I	U	C
Arizona	I	I	I	C	C	C	U
Arkansas	C	C	C	C	U	U	U
California	C	C	C	I	U	C	U
Colorado	U	U	C	I	U	I	C
Connecticut	C	NA	C	I	C	C	C
Delaware	I	NA	I	I	U	I	C
Florida	U	U	D	D	C	I	C
Georgia	C	C	C	C	U	I	C
Idaho	U	U	I	I	U	C	U
Illinois	I	I	C	I	U	C	U
Indiana	I	D	I	I	I	U	U
Iowa	C	NA	C	C	U	U	C
Kansas	C	C	I	C	U	C	C
Kentucky	D	C	I	C	I	C	C
Louisiana	C	I	C	I	U	U	D
Maine	U	U	I	I	C	C	C
Maryland	C	C	I	I	U	I	C
Massachusetts	U	NA	I	I	U	C	U
Michigan	D	D	D	D	I	D	I
Minnesota	U	U	U	C	U	C	C
Mississippi	C	C	I	I	C	C	C
Missouri	C	C	I	I	U	C	U
Montana	U	U	U	U	I	C	C
Nebraska	U	U	I	C	U	C	U
Nevada	U	U	D	D	U	I	C
New Hampshire	C	C	I	I	I	C	I
New Jersey	D	NA	I	I	I	C	C
New Mexico	D	D	I	I	U	I	U
New York	U	U	I	I	C	C	U
North Carolina	D	I	I	C	U	C	C
North Dakota	I	I	I	I	U	I	C
Ohio	I	I	I	I	U	C	C
Oklahoma	C	C	C	C	I	C	C
Oregon	D	C	I	I	I	I	U
Pennsylvania	C	C	D	I	I	C	D
Rhode Island	C	NA	I	I	U	C	C
South Carolina	C	C	D	I	U	I	C
South Dakota	C	C	I	D	C	C	D
Tennessee	C	C	I	C	U	C	C
Texas	U	U	U	U	I	I	U
Utah	D	C	D	D	I	I	D
Vermont	U	U	I	I	C	I	C
Virginia	U	U	I	I	U	U	U
Washington	D	D	D	D	C	I	C
West Virginia	C	C	I	I	U	U	D
Wisconsin	C	I	I	I	C	I	C
Wyoming	C	C	C	C	D	I	C

C = CONSTANT   I = INCREASED   D = DECREASED   U = UNKNOWN   NA = NOT ALLOWED

FIREARM HUNTING INFORMATION
In Alphabetical Order By State

State	Firearm Season Dates[1]	Number Of Firearm Season Days[2]	How Many Resident Firearms Hunters?	How Many Non-Resident Firearms Hunters?[3]	Number Of Deer Harvested By Firearms	Are Rifles Permitted?[4]	Are Handguns Permitted?[4]
Alabama	11/20 - 1/31	83	205,000	20,500	270,000	Yes	Yes
Arizona	10/29 - 12/31	46	63,066	3,670	17,519	Yes	Yes
Arkansas	11/13 - 12/18	36	Unknown	Unknown	79,385	Yes	Yes
California	8/13 - 10/9	58	303,720	Combined	27,553	Yes	Yes
Colorado	8/28 - 12/31	122	96,500	61,100	54,100	Yes	Yes
Connecticut	11/21 - 12/10	18	24,000	1,100	6,629	Yes	No
Delaware	11/11 - 1/21	11	17,450	1,236	5,872	No	No
Florida	10/30 - 2/16	72	184,910	3,061	Combined	Yes	Yes
Georgia	10/22 - 1/8	79	330,000	20,000	345,100	Yes	Yes
Idaho	9/15 - 11/20	65	142,000	16,877	61,200	Yes	Yes
Illinois	11/18 - 1/15	13	143,308	Combined	92,000	No	Yes
Indiana	11/13 - 11/28	16	165,000	4,000	74,800	No	Yes
Iowa	12/3 - 12/18	16	131,188	700	61,663	No	No
Kansas	12/1 - 12/12	12	52,604	Just Started	30,000	Yes	Yes
Kentucky	11/12 - 11/21	10	141,960	2,839	68,000	Yes	Yes
Louisiana	10/30 - 1/17	68	189,100	2,142	189,100	Yes	Yes
Maine	10/30 - 11/27	25	160,250	31,300	26,608	Yes	Yes
Maryland	11/26 - 12/10	13	106,000	14,000	33,785	Yes	Yes
Massachusetts	11/28 - 12/10	13	70,000	1,350	6,300	No	No
Michigan	11/15 - 11/30	16	738,200	17,800	251,410	Yes	Yes
Minnesota	11/6 - 11/26	21	443,000	8,500	188,109	Yes	Yes
Mississippi	11/20 - 1/19	47	175,000	16,858	220,000	Yes	Yes
Missouri	11/12 - 11/20	9	436,341	10,390	154,159	Yes	Yes
Montana 5	9/15 - 12/31	36	143,100	15,000	153,928	Yes	Yes
Nebraska	11/12 - 11/20	9	53,967	1,621	30,767	Yes	Yes
Nevada	9/11 - 1/2	97	45,000	10,000	5,991	Yes	Yes
New Hampshire	11/10 - 12/5	26	66,872	10,028	6,643	Yes	Yes
New Jersey	12/6 - 1/22	9	108,116	2,358	27,197	No	No
New Mexico	10/17 - 11/15	22	59,000	5,100	16,820	Yes	Yes
New York	10/22 - 12/13	53	600,000	30,000	Combined	Yes	Yes
North Carolina	10/17 - 1/2	67	260,000	14,000	150,000	Yes	Yes
North Dakota	11/4 - 11/20	17	89,691	669	65,375	Yes	Yes
Ohio	11/28 - 12/3	6	350,000	3,000	104,400	No	Yes
Oklahoma	11/19 - 11/27	9	151,002	606	40,033	Yes	Yes
Oregon 5	9/3 - 12/18	91	233,100	2,086	64,000	Yes	Yes
Pennsylvania	11/29 - 1/22	42	1,044,634	75,777	351,544	Yes	Yes
Rhode Island	11/26 - 12/4	9	7,758	200	313	No	No
South Carolina 5	8/15 - 1/2	141	147,500	29,500	Combined	Yes	Yes
South Dakota 5,6	9/18 - 12/19	56	Combined	Combined	63,100	Yes	Yes
Tennessee	11/20 - 1/9	34	190,200	5,228	85,568	Yes	Yes
Texas 5	11/6 - 1/30	85	588,000	12,000	456,000	Yes	Yes
Utah	10/17 - 10/23	7	97,000	9,500	21,822	Yes	Yes
Vermont	11/12 - 11/27	16	89,423	17,082	10,043	Yes	Yes
Virginia	11/21 - 1/7	42	278,562	14,307	158,361	Yes	Yes
Washington	9/15 - 11/20	48	168,156	1,083	47,701	Yes	Yes
West Virginia	11/21 - 12/17	21	329,472	46,065	132,820	Yes	Yes
Wisconsin	11/20 - 11/28	9	639,964	26,606	217,584	Yes	Yes
Wyoming 5	9/10 - 11/30	52	72,272	50,117	69,415	Yes	Yes
TOTALS			**10,131,386**	**619,356**	**4,542,717**		

Leading Firearm Hunting States
Licensed Gun Hunters (1993-94)

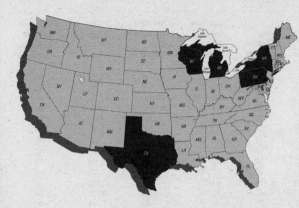

Pennsylvania
1,044,634

Michigan
738,200

Wisconsin
639,964

New York
600,000

Texas
588,000

Leading Firearm Deer Kill States
Total Whitetail Kill Using Gun

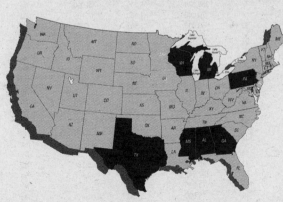

Texas
456,000

Wisconsin
398,002

Pennsylvania
351,544

Georgia
345,100

Michigan
251,410

Alabama
270,000

1. Dates for the firearm season as listed here are in the broadest context due to space limitations. These dates reflect the first day to the last day of firearm activity within the state. While some states have statewide seasons, others have varying seasons for different management units within the state. Some of the dates listed were for the 1993 - 1994 season, and some are for the 1994 - 1995 season.

2. The number of firearm season days is the total number of available firearm hunting days in each state. Some states do not allow hunting on Sundays, while some states break seasons into "early" and "late" seasons.

3. "Combined" means that the non-resident hunter figure is included with the resident hunter figure.

4. Indicates types of weapons that may be used to hunt deer at some time period during the year. "Yes" signifies that the firearm is allowed in at least some parts of the state, but not necessarily all parts. Check regulations for restrictions.

5. The number of resident firearm hunters, non-resident firearm hunters, and total deer harvested by firearms includes both the firearm totals and the muzzleloader totals.

6. Refer to the "State Deer Hunting Statistics" chart for hunter numbers.

BOW-HUNTING INFORMATION

In Alphabetical Order By State

State	Bow Season Dates (1)	Bow Season Days (2)	How Many Resident Bow-Hunters?	How Many Non-Resident Bow-Hunters? (3)	Number Of Deer Harvested By Bow (4)	May General Public Hunt Deer With A Crossbow? (5)
Alabama	10/15 - 1/31	108	62,000	6,200	32,000	No
Arizona	8/20 - 1/31	74	18,262	621	758	Yes
Arkansas	10/1 - 2/28	151	Unknown	Unknown	14,797	Yes
California	7/9 - 9/11	65	31,870	Combined	1,682	Yes
Colorado	8/28 - 11/26	30	14,300	9,100	4,900	Yes
Connecticut	9/15 - 12/31	108	13,000	2,000	2,165	No
Delaware	9/1 - 1/31	107	6,725	402	507	Yes
Florida	9/11 - 11/14	75	30,613	515	Combined	Yes
Georgia	9/17 - 10/21	35	95,000	2,000	21,450	No
Idaho	8/30 - 12/19	26	23,000	2,734	3,000	Yes
Illinois	10/1 - 1/12	104	81,000	Combined	21,000	No
Indiana	10/1 - 12/31	87	92,500	1,500	23,933	No
Iowa	10/1 - 1/10	86	34,165	450	8,814	No
Kansas	10/1 - 12/31	81	15,000	Just Started	5,500	No
Kentucky	10/1 - 1/15	107	94,640	1,800	8,400	Yes
Louisiana	10/1 - 1/20	112	50,800	345	22,600	No
Maine	9/30 - 10/29	26	12,000	1,175	682	No
Maryland	9/15 - 1/31	118	46,000	7,000	11,043	No
Massachusetts	11/7 - 11/26	20	17,500	337	1,370	No
Michigan	10/1 - 1/1	77	338,320	6,200	99,990	No
Minnesota	9/18 - 12/31	104	70,000	1,100	12,730	No
Mississippi	10/1 - 1/31	62	58,000	5,587	41,000	No
Missouri	10/1 - 12/31	92	92,031	1,544	14,696	No
Montana (8)	9/3 - 10/16	44	16,900	8,000	3,473	Yes
Nebraska	9/15 - 12/31	99	13,177	621	3,581	No
Nevada	8/14 - 1/2	42	1,954	320	285	No
New Hampshire	9/15 - 12/15	91	17,804	3,761	877	No
New Jersey	10/2 - 1/26	76	50,685	2,002	17,006	No
New Mexico	9/1 - 1/15	96	5,314	511	755	No
New York	9/27 - 12/31	96	160,000	5,000	20,048	No
North Carolina	9/12 - 11/19	54	100,000	5,385	10,000	No
North Dakota	9/3 - 12/31	121	11,400	669	4,473	No
Ohio	10/2 - 1/31	122	192,000	2,000	23,160	Yes
Oklahoma	10/1 - 12/31	78	53,106	403	7,837	No
Oregon	8/27 - 12/4	53	26,555	1,308	5,391	No
Pennsylvania	10/2 - 1/8	49	292,247	22,857	49,407	No
Rhode Island	10/1 - 1/31	123	3,800	200	378	No
South Carolina (8)	8/15 - 10/10	41	25,000	5,000	Combined	Yes
South Dakota	10/1 - 12/31	92	Combined	Combined	3,400	No
Tennessee	9/25 - 11/14	44	82,040	5,228	18,691	No
Texas	10/1 - 10/31	31	78,000	2,000	19,500	No
Utah	8/21 - 9/17	28	22,332	1,390	4,704	No
Vermont	10/1 - 12/11	32	23,110	5,592	2,999	No
Virginia	10/1 - 1/7	43	63,273	2,287	15,900	No
Washington	9/15 - 12/15	51	22,013	155	4,856	No
West Virginia	10/15 - 12/31	67	107,160	18,047	26,425	No
Wisconsin	9/18 - 12/31	86	215,292	5,535	52,623	No
Wyoming	9/1 - 9/30	30	8,111	2,669	1,538	Yes
TOTALS			**2,887,999**	**151,550**	**650,324**	

Leading Bow-Hunting States
Licensed Resident Bow Hunters (1993-94)

Michigan
338,320

Pennsylvania
292,247

Wisconsin
215,292

Ohio
192,000

New York
160,000

Leading Bow Deer Kill States
Total Whitetail Kill Using Bow

Michigan
99,990

Wisconsin
69,269

Pennsylvania
49,407

Mississippi
41,000

Alabama
32,000

1. Dates for the bow hunting season as listed here are in the broadest context due to space limitations. These dates reflect the first day to the last day of bow hunting activity within the state. While some states have statewide seasons, others have varying seasons for different management units within the state. Some of the dates listed were for the 1993 - 1994 season, and some are for the 1994 - 1995 season.
2. The number of bow season days is the total number of available bow hunting days in each state. Some states do not allow hunting on Sundays, while some states break seasons into "early" and "late" seasons.
3. "Combined" means that the non-resident hunter figure is included with the resident hunter figure.
4. "Combined" means that the deer harvested by bow are included with the number of deer harvested by regular firearms. The total may be found in the chart entitled "State Deer Hunting Statistics."
5. Indicates states that allow the use of a crossbow to hunt deer. Some states classify a crossbow as a firearm, some as a bow, and others outlaw them.
6. Indicates the general statewide bag limit for the majority of bow hunters in the state.
7. "Yes" signifies that a special bow hunting license, stamp, or tag is required to go bowhunting in the state.
8. The general population may use a crossbow during the firearms season, but there are no special archery permits available for the handicapped.
9. Rules of the regular firearms season will usually apply in these states during the bow season. Use of blaze orange, and getting a special permit may be required, among other restrictions.

MUZZLELOADER INFORMATION

In Alphabetical Order By State

State	Muzzle-loader Season Dates (1)	Special Muzzle-loader Season Days (2)	Are There Special Muzzle-loader Restrictions? (5)	How Many Resident Muzzle-loader Hunters? (6)	How Many Non-Resident Muzzle-loader Hunters? (7)	Number Of Deer Harvested By Muzzle-loaders (8)
Alabama	11/20 - 1/31	0	Yes	23,000	2,300	Combined
Arizona	10/29 - 12/31	32	Yes	1,380	60	288
Arkansas	10/23 - 1/2	21	Yes	Unknown	Unknown	16,219
California	10/22 - 1/29	48	Yes	2,071	Combined	86
Colorado	9/11 - 9/19	9	Yes	6,500	1,300	2,500
Connecticut	12/12 - 12/24	12	Yes	6,000	250	367
Delaware	10/10 - 1/25	9	Yes	7,352	603	1,045
Florida	10/15 - 2/27	20	Yes	14,089	237	Combined
Georgia	9/23 - 1/12	57	Yes	20,000	1,212	Combined
Idaho	11/10 - 12/9	20	Yes	12,600	1,498	6,000
Illinois	12/9 - 12/11	3	Yes	3,017	Combined	Combined
Indiana	11/13 - 12/19	16	Yes	45,400	225	13,621
Iowa	10/15 - 1/10	32	Yes	19,000	50	6,564
Kansas	9/18 - 12/12	21	Yes	2,575	Just Started	1,100
Kentucky	10/15 - 12/16	9	No	35,000	1,000	8,200
Louisiana	12/6 - 12/10	5	Yes	4,197	50	3,200
Maine	11/29 - 12/4	6	No	5,000	160	112
Maryland	10/20 - 12/31	16	Yes	34,717	5,283	5,174
Massachusetts	12/19 - 12/21	3	Yes	12,500	241	580
Michigan	12/3 - 12/19	17	Yes	172,250	4,153	23,240
Minnesota	11/27 - 12/12	16	Yes	3,000	58	1,097
Mississippi	12/2 - 12/15	14	Yes	64,000	6,165	39,000
Missouri	11/12 - 12/11	9	Yes	13,116	Just Started	2,566
Montana	9/15 - 12/31	0	Yes	Combined	Combined	Combined
Nebraska	12/4 - 12/19	16	Yes	5,819	127	2,282
Nevada	9/11 - 1/2	0	Yes	1,200	200	139
New Hampshire	10/30 - 11/9	11	No	20,608	2,875	2,369
New Jersey	12/13 - 1/1	14	Yes	20,000	436	5,739
New Mexico	9/10 - 9/20	11	Yes	4,727	822	1,692
New York	10/15 - 12/20	14	Yes	43,000	900	3,407
North Carolina	10/10 - 11/19	18	No	96,000	5,169	13,000
North Dakota	11/26 - 12/6	11	Yes	646	0	299
Ohio	1/5 - 1/7	3	Yes	107,000	1,000	10,396
Oklahoma	10/22 - 10/30	9	Yes	42,556	202	10,255
Oregon	10/1 - 12/11	72	Yes	Combined	Combined	868
Pennsylvania	12/27 - 1/8	12	Yes	70,941	5,548	7,606
Rhode Island	10/31 - 12/24	36	Yes	4,500	250	624
South Carolina 9	10/1 - 10/10	10	Yes	Combined	Combined	Combined
South Dakota 9	10/27 - 12/19	42	Yes	Combined	Combined	300
Tennessee	10/16 - 12/12	30	Yes	94,662	5,228	27,858
Texas	1/7 - 1/15	9	No	Combined	Combined	Combined
Utah	11/6 - 11/15	10	Yes	16,075	1,020	3,442
Vermont	12/3 - 12/11	9	Yes	13,288	1,589	291
Virginia	11/7 - 1/7	29	Yes	58,617	3,639	25,995
Washington	10/1 - 12/15	34	Yes	9,161	69	2,740
West Virginia	11/21 - 12/17	6	Yes	72,236	7,378	9,769
Wisconsin	11/29 - 12/5	7	Yes	2,500	Combined	385
Wyoming	9/10 - 11/30	0	Yes	Combined	Combined	Combined
TOTALS				**1,190,300**	**61,297**	**260,415**

Boone & Crockett Record Whitetails

The information in this chapter is taken from the Boone and Crockett Club's *Records of North American Whitetail Deer*, third edition, 1995, with the permission of B&C. What follows is only a partial listing of the top whitetails. The history behind several of the bucks listed in this chapter is included in the club's *22nd Big Game Awards*. For more information on the club and these books, write: Boone and Crockett Club, 250 Station Drive, Missoula, MT 59801.

All-Time Top 20 White-Tailed Deer

Typical Antlers

Place	Locality killed	Score
World Record	Saskatchewan	213 5/8
Second Place	Wisconsin	206 1/8
Third Place	Missouri	205
Fourth Place	Illinois	204 4/8
Fifth Place	Alberta	204 2/8
Sixth Place	Saskatchewan	202 6/8
Seventh Place	Minnesota	202
Eighth Place	Iowa	201 4/8
Ninth Place	Minnesota	201
Tenth Place	Saskatchewan	200 2/8

Non-Typical Antlers

Place	Locality killed	Score
World Record	Missouri	333 7/8
Second Place	Ohio	328 2/8
Third Place	Texas	286
Fourth Place	Iowa	282
Fifth Place	Louisiana	281 6/8
Sixth Place	Kansas	280 4/8
Seventh Place	Alberta	279 6/8
Eighth Place	Alberta	277 5/8
Ninth Place	Nebraska	277 3/8
Tenth Place	Nova Scotia	273 6/8

Number of Boone & Crockett White-Tailed Deer Entries by State and Year Taken

State	1830 to 1993	1984 to 1993	1991 to 1993
Alabama	11	4	0
Arkansas	50	17	10
Colorado	15	12	5
Connecticut	4	3	1
Delaware	3	2	1
Florida	1	0	0
Georgia	65	24	7
Idaho	35	19	7
Illinois	224	175	81
Indiana	50	38	15
Iowa	317	190	56
Kansas	128	89	29
Louisiana	27	5	1
Maine	62	16	4
Maryland	21	11	2
Massachusetts	1	1	1
Michigan	77	38	13
Minnesota	420	125	42
Mississippi	28	8	0
Missouri	119	69	29
Montana	78	24	11
Nebraska	77	23	6
New York	34	5	2
New Hampshire	4	3	3
North Carolina	5	5	1
North Dakota	34	11	5
Ohio	109	60	24
Oklahoma	23	14	4
Oregon	1	0	0
Pennsylvania	19	3	1
South Carolina	1	0	0
South Dakota	67	10	3
Tennessee	16	6	2
Texas	203	52	28
Vermont	2	1	0
Virginia	26	13	3
Washington	36	11	5
West Virginia	7	1	0
Wisconsin	272	97	28
Wyoming	27	13	5
Totals	**2,699**	**1,198**	**435**

Alabama

Typical

Score	Locality Killed / By Whom Killed	Date Killed
186 3/8	Lee County/Picked Up	1986
182 7/8	Hale County/ James C. Bailey	1974
172 1/8	Pickens County/Walter Janes	1968
170 2/8	Lee County/George P. Mann	1980
168 2/8	Marengo County/William Wright	1979

Non-Typical

Score	Locality Killed / By Whom Killed	Date Killed
259 7/8	Perry County/Jon G. Moss	1989
114 5/8	Perry County/Robert E. Royster	1976
223 1/8	Sumter County/James Spidle Sr.	1952
217 2/8	Dallas County/Robert Tate	1988
200 1/8	Dallas County /H.Lloyd Morris	1989

Arkansas

Typical

Score	Locality Killed / By Whom Killed	Date Killed
189	Crawford County/Tom Sparks Jr.	1975
186 7/8	Arkansas County/Walter Spears	1952
184 6/8	Desha County/Lee Perry	1961
184	Arkansas County/Willard L. Harper	1946
183 7/8	White County/W. Harden, C. Craven	1993

Non-Typical

Score	Locality Killed / By Whom Killed	Date Killed
223 1/8	Cross County/Randal Harris	1986
216	Prairie County/Cecil M. Miller	1973
210 1/8	White County/Chester Weathers Sr.	1973
208 7/8	Bradley County/Carthel Forte	1971
2085/8	St. Francis County/George Hobson	1987

Colorado

Typical

Score	Locality Killed / By Whom Killed	Date Killed
182 5/8	Yuma County/Ivan W. Rhodes	1978
180 2/8	Yuma County/Jeff L. Mekelburg	1989
178 4/8	Yuma County/Terry M. Scheidecker	1979
176 3/8	Boulder County/Picked Up	1989
175 7/8	Logan County/Picked Up	1971

Non-Typical

Score	Locality Killed / By Whom Killed	Date Killed
258 2/8	Cheyenne County/Michael J. Okray	1992
204 2/8	Yuma County/Jeff L. Mekelburg	1986
201 3/8	Kiowa County/Dale A. Dilulo	1991
200 3/8	Logan County/Picked Up	1994
197 6/8	Prowers County/Samuel S. Pittillo	1988

Connecticut

Typical

Score	Locality Killed / By Whom Killed	Date Killed
179 4/8	Litchfield County/Garry J. Lovrin	1993
177 2/8	Litchfield County/Picked Up	1984
176 2/8	Litchfield County/Frederick Clymer	1987

Non-Typical

Score	Locality Killed / By Whom Killed	Date Killed
195	Windham County/Harold Tanner	1970

Delaware

Typical

Score	Locality Killed / By Whom Killed	Date Killed
185 4/8	Sussex County/Herbert N. Milam	1978
181 6/8	Sussex County/Donald L. Betts	1989
172 2/8	Sussex County/David T. Murray	1992
163 1/8	Kent County/Austin M. Carney	1989
162 7/8	Kent County/Michael J. Biggs	1991

Florida

Non-Typical

Score	Locality Killed / By Whom Killed	Date Killed
201 3/8	Wakulla County/Clark Durrance	1941
186 1/8	Jackson County/Henry Brinson	1959

Georgia

Typical

Score	Locality Killed / By Whom Killed	Date Killed
184 3/8	Paulding County/Floyd Benson	1962
184 2/8	Dooly County/Joe Morgan	1985
184	Newton County/Gene Almand	1966
184	Hart County/Kenton L. Adams	1986

Indiana

Typical

Score	Locality Killed / By Whom Killed	Date Killed
195 1/8	Parke County/B. Dodd Porter	1985
194 2/8	Vigo County/D. Bates & S. Winkler	1983
192 3/8	Monroe County/Donald L. Fritch	1992
190 5/8	Parke County/Tony A. Trotter	1992
190 2/8	Pike County/Vince Brock	1993

Non-Typical

Score	Locality Killed / By Whom Killed	Date Killed
248 4/8	Fulton County/Robert S. Sears	1990
233 2/8	Switzerland County/Henry Mitchell	1972
229 7/8	Jackson County/Larry E. Deaton	1990
226 3/8	Clark County/Robert L. Bromm Sr.	1985
225 6/8	La Porte County/David Grundy	1987

Iowa

Typical

Score	Locality Killed / By Whom Killed	Date Killed
201 4/8	Hamilton County/Wayne A. Bills	1974
196 4/8	Des Moines County/Michael R. Edle	1989
296 3/8	Plymouth County/Picked Up	1952
194 4/8	Monroe County/Lloyd Goad	1962
194 3/8	Warren County/Forest H. Richardson	1989

Non-Typical

Score	Locality Killed / By Whom Killed	Date Killed
282	Clay County/Larry Raveling	1973
258 1/8	Cedar County/Picked Up	1988
256 7/8	Jackson County/David Manderscheid	1977
256 2/8	Monona County/Carroll E. Johnson	1968
252	Lee County/Carl Wenke	1972

Kansas

Typical

Score	Locality Killed / By Whom Killed	Date Killed
198 2/8	Nemaha County/Dennis P. Finger	1974
197 2/8	Comanche County/Picked Up	1991
194 7/8	Leavenworth County/Wm. Mikijanis	1985
191 4/8	Chautauqua County/Michael Young	1973
190 7/8	Lyon County/Jamie Fowler	1992

Non-Typical

Score	Locality Killed / By Whom Killed	Date Killed
240⅜	Monroe County/John L. Hattan Jr.	1973
215⅞	Putnam County/Thomas H. Cooper	1974
211 4/8	Worth County/Wade Patterson	1988
208⅜	Decatur County/James L. Darley	1964
206⅜	Colquitt County/Picked Up	1990

Idaho

Typical

Score	Locality Killed / By Whom Killed	Date Killed
182⅝	Boundary County/Aaron M. McNall	1993
181⅞	Clearwater County/Richard Carver	1985
177⅝	Idaho County/Donna M. Knight	1986
176 6/8	Idaho County/Edward D. Moore	1986
176 6/8	Idaho County/Frank J. Loughran	1987

Non-Typical

Score	Locality Killed / By Whom Killed	Date Killed
267 4/8	Idaho/Unknown	1923
257 6/8	Nez Perce/County John D. Powers	1983
226⅜	Nez Perce County/Mrs. Ralph Bond	1964
219⅞	Clearwater County/Kipling Manfull	1989
213⅝	Bonner County/Rodney Thurlow	1968

Illinois

Typical

Score	Locality Killed / By Whom Killed	Date Killed
204 4/8	Peoria County/M.J. Johnson	1965
200 2/8	Macon County/Brian S. Damery	1993
197⅛	Macoupin County/Kevin L. Naugle	1988
192⅞	Williamson County/A. & J. Albers	1991
191⅞	Wayne County/Leo E. Elliott	1990

Non-Typical

Score	Locality Killed / By Whom Killed	Date Killed
267⅜	Peoria County/Richard A. Pauli	1983
256⅛	McDonough County/Brian E. Bice	1992
244⅛	Sangamon County/William E. Hood	1991
242⅞	Pope County/William E. Henderson	1991
239⅛	Illinois/William Scidel	1987

Non-Typical

Score	Locality Killed / By Whom Killed	Date Killed
280 4/8	Shawnee County/Joseph H. Waters	1987
258 6/8	Republic County/John O. Band	1965
251 1/8	Mitchell County/Theron E. Wilson	1974
250 2/8	Washington County/Picked Up	1988
248 7/8	Greenwood County/Clifford G. Pickell	1968

Kentucky

Typical

Score	Locality Killed / By Whom Killed	Date Killed
191 3/8	Meade County/Picked Up	1977
188 5/8	Lewis County/Ben C. Johnson	1993
187 6/8	Union County/Charles Meuth	1964
187 1/8	Pulaski County/Scott Abbott	1982
186 2/8	Carter County/Herman G. Holbrooks	1989

Non-Typical

Score	Locality Killed / By Whom Killed	Date Killed
236 3/8	Union County/Wilbur E. Buchanan	1970
232 3/8	Breathitt County/Delmar R. Hounshell	1990
226 5/8	Pulaski County/H.C. Sumpter	1984
223 1/8	McCreary County/James H. Sanders	1957
222 5/8	Henderson County/Ronnie D. Stacy	1992

Louisiana

Typical

Score	Locality Killed / By Whom Killed	Date Killed
184 6/8	Madison Parish/John Lee	1943
184	Bossier County/Earnest O. McCoy	1961
180 5/8	St. Landry Parish/Shawn P. Ortego	1975
180 4/8	Madison Parish/Buford Perry	1961

Non-Typical

Score	Locality Killed / By Whom Killed	Date Killed
281 6/8	Tenas Parish/James H. McMurray	1994
252 2/8	Concordia Parish/J.O. Shields	1948
227	Concordia Parish/Picked Up	1969
219 6/8	Caddo Parish/William D. Ethredge, Jr.	1988
218 4/8	St. Martin Parish/Drew Ware	1941

Maine

Typical

Score	Locality Killed / By Whom Killed	Date Killed
193 2/8	Aroostock County/Ronnie Cox	1965
192 7/8	York County/Alphonse Chase	1920
186 2/8	Hancock County/Gerald C. Murray	1984
184 5/8	Washington County/Unknown	1944
184 1/8	Waldo County/Christopher Ramsey	1983

Non-Typical

Score	Locality Killed / By Whom Killed	Date Killed
259	Washington County/Hill Gould	1910
248 1/8	Penobscot County/Unknown	1945
228 7/8	Cherryfield/Flora Campbell	1953
228 1/8	Maine/Henry A. Caesar	1911
224	Hancock County/Picked Up	1975

Maryland

Typical

Score	Locality Killed / By Whom Killed	Date Killed
184	St. Marys County/Larry O. Day	1990
183 3/8	Dorchester County/John R. Seifert, Jr.	1973
181 6/8	Montgomery County/Gary F. Menso	1985
178 1/8	Kent County/Herman Gravatt	1955
177 7/8	St. Marys County/Timothy B. Moore	1990

Non-Typical

Score	Locality Killed / By Whom Killed	Date Killed
228 4/8	Montgomery County/John W. Poole	1987
221 3/8	Anne Arundel County/Unknown	1979
217 2/8	Talbot County/Vincent L. Jordan, Sr.	1974
216 6/8	Charles County/Brian G. Klaas	1993

Massachusetts

Typical

175 3/8	Worcester County/Thomas W. Bombard	1992

Michigan

Typical

Score	Locality Killed / By Whom Killed	Date Killed
193 2/8	Jackson County/Craig Calderone	1986

186 3/8	Ontonagon County/Unknown	1980
184 7/8	Baraga County/Louis J. Roy	1987
182 7/8	Iosco County/Harvey H. Keast	1938
181 5/8	Ionia County/Lester Bowen	1947

Non-Typical

Score	Locality Killed / By Whom Killed	Date Killed
238 2/8	Bay County/Paul M. Mickey	1976
221 2/8	Lapeer County/Picked Up	1993
218 7/8	St. Joseph County/Picked Up	1989
218 3/8	Keweenaw County/Bernard J. Murn	1980
215 5/8	Iron County/C. & R. Lester	1970

Minnesota

Typical

Score	Locality Killed / By Whom Killed	Date Killed
202	Beltrami County/John A. Breen	1918
201	Kittson County/Wayne G. Stewart	1961
199 2/8	Lake of the Woods County/V. Jensen	1954
197 6/8	Wright County/Curtis F. Van Lith	1986
195 5/8	Marshall County/Robert Sands	1960

Non-Typical

Score	Locality Killed / By Whom Killed	Date Killed
268 5/8	Norman County/Mitchell A Vakoch	1974
258 2/8	Becker County/J.J. Matter	1973
251 4/8	Beltrami County/Rodney Rhineberger	1976
249 2/8	Fillmore County/Dallas R. Henn	1961
245 5/8	Itasca County/Peter Rutkowski	1942

Mississippi

Typical

Score	Locality Killed / By Whom Killed	Date Killed
182 7/8	Noxubee County/Glen D. Jourdon	1986
182 2/8	Claiborne County/R.L. Bobo	1955
181 5/8	Wilkinson County/Ronnie P. Whitaker	1981
180 4/8	Leflore County/W.F. Smith	1968
179 2/8	Hinds County/Marlon Stokes	1988

Non-Typical

Score	Locality Killed / By Whom Killed	Date Killed
225	Londes County/Richard Herring	1988
221 2/8	Holmes County/Milton Parrish	1970

217 5/8	Carroll County/Mark T. Hathcock	1978
209 6/8	Franklin County/Ronnie Strickland	1981
205 6/8	Lowndes County/Joe W. Shurden	1976

Missouri

Typical

Score	Locality Killed / By Whom Killed	Date Killed
205	Randolph County/Larry W. Gibson	1971
199 4/8	Clark County/Jeffrey A. Brunk	1969
190 3/8	Pettis County/Jesse A. Perry	1986
187 2/8	Scotland County/Robin Berhorst	1971
187 1/8	Cooper County/Joe Ditto	1974

Non-Typical

Score	Locality Killed / By Whom Killed	Date Killed
333 7/8	St. Louis County/Picked Up	1981
259 5/8	Chariton County/Duane R. Linscott	1985
225 1/8	Nodaway County/Ken Barcus	1982
221 4/8	Pike County/Billy J. Schanks	1991
219 5/8	Warren County/James E. Williams	1959

Montana

Typical

Score	Locality Killed / By Whom Killed	Date Killed
199 3/8	Missoula County/Thomas H. Dellwo	1974
191 5/8	Flathead County/Earl T. McMaster	1963
189 1/8	Blaine County/Kenneth Morehouse	1959
188 5/8	Flathead County/Len E. Patterson	1992
186 3/8	Flathead County/Unknown	1973

Non-Typical

Score	Locality Killed / By Whom Killed	Date Killed
252 1/8	Hill County/Frank A. Pleskac	1968
248 5/8	Snowy Mountains/Unknown	1980
241 7/8	Flathead County/George Woldstad	1960
234 1/8	Glacier County/Unknown	1968
232 7/8	Montana/Unknown	1950

Nebraska

Typical

Score	Locality Killed / By Whom Killed	Date Killed
194 1/8	Dakota County/E. Keith Fahrenholz	1966

189 1/8	Nuckolls County/Van Shotzman	1968
185 5/8	Nenzel/Richard Kehr	1965
1855/8	Polk County/Keith Houdersheldt	1985
1921/8	Frontier County/Robert G. Bortner	1985

Non-Typical

Score	Locality Killed / By Whom Killed	Date Killed
277 3/8	Hall County/Del Austin	1962
242 5/8	Nance County/Robert E. Snyder	1961
238	Keya Paha County/Donald B. Phipps	1969
234 5/8	Nebraska/Picked Up	1972
233 6/8	Custer County/Lonnie E. Poland	1986

New Hampshire

Typical

Score	Locality Killed / By Whom Killed	Date Killed
172 7/8	Sullivan County/Gordon E. Adams	1992
172 6/8	Cheshire County/Peter J. Krochunas	1991
170 3/8	Grafton County/William M. Gordon	1993
168 3/8	Cheshire County/Richard J. Jarvis	1988
164 6/8	Belknap County/Picked Up	1981

Non-Typical

Score	Locality Killed / By Whom Killed	Date Killed
211 4/8	Hillsborough County/Curtiss Whipple	1947
193 2/8	Rockingham County/A.E. Field	1991
191 1/8	Rockingham County/Theron Young Sr.	1945

New York

Typical

Score	Locality Killed / By Whom Killed	Date Killed
198 3/8	Allegany County/Roosevelt Luckey	1939
181 3/8	Orange County/Roy Vail	1960
180 3/8	Livingston County/Edward Beare	1943
179 3/8	Essex County/Herbert Jaquish	1953
178 5/8	Monroe County/David P. Ives	1993

Non-Typical

Score	Locality Killed / By Whom Killed	Date Killed
244 2/8	Allegany County/Homer Boylan	1939
225 2/8	St. Lawrence County/Kenneth M. Locy	1992
219 7/8	Genesee County/Robert Wood	1944
270 7/8	Suffolk County/George Hackal	1950

207 4/8	Portageville/Howard W. Smith	1959

North Carolina

Typical

Score	Locality Killed / By Whom Killed	Date Killed
181 7/8	Guilford County/Terry E. Faffron	1987
178	Caswell County/Picked Up	1988
172 4/8	Guilford County/Rodney D. Summers	1993
172 1/8	Granville County/Dudley Barnes	1985
170 4/8	Rockingham County/Lindsey H. Watkins	1987

North Dakota

Typical

Score	Locality Killed / By Whom Killed	Date Killed
189 3/8	McKenzie County/Gene Veeder	1972
187 5/8	Emmons County/Joseph F. Bosch	1959
187 2/8	McLean County/Frank O. Bauman	1986
182	Zap/Wally Duckwitz	1962
178 2/8	Richland County/Jeffrey Krabbenhoft	1993

Non-Typical

Score	Locality Killed / By Whom Killed	Date Killed
254 6/8	Stanley/Roger Ritchie	1968
232 1/8	McLean County/Olaf P. Anderson	1886
220 7/8	Pembina County/Gary F. Bourbanis	1985
216 6/8	Kathryn/Gerald R. Elsner	1963
210 5/8	Renville County/Glen Southam	1978

Ohio

Typical

Score	Locality Killed / By Whom Killed	Date Killed
186 6/8	Logan County/Bernard R. Hines	1990
184 6/8	Muskingum County/Dale Hartberger	1981
184 1/8	Vinton County/Dan F. Allison	1965
184 1/8	Carroll County/Timothy F. Treadway	1989
183	Piedmont Lake/J. Rumbaugh & J. Ruyan	1958

Non-Typical

Score	Locality Killed / By Whom Killed	Date Killed
328 2/8	Portage County/Picked Up	1940
256 5/8	Holmes County/Picked Up	1975

250%	Richland County/David D. Dull	1987
243%	Mahoning County/David L. Klemm	1980
238%	Mahoning County/Ronald K. Osborne	1986

Oklahoma

Typical

Score	Locality Killed / By Whom Killed	Date Killed
177⅝	Harper County/Scott Davis	1993
177%	Atoka County/Skip Rowell	1972
174%	Beaver County/Tanner Alexander	1990
173%	Woods County/Jack Clover	1983
173%	Rodgers County/Marc Thompson	1991

Non-Typical

Score	Locality Killed / By Whom Killed	Date Killed
247%	Johnston County/Bill M. Foster	1970
234%	Alfalfa County/Loren Tarrant	1984
229%	Dewey County/Ricky C. Watt	1987
225⅛	Comanche County/Michael C. Apoka	1993
223%	Woods County/Monty E. Pfleider	1987

Oregon

Typical

Score	Locality Killed / By Whom Killed	Date Killed
178⅔	Wallowa County/Sterling K. Shaver	1982
165%	Wallowa County/James H. Hambleton	1992
163⅛	Umatilla County/Jeffrey A. Koorenny	1987
161⅛	Wallowa County/Larry V. Haney	1992

Pennsylvania

Typical

Score	Locality Killed / By Whom Killed	Date Killed
184%	Greene County/Ivan Parry	1974
182%	Sullivan County/Floyd Reibson	1930
177%	Bedford County/Raymond Miller	1957
176%	Miffin County/John Zerba	1936
176	Bradford County/Clyde H. Rinehuls	1944

Non-Typical

Score	Locality Killed / By Whom Killed	Date Killed
213%	Lycoming County/Al Prouty	1949
209	York County/Kevin R. Brumgard	1992

207 7/8	Port Royal/C. Ralph Landis	1951
201 1/8	Westmoreland County/Richard K. Mellon	1966
196 6/8	Perry County/Kenneth Reisinger	1949

South Carolina

Typical

Score	Locality Killed / By Whom Killed	Date Killed
167 3/8	Saluda County/Tristan A. DuBose	1993

Non-Typical

Score	Locality Killed / By Whom Killed	Date Killed
208 5/8	Beaufort County/John M. Wood	1971

South Dakota

Typical

Score	Locality Killed / By Whom Killed	Date Killed
193	South Dakota/Unknown	1964
192	Lyman County/Bob Weidner	1957
189 5/8	Tabor/Duane Graber	1954
184 3/8	Kingsbury County/Rudy F. Weigel	1960
182 5/8	Jones County/Richard A. Gordon	1989

Non-Typical

Score	Locality Killed / By Whom Killed	Date Killed
256 1/8	Marshall County/Francis Fink	1948
250 6/8	South Dakota/Howard Eaton	1870
249 1/8	Lily/Jerry Roitsch	1965
238 2/8	Potter County/Larry Nylander	1963
235 3/8	Harding County/J. Krueger & R. Keeton	1965

Tennessee

Typical

Score	Locality Killed / By Whom Killed	Date Killed
186 1/8	Roane County/W.A. Foster	1959
184 4/8	Fayette County/Benny M. Johnson	1979
178 5/8	Scott County/Charles H. Smith	1978
173 4/8	Shelby County/John J. Heirigs	1962
173 2/8	Decatur County/Glen D. Odle	1972

Non-Typical

Score	Locality Killed / By Whom Killed	Date Killed
223 4/8	Hawkins County/Luther E. Fuller	1984

209 7/8	Hawkins County/Johnny W. Byington	1982
198 3/8	Montgomery County/Clarence McElhaney	1978
196 6/8	Unicoi County/Elmer Payne	1972
196	McNairy County/Bradley S. Koeppel	1993

Texas

Typical

Score	Locality Killed / By Whom Killed	Date Killed
196 4/8	Maverick County/Tom McCulloch	1963
196 1/8	McMullen County/Milton P. George	1906
192 2/8	Frio County/Basil Dailey	1903
190 2/8	Shackelford County/Steven W. O'Carroll	1991
190	Dimmit County/C.P. Howard	1950

Non-Typical

Score	Locality Killed / By Whom Killed	Date Killed
286	Brady/Jeff Benson	1892
272	Junction/Picked Up	1925
247 7/8	Frio County/Raul Rodriquez II	1966
244 2/8	Zavala County/John R. Campbell	1947
240	Kerr County/Walter R. Schreiner	1905

Vermont

Typical

Score	Locality Killed / By Whom Killed	Date Killed
171	Windsor County/Picked Up	1935
170 1/8	Essex County/Kevin A. Brockney	1986

Virginia

Typical

Score	Locality Killed / By Whom Killed	Date Killed
188 6/8	Shenandoah County/Gene Wilson	1985
178 3/8	Goochland County/Edward W. Fielder	1981
177 2/8	August County/Donald W. Houser	1963
176 7/8	Prince George County/Fred W. Collins	1949
176 2/8	Rappahannock County/George Beahm	1959

Non-Typical

Score	Locality Killed / By Whom Killed	Date Killed
257 4/8	Warren County/James W. Smith	1992
249 3/8	Rockingham County/Jeffery W. Hensley	1990

242%	Bedford County/Walter Hatcher	1993
232%	Buckingham County/James R. Shumaker	1986
221% ·	Louisa County/Picked Up	1981

Washington

Typical

Score	Locality Killed / By Whom Killed	Date Killed
181%	Whitman County/George A. Cook III	1985
180%	Okanogan County/Joe Peone	1983
179%	Spokane County/Bert E. Smith	1972
178%	Addy/Irving Naff	1957
176%	Washington/Unknown	1953

Non-Typical

Score	Locality Killed / By Whom Killed	Date Killed
234%	Stevens County/Larry G. Gardner	1953
233%	Thompson Creek/George Sly Jr.	1964
231	Stevens County/Joe Bussano	1946
227%	Pullman/Glenn C. Paulson	1965
223%	Stevens County/Mike W. Naff	1992

West Virginia

Typical

Score	Locality Killed / By Whom Killed	Date Killed
182%	Braxton County/William D. Given	1976
180%	Cheat Mt./Joseph V. Volitis	1969
175%	Wetzel County/Matthew Scheibelhood	1984
171	Hampshire County/Conda L. Shanholtz	1958

Non-Typical

Score	Locality Killed / By Whom Killed	Date Killed
205%	Ritchie County/Charles E. Bailey, Jr.	1979
204%	Gilmer County/Brooks Reed	1960
203%	Wetzel County/Tom Kirkhart	1981
187%	Hancock County/Shawn J. Sargent	1990

Wisconsin

Typical

Score	Locality Killed / By Whom Killed	Date Killed
206%	Burnett County/James Jordan	1914
197%	Wood County/Joe Haske	1945
191%	Vilas County/Robert Hunter	1910

189 7/8	Trempealeau County/Emil Stelmach	1959
189 1/8	Douglas County/Bryan Lawler	1946

Non-Typical

Score	Locality Killed / By Whom Killed	Date Killed
245	Buffalo County/Elmer F. Gotz	1973
241 3/8	Wisconsin/Unknown	1940
233 7/8	Loraine/Homer Pearson	1937
233	Burnett County/Victor Rammer	1949
232	Waukesha County/John Herr Sr.	1955

Wyoming

Typical

Score	Locality Killed / By Whom Killed	Date Killed
191 4/8	Albany County/Robert D. Ross	1986
177 1/8	Newcastle/H.W. Julien	1954
176 2/8	Converse County/Basil C. Bradbury	1990
174 3/8	Goshen County/Casey L. Hunter	1984
173	Big Horn County/Daniel D. Wood	1989

Non-Typical

Score	Locality Killed / By Whom Killed	Date Killed
238 7/8	Crook County/Picked Up	1962
224 1/8	Crook County/John S. Mahoney	1947
217 7/8	Washakie County/Kenneth A. Fossum	1991
217 3/8	Weston County/Harry Phillips	1957
214 7/8	Big Horn County/Michael K. Smith	1987

Alberta

Typical

204 2/8	Beaverdam Creek/Stephen Jansen	1967
199 5/8	Edmonton/Don McGarvey	1991
197 3/8	Mann Lakes/Lawrence J. Youngman	1992
192 7/8	Wabatansik Creek/Norman Trudeau	1992
190 5/8	Buffalo Lake/Eugene L. Boll	1969

Non-Typical

Score	Locality Killed / By Whom Killed	Date Killed
279 6/8	Whitemud Creek/Neil J. Morin	1991
277 5/8	Hardisty/Doug Klinger	1976
267 7/8	Shoal Lake/Jerry Froma	1984
255 4/8	Pigeon Lake/Leo Eklund	1973
241 1/8	Bighill Creek/Donald D. Dwernychuk	1984

British Columbia

Typical

Score	Locality Killed / By Whom Killed	Date Killed
184⅞	Aitken Creek/Guyle Cox	1990
183⅜	Holmes River/Randy Lloyd	1991
180	Dawson Creek/H. Peter Bruhs	1989
177⅞	Ymir/Frank Gowing	1961
175⅞	Pouce Coupe River/Dale Callahan	1986

Non-Typical

Score	Locality Killed / By Whom Killed	Date Killed
245⅞	Elk River/James I. Brewster	1905
230⅞	West Kootenay/Karl H. Kast	1940
219⅜	Midway/Gordon Kamigochi	1980
218⅝	Dawston Creek/John D. Todd	1992
203⅜	Upper Cutbank/William E. Eckert	1990

Manitoba

Typical

Score	Locality Killed / By Whom Killed	Date Killed
197⅞	Assiniboine River/Larry H. MacDonald	1980
189	Red Deer Lake/Will Bigelow	1986
188⅜	Souris River/Wes Todoruk	1986
188⅜	Sanford/Picked Up	1982
187⅜	Mantagao Lake/Picked Up	1988

Non-Typical

Score	Locality Killed / By Whom Killed	Date Killed
258⅜	Steep Rock/Unknown	1973
257⅜	Elkhorn/Harvey Olsen	1973
241⅝	Manitoba/Unknown	1984
238⅜	Assiniboine River/Doug Hawkins	1981
237⅜	Whiteshell/Angus McVicar	1925

New Brunswick

Typical

Score	Locality Killed / By Whom Killed	Date Killed
182⅞	Oromocto River/Bruce MacGougan	1984
180⅜	New Brusnwich/Unknown	1937
178⅜	Queens County/Bert Bourque	1970
176⅜	Charlotte County/Albert E. Dewar	1960
175⅜	Nine Mile Brook/Leopold Leblanc	1973

Non-Typical

Score	Locality Killed / By Whom Killed	Date Killed
249 7/8	Kings County/Ronald Martin	1946
243 7/8	Wirral/H. Glenn Johnston	1962
224 2/8	Salmon River/Ford Fulton	1966
214 7/8	St. John County/T. Emery	1968

Nova Scotia

Typical

Score	Locality Killed / By Whom Killed	Date Killed
193 6/8	Antigonish County/Unknown	1987
179	Pictou County/Earl Perry	1990
174 6/8	Lake William/Neil G. Oickle	1985
170 7/8	McDonald Lake/Frederick Zwarum	1976
170 6/8	Guysborough County/Roy B. Simpson	1968

Non-Typical

Score	Locality Killed / By Whom Killed	Date Killed
273 6/8	West Afton River/Alexander C. MacDonald	1960
253	Goildenville/Neil MacDonald	1945
233 1/8	Condon Lakes/Don McDonnell	1987
222 4/8	Ostrea Lake/Verden M. Baker	1949
218 7/8	Bay of Fundy/Basil S. Lewis	1983

Ontario

Typical

Score	Locality Killed / By Whom Killed	Date Killed
177	Rainey River/Robert K. Hayes	1949
174 1/8	Amherstview/Tony H. Stranak	1987
172 2/8	Rainy Lake/Andrew Brigham	1989
171 2/8	Macintosh/Richard Kouhi	1967
171 1/8	Perth/Robert J. Moir	1992

Non-Typical

Score	Locality Killed / By Whom Killed	Date Killed
234 5/8	Round Lake/Picked Up	1990
208 7/8	Rideau River/Harry Rathwell	1988

Saskatchewan

Typical

Score	Locality Killed / By Whom Killed	Date Killed
213 5/8	Biggar/Milo N. Hanson	1993
202 6/8	Barrier Valley/Bruce Ewen	1992
200 2/8	Whitkow/Peter J. Swistun	1983
195 4/8	Porcupine Plain/Philip Philipowich	1985
195 1/8	Brightsand Lake/Larry Pellerin	1993

Non-Typical

265 3/8	White Fox/Elburn Kohler	1957
251 4/8	Meeting Lake/Greg Brataschuk	1987
248 4/8	Moose Mt. Park/Walter Bartko	1964
245 4/8	Carrot River/Picked Up	1962
243 5/8	Govan/A.W. Davis	1951

Mexico

Typical

Score	Locality Killed / By Whom Killed	Date Killed
184 5/8	Nuevo Leon/Charles H. Priess	1985
183 1/8	Nuevo Leon/Thomas D. Brittingham	1990
182 6/8	Coahuila/Manuel A. Flores Rojas	1990
181 7/8	Coahuila/German Lopez Flores	1986
181 6/8	Nuevo Leon/J.P. Davis	1985

Non-Typical

Score	Locality Killed / By Whom Killed	Date Killed
223 6/8	Nuevo Leon/Ron Kolpin	1983
210 6/8	Coahuila/Picked Up	1981
208 1/8	Mexico/Unknown	1959
200 6/8	Coahuila/Biff MacCollum	1992
196 3/8	Coahuila/Jeanie D. Willard	1993

Records of the Pope & Young Club

Your 1997 *Deer Hunters' Almanac* includes the top 10 white-tailed deer listings of the Pope and Young Club. The records listed here are taken from the club's *Bowhunting Big Game Records of North America*, fourth edition 1993, with the permission of the Pope and Young Club. The records appearing here are only a partial listing of the top whitetails. For information on the complete record book, write Pope and Young Club Inc., Box 548, Chatfield, MN 55923.

WHITE-TAILED DEER (Typical Antlers)
Top Ten

Score	Area	State	Hunter's Name	Date	Rank
204 4/8	Peoria County	IL	M.J. Johnson	1965	1
197 6/8	Monroe County	IA	Lloyd Goad	1962	2
197 6/8	Wright County	MN	Curt Van Lith	1966	2
197 1/8	Edmonton	ALB	Don McGarvey	1961	4
194 2/8	Jones County	IA	Robert L. Miller	1977	5
194 0/8	Logan County	CO	Stuart Clodfielder	1981	6
193 2/8	Jackson County	MI	Craig Calderone	1986	7
190 5/8	Warren County	IA	Richard Swim	1981	8
190 4/8	Parke County	IN	B. Dodd Porter	1985	9
189 1/8	Kearney County	NE	Robert Vrbsky	1978	10

WHITE-TAILED DEER (Non-typical Antlers)
Top Ten

Score	Area	State	Hunter's Name	Date	Rank
279 7/8	Hall County	NE	Del Austin	1962	1
257 0/8	Reno County	KS	Ken Flowler	1988	2
249 6/8	Greenwood Cty.	KS	Clifford Pickell	1968	3
245 5/8	Vermilion Cty.	IL	Robert Chestnut	1981	4
245 4/8	Chase County	KS	Douglas Siebert	1988	5
241 2/8	Cochrane	ALB	Dean Dwernuchuk	1984	6
238 6/8	Mahoning Cty.	OH	Ronald K. Osborne	1986	7
237 5/8	Wilson County	KS	Gilbert Boss	1986	8
233 7/8	Greenwood Cty.	KS	Randy Young	1989	9
232 7/8	Kiowa County	KS	Royce E. Frazier	1978	10

Hard Questions

To hunters, there is a division between the poachers and the law-abiding hunter. ... But to an outside observer, especially a non-hunter or an anti-hunter, the line is blurred, especially considering most of the poaching goes on during the legal hunting season.

■ *Joel Spring*

tem one: While crossing the brushy woodlot, my father-in-law, Howard, and I came upon a pair of hunters following a blood trail on our property. We chatted with the two men, and discovered they were our new neighbors. They explained that they had shot a buck, and that it ran onto our land. We told them they were welcome to trail wounded deer onto our land any time. We've all been in that situation.

Moments later, the four of us found the 4-pointer, which had two hits to the chest cavity. The two men dressed the buck and dragged it back to their land after politely thanking us. Howard headed toward his stand and I, out of

curiosity, followed the bright blood trail back to a huge, homemade tree stand nestled in a tree that displayed our posted sign. The tree wasn't anywhere near the new neighbor's property line, but it was within sight of the road. Two .270 cases were still inside.

No big deal, right?

Item two:
A hunter wandered beneath my overlook on a rocky ridge. He seemed lost. I waved my hand to attract his attention.

"Are you lost?" I asked.

He told me that "Danny" said it was OK to hunt here.

"Danny who?" I asked.

He gave me a dirty look and walked away, mumbling to himself.

No big deal, right?

Item three:
I looked down at my watch, waiting to start our simple two-man push. Hidden in the thick brush to my left, my partner was also anxious. While other hunters in our group got into position for the "The Pasture Drive," I sat on an ancient stone wall with my back to the big field and road. I was amused by a button buck feeding in the center of the field, oblivious to the hunting season. I heard a truck coming up the

road and turned around to see the bright blue, brand-new truck stop about 200 yards away. The driver's door popped open, and the driver emerged with a gun. He loaded it and leaned across the hood to shoot. A puff of dirt flew near the little buck's feet, but the deer stood still. I couldn't believe it. I was fully clad in hunter orange. The man had to see me. I headed out of shooting range and toward the road. I circled around to the truck and yelled at the shooter.

"Stop shooting! What's wrong with you? We've got men down there in the woods!"

"— — you," he shouted defiantly, and then jumped into his truck and sped away before I could read his license plate. I headed back into the woods to let my confused hunting partners know what all the shooting was about.

No big deal, right?

Wrong. All the situations were wrong.

The above items are true. They contain no exaggerations or embellishments. As hunters, most of us have probably had similar experiences. What disturbs me the most is that these three encounters didn't take place years apart. They occurred during the first two days of a recent rifle season.

Our property doesn't border public land, and we post the

Unfortunately, the outlaws too often become the poster-children of hunting. Their bold, disgraceful acts are far more visible than the honest hunter's quiet pursuits.

area heavily. We've never denied anyone permission to hunt, yet we have rarely been asked.

So, what's the problem? It's easy to blame the "city" hunters or the "out-of-staters," but that's often nonsense. The culprits might be closer than you think. In fact, unfortunately, they might be staying in your hunting cabin each fall. Maybe they even live in your house. Whoever they are, and wherever they come from, they gut-shoot deer hunting every fall.

Period.

If these outlaws make hunting less enjoyable for serious hunters, consider how they affect our image outside of the hunting community. Trespassing is always a concern, but I have trouble labeling someone a "poacher" merely because he or she crossed an old fence and 50 yards of brush. But when these people trespass onto lands owned by those who don't want hunters on their property, hunting suffers serious damage. The public's perception of us is much more important than our own perception of each other.

To hunters, there is a division between the poachers and the law-abiding hunter. To a true hunter, there is a lot of difference between a hunter who sits in a tree to kill his deer and one who sits in his truck on the edge of the road. But to an outside observer, especially a non-hunter or an anti-hunter, the line is blurred, especially since most of the poaching goes on during the legal hunting season. If "they" are so different from us, why isn't their presence felt more heavily year-round?

The fact that so much poaching occurs during deer season might be a case of mere opportunity. As with the criminal who finds it easier to snatch purses in crowded airports than on quiet streets, poachers find it easier to kill their prey while disguising themselves as hunters.

Unfortunately, the outlaws too often become the poster-children of hunting. Their bold, disgraceful acts are far more visible than the honest hunter's quiet pursuits.

It's up to us to show the

> *Chances are, you know them well, and you've found many excuses not to report them.*

good things hunters are doing. We see it in programs like Hunters Helping the Hungry, and in the rich principles that guide North America's wildlife management. But for every success story we hear, we seem to get a garbage truck full of bad attention.

We could blame the media or the scapegoat of your choice, but what are we doing to protect hunting? Who are the outlaws and poachers? Chances are, you know them well, and you've found many excuses not to report them, even though you can do it anonymously. Show them the door with no apologies.

Does that mean reporting the license plate of road warriors? Does it mean kicking an old friend out of camp? Or does it mean calling the poacher's hotline, and volunteering to fill out a complaint and appear in court?

Hard questions? You bet.

Contacts for Hunting Information

STATE
DEPT/ADDRESS

Alabama
Dept. of Conservation
64 North Union St.
Montgomery, AL 36130

Alaska
Dept. of Fish & Game
Div. of Fish & Wildlife Protection
Box 3-2000
Juneau, AK 99802

Arizona
Game & Fish Dept.
2221 W. Greenway Road
Phoenix, AZ 85023

Arkansas
Game & Fish Commission
No. 2 Natural Resources Drive
Little Rock, AR 72205

California
California Fish & Game
Box 944209
Sacramento, CA 94244

Colorado
Dept. of Natural Resources
Division of Wildlife
6060 Broadway
Denver, CO 80216

Connecticut
Dept. of Environment Protection
391 Route 32
North Franklin, CT 06254

Delaware
Dept. of Natural Resources
89 Kings Hwy.
Box 1401
Dover, DE 19903

STATE
DEPT/ADDRESS

Florida
Game & Fresh Water Fish Comm.
Bureau Staff Office
620 S. Meridian
Farris Bryant Blvd.
Tallahassee, FL 32399

Georgia
Dept. of Natural Resources
Wildlife Resources Division
Game Management Section
2070 US Hwy. 278 SE
Social Circle, GA 30279

Hawaii
Dept. of Land & Natural
Resources
Div. of Forestry & Wildlife
1151 Punchbowl St.
Honolulu, HI 96813

Idaho
Dept. of Fish & Game
600 S Walnut St.
Box 25
Boise, ID 83707

Illinois
Dept. of Conservation
524 S Second St.
Springfield, IL 62701

Indiana
Dept. of Natural Resources
402 W. Washington
Room 255D
Indianapolis, IN 46204

Iowa
Dept. of Natural Resources
Wallace State Office Bldg.
Des Moines, IA 50319

Contacts for Hunting Information

STATE
DEPT/ADDRESS

STATE
DEPT/ADDRESS

Kansas
Dept. of Wildlife & Parks
Route 2 Box 54A
Pratt, KS 67124

Kentucky
Dept. of Fish & Wildlife
#1 Game Farm Road
Frankfort, KY 40601

Louisiana
Dept. of Wildlife & Fisheries
Box 98000
Baton Rouge, LA 70898

Maine
Dept. of Inland Fisheries
284 State St.
State House Station 41
Augusta, ME 04333

Maryland
Department of
Natural Resources
3 Pershing St., Room 110
Cumberland, MD 21502

Massachusetts
Division of Fisheries
& Wildlife
100 Nashua St.
Boston, MA 02114

Michigan
Department of Natural Resources
Wildlife Division
Box 30028
Lansing, MI 48909

Minnesota
Dept. of Natural Resources
Division of Fish & Wildlife
Box 7 DNR Bldg.
500 Lafayette
St. Paul, MN 55155

Mississippi
Dept. of Wildlife Conservation
Southport Mall
Box 451
Jackson, MS 39205

Missouri
Dept. of Conservation
1110 S. College Avenue
Columbia, MO 65203

Montana
Department of Wildlife
1420 E. 6th Avenue
Helena, MT 59620

Nebraska
Game & Parks Commission
2200 N 33rd St.
Box 30370
Lincoln, NE 68508

Nevada
Department of Wildlife
Box 10678
1100 Valley Road
Reno, NV 89520

New Hampshire
Fish & Game Dept.
Region 1 Ofc, Rd 2
Route 3N, Box 241
Lancaster, NH 03584

New Jersey
Division of Fish,
Game &Wildlife
5 Station Plaza CN400
Trenton, NJ 08625

New Mexico
Department of
Natural Resources
Villagra Bldg 408 Galisteo
Santa Fe, NM 87503

Contacts for Hunting Information

STATE
DEPT/ADDRESS

New York
Dept. of Environ. Conservation
50 Wolf Road
Albany, NY 12233

North Carolina
Wildlife Resources Commission
512 N. Salisburg St.
Raleigh, NC 27604-1188

North Dakota
Game & Fish Dept.
100 N. Bismarck Expy.
Bismarck, ND 58501

Ohio
Dept. of Natural Resources
1840 Belcher Drive
Columbus, OH 43224

Oklahoma
Dept. of Wildlife Conservation
1801 N. Lincoln, Box 53465
Oklahoma City, OK 73105

Oregon
Dept. of Fish & Wildlife
400 Public Service Bldg.
Salem, OR 97310

Pennsylvania
Pennsylvania Game Commission
Enforcement
2001 Elmerton Avenue
Harrisburg, PA 17110

Rhode Island
Dept. of Environmental Mgmt.
83 Park St.
Providence, RI 02903

South Carolina
Dept. of Natural Resources
Box 167
Columbia, SC 29202

STATE
DEPT/ADDRESS

South Dakota
Division of Wildlife
Bldg. 445 E. Capital
Pierre, SD 57501

Tennessee
Wildlife Resources
Box 40747
Nashville, TN 37204

Texas
Parks & Wildlife Dept.
4200 Smith School Road
Austin, TX 78744

Utah
Division of Wildlife Resources
1596 W. N. Temple
Salt Lake City, UT 84116

Vermont
Dept. of Fish & Wildlife
103 S. Main St., 10 S.
Waterbury, VT 05671

Virginia
VA Dept. of Game&Inland Fish.
4010 W. Broad St., Box 11104
Richmond, VA 23230

Washington
Dept. of Wildlife
600 Capitol Way N.
Olympia, WA 98501

West Virginia
Wildlife Resources
State Capital Complex
Bldg. 3
Charleston, WV 25305

Wisconsin
Dept. of Natural Resources
101 S. Webster St.
Madison, WI 53707

Contacts for Hunting Information

STATE
DEPT/ADDRESS

Wyoming
Game & Fish Department
5400 Bishop Blvd.
Cheyenne, WY 82002

Canada
Alberta Fish & Wildlife
Bramalea Building
9920 108th St.
Edmonton AB T5K 2M4
CANADA

Dept. of Natural Resources
Box 6000
Fredericton NB E3B 5H1
CANADA

Quebec
Jean-Yves Desbiens 150 Blvd.
Rene LaVefque E. 5th Floor
Quebec City PQ G1R 4Y1
CANADA

British Columbia
Fish & Wildlife Branch
Parliament Bldgs.
Victoria BC V8V 1X5
CANADA

Provincial Building
136 Exhibition St.
Kentville, King Country
Novia Scotia B4N 4E5

STATE
DEPT/ADDRESS

QUEBEC Wildlife Federation
Castelneau St. La Tuque PQ G9X
2P4
CANADA

Energy & Natural Resources
Mail Floor, N. Tower 9945-108 St.
Edmonton AB T5K 2G6
CANADA

Wildlife Branch
Dept. of Natural Resources
Box 24, 1495 St. James St.
Winnipeg MB R3H OW9
CANADA

ON Federation of Anglers &
Hunters
2740 Queensview Drive
Ottawa ON K2B 1A2
CANADA

SK Dept. of Environment &
Resource Management
Box 3003
Prince Albert, SK S6V 6G1
CANADA

Venison Recipes

A few years back, the editors of *Deer & Deer Hunting* asked the magazine's readers to send their favorite venison recipes. The response was incredible. In fact, the magazine received enough recipes to fill a book: *301 Venison Recipes: The Ultimate Deer Hunter's Cookbook*.

To pass along some of the better dishes, we include several pages of recipes annually in the *Deer Hunters' Almanac*. This year's selections include a wonderful variety, and every section is indexed!

Use this list to reference your favorite venison recipes:

Venison Marinade

1½ inch thick venison steak (hind quarters) or 4½ inch thick slices from tenderloin, or 2 cups cubed meat for stews or stir-fry

ADD:
1 cup dry red wine (burgundy preferred)
3 tablespoons light soy sauce
2 tablespoons balsamic vinegar
1 tablespoon fresh ground pepper

¼ cup apple juice (cider or applejack)
2 tablespoons dry garlic chips
½ teaspoon powdered fennel

Marinate for 24 hours, turning 3 or 4 times. Remove meat and cook as you would for the recipe you prefer. My favorite is below.
For tenderloin sauce:
Remove tenderloins from solid piece cutting them in 1 inch slices. Flatten to ½ inch and roll with a rolling pin to give a bigger cooking surface. Marinate 4 hours in above marinade. Remove meat; reserve liquid for sauce. Saute in 1 tablespoon butter or margarine and 2 tablespoons olive oil that has been heated to HOT. Sear each piece on both sides. Salt and pepper each side. Remove meat and keep warm. Add reserve marinade, ¼ cup beef or veal stock or just plain water. Reduce to ½ volume. Add 1 pat of butter or margarine to slightly thicken. Pour over tenderloins.

— *H. M. Balch, Edo, PA*

Favorite Steak Sandwiches

2 pounds venison round steak, cut into serving size pieces. Marinate overnight in:

Milk
Flour
Salt and pepper
Garlic powder

Minced onion flakes
Stick of butter or margarine
1 long loaf French bread

Salt & pepper meat; dredge in flour. Brown in small amount of oil in skillet over medium heat. After meat is browned add ½ cup water and cook over low heat until tender.
Slice bread lengthwise, spread butter or margarine on each side.
Sprinkle with garlic powder and minced onion flakes.
Lay slices of meat on bottom half; top with other half of bread. Wrap

in foil. Heat in 300 degree oven until bread is heated through and margarine is melted. Cut into serving size sandwiches. Serve with sliced onions, pickles and peppers.

— *Donna Toms, Danville, Ill.*

Grilled Tenderloin

Marinade:
¼ cup red wine vinegar
1 tablespoon ketchup
1 tablespoon soy sauce

1 tablespoon olive oil
Nature's Seasoning to taste
Pepper to taste

Cut tenderloin across grain of meat approximately ½-inch thick. Soak steaks in marinade for 2 hours at room temperature. Place on hot charcoal grill and cook accordingly.

— *Michael L. Bankhead, Great Falls, S.C.*

Venison Steak

4-5 pieces of venison steak per person
6-8 pieces of bacon
2 large onions, sliced

½ teaspoon sugar
Lemon and pepper seasoning to taste

Fry the bacon. Set aside in a heated dish. In the pan, leave 2-3 tablespoons bacon drippings. Add the onions and sugar. Simmer until tender, add the bacon slices to rewarm if necessary. Remove both to heated covered dish. Sprinkle both sides of meat liberally with lemon and pepper seasoning. Add 1-2 tablespoons bacon drippings to electric frying pan and heat to about 300 or medium high heat. The flavor of venison is best when it's slightly pink. Have your watch with the second hand ready. Your timing depends on the thickness of your steaks. For ½-inch tenderloins, fry them about 1 minute on each side. Your timing begins as you place them in the frying pan, turn them in the same order. I always check the first piece to see if it's cooked sufficiently.
It's better to under cook. Remove steak to heated, covered serving dish.

— *Maren Wegner, Blue Mounds, Wis.*

Venison Barbecue

1 medium venison roast
3-4 venison chops
1 medium round steak

3 medium onions, sliced
1 18-ounce bottle barbecue sauce

Soak meat 3 to 4 hours in saltwater. Drain water and place meat in
slow cooker or Crock-Pot and add onions and water. Cook 7 to 8 hours
on medium heat until done. Strain water and remove onions. Shred
meat, removing all fat. Add your favorite barbeque sauce and stir
together. Place back in Crock-Pot and heat.

— *B. Moore, Igsport, Tenn.*

Grilled Deer Ribs

Cut rack of ribs into hand-size pieces using a meat saw or hack saw. Rib
bones fragment easily; therefore, a hatchet or meat cleaver should
never be used to divide ribs. Season ribs with powdered garlic, black
pepper, Lawry's seasoning salt and thyme leaves. Tenderize ribs in a
pressure cooker for 20-30 minutes. Add your favorite barbecue sauce
(mine below) and cook over charcoal or broil in oven. A thick sauce is
desirable when cooking with charcoal.

Barbecue Sauce

2 bottles (34-ounce) ketchup
½ cup yellow mustard
Add a few drops of hot sauce if desired

½ cup apple cider vinegar
½ cup sugar
2 squirts of lemon juice

— *Joe Hamilton, Biologist, S.C. Wildlife & Marine Resources Dept.*

Venison Crock-Pot Barbecue

Put 3½ to 4 pounds venison in Crock-Pot. Then pour water over venison
with ⅔ cup of vinegar. Cook on high temperature until venison is done,
about 1½ hours. Pour off water, cut venison into little pieces and return
to Crock-Pot. Dice onion and celery (enough to make a ½ cup of each),
and add to venison. Put 1 cup of barbecue sauce, 2 or 3 tablespoons of
brown sugar, 2 tablespoons of A-1 sauce into Crock-Pot and cook for 1
hour.

— *Terry Pickett, Cicero, Ind.*

Venison Barbecue

4-6 pounds venison
Vinegar for marinade
1 teaspoon pickling spice
2 tablespoons sugar
1 clove garlic
Salt and pepper
2 slices of salt pork
1 cup water

½ cup vinegar
2 tablespoons Worcestershire sauce
½ teaspoon dry mustard
1 teaspoon Tabasco sauce
1 clove garlic, mashed
½ cup mayonnaise
1 teaspoon prepared mustard

Cover venison with vinegar. Add one clove garlic, 1 teaspoon pickling spice, 2 tablespoons sugar, salt and pepper to taste. Marinate overnight. Take venison out. Do not rinse. Place in pan with two slices of salt pork. Brown the venison, add one cup water, cook slowly until almost done. Combine remaining ingredients for sauce, mix thoroughly and pour over venison. Put in hot oven and cook until golden brown.

— *Michael Ramach, Jacksonville, N.C.*

Barbecue Venison

2 pounds boneless venison
½ pound bacon
1 cup onions, chopped
2 garlic cloves, minced
1 cup ketchup

½ cup red wine vinegar
¼ cup Worcestershire sauce
¼ cup brown sugar
Rice, salt and pepper

Cut venison into pieces no larger than 1 inch cubes. In the bottom of a Dutch oven, or large frying pan, cook bacon until crisp.
Remove bacon, crumble and set aside.
In a bowl, mix all ingredients except venison and rice. Salt or pepper to taste. Brown venison in bacon drippings. Add bowl of ingredients to venison. Stir well. Cover tightly and simmer about 1 hour or until meat is tender. Stir occasionally. Serve over rice.

— *Bonnie Streff, Fredonia, Wis.*

Roast Leg of Venison Unmarinated

10 bacon slices
6-pound leg of venison
2 cloves garlic, sliced thin
1 teaspoon powdered thyme
(or thyme mixed with rosemary)
2¼ cups stock of beef broth
¼ pound butter, softened
3 tablespoons flour
Salt and pepper

Put slices of bacon under the meat and, affixed with wooden toothpicks, place other slices on top of the leg. Rub all surfaces of leg with soft butter and dust with the powdered herb or herb mixture over all.
Put the roast in uncovered roasting pan, add one-half cup liquid and roast at 325 degrees for about two hours. If you use a meat thermometer, make sure that it does not touch the bone. Venison should be served rare but not bloody. Allow 16 minutes to the pound.
Watch the meat and add liquid from time to time. Because the venison has been roasted with some liquid you may wish to turn the oven to 450 to 500 degrees for the last 10 minutes to brown the roast.
Turn off the oven, open the door and wave it open and shut a few times to reduce the heat. Then place the leg on a metal pan and keep it hot in the oven. Just hot; don't roast it any more. Serves 10.

Venison Roast

3-4 pound venison roast
6-8 strips of bacon
1 cup burgundy wine

Remove all fat from roast. Wrap bacon around roast and secure with toothpicks. Bake in an uncovered pan for about 2 hours at 325 degrees for a medium roast. During the last hour of cooking, pour the burgundy wine over the roast and baste frequently with pan juices. Use the pan juices for gravy (Don't overbake; best when pink).
Leftovers: Slice it thin and simmer it in barbecue sauce for 10 minutes. Serve on hamburger buns.

— *Maren Wegner, Blue Mound, Wis.*

Deer Roast

Soak roast ½ hour in ¼ cup salted water. Add enough water to cover, then drain and pat dry. Brown in ¼ cup fat on all sides. Add beef roast, spices, 1 8-ounce can tomato sauce and 8 ounces water. Put in roasting bag. Bake for about an hour, depending on size of roast.

— *Everitt Chesser, Springfield, Ky.*

Venison Roast

6-pound venison roast
3 tablespoons garlic, minced
2 large bell peppers, chopped
Salt, pepper, and cayenne pepper to taste
3 large onions, chopped
3 cups brewed coffee
2 6-ounce cans apple juice
1 cup white wine

Season venison with salt, black pepper, cayenne pepper and garlic.
Place in roasting pan and add bell pepper and onion.
Pour coffee, wine and apple juice over roast. Bake covered at 325
degrees for approximately 2 hours, baste often. Serves 8.

— *Don B. Adams, Newborn, Ga.*

Venison Shoulder Roast

Season meat with black pepper, garlic powder, ground ginger, rosemary,
thyme and Lawry's seasoning salt. Then brown shoulder (with or with-
out flour) in large pan.
Saute: mushrooms, onions, chopped celery and peppers. Add this to meat.
Mix 1 can cream of mushroom and cream of celery soup and 1 packet of
Lipton onion-mushroom soup mix. Add this to meat.
Vegetables: 8 small red or new potatoes, 6-8 small yellow onions, 2-3
bell peppers, and 6-8 chopped carrots. Spread over meat.
Additional seasonings: white pepper, Kitchen Bouquet, chunks of ginger
root and celery seed. Bake at 250 degrees for 4-6 hours.

— *Joe Hamilton, Biologist, S.C. Wildlife & Marine Resources Dept.*

Venison Roast

3 pounds venison
1 cup onion, chopped
4 slices bacon
1 red pepper or dash of red pepper
3 tablespoons flour
3 tablespoons red wine
Salt and pepper

Cook venison until tender in water. Add salt and pepper. Cool.
Cut into small pieces and put in pan and cover with the stock it was in.
Put onion, flour, wine and bacon strips on top. Cook for 2 hours in low
oven.

— *Michael Ramach, Jacksonville, N.C.*

Venison Stroganoff

2 pounds venison steak or roast cut into ¾-inch pieces
4-8 tablespoons margarine
½ pound mushrooms, sliced
1 12-ounce can tomato juice

1 clove garlic pressed (optional)
¼ teaspoon salt
⅛ teaspoon pepper
2 cups sour cream

Dredge meat into flour and lemon pepper; brown in margarine in Dutch oven. Add tomato juice and mushrooms. Cover and simmer 30 minutes. Add garlic and salt to taste and simmer 1 hour more. Before serving add sour cream and heat through. Serve over rice.
*Hint: the flavor of the venison improves dynamically when this is made in advance, frozen, thawed, slowly warmed and served.

— *Denny Grueneberg*
  Neenah, Wis.

Venison Paprika

¼ cup shortening
2 pounds cubed venison
1 cup onion, sliced
1 small clove garlic, minced
¾ cup ketchup
2 tablespoons Worcestershire sauce

1 tablespoon brown sugar
2 teaspoons salt
2 teaspoons paprika
½ teaspoon dry mustard
¼ cup water
Dash hot pepper

Melt shortening in large skillet. Add meat, onion and garlic.
Cook and stir until meat is brown and onion is tender.
Stir in ketchup, Worcestershire sauce, sugar, salt, paprika, mustard, hot pepper and 1½ cups water.
Cover and simmer for 2 to 2½ hours.
Blend flour and ¼ cup water, stir gradually into meat mixture. Heat to boiling, stirring constantly. Boil and stir 1 minute. Serve over noodles.

— *John D. Klinger*
  Valley View, Pa.

Venison Pilaf

4 pounds ground venison
3 cans cream of mushroom soup
3 cans cream of celery soup
1 large yellow onion
2 green bell peppers
1 red bell pepper

1 package Lipton onion-mushroom soup mix
1 large container of fresh mushrooms
4 strips bacon
3 packs yellow rice
¾ cup water

Seasonings:
Black pepper
Ground ginger
Rosemary leaves
Thyme leaves
Lawry's seasoning salt
Salt
Celery Seeds
Soy sauce
Worcestershire sauce
Garlic powder

Fry bacon until crisp and saute chopped onion, bell peppers and mushrooms in bacon drippings. Mix soups in large pot and add rice. Brown ground venison in frying pan and add to soup and rice mixture. Season soup mixture and venison separately. Add Kitchen Bouquet for darker color.

— *Joe Hamilton, Biologist, S.C. Wildlife & Marine Resources Dept.*

Deer Meat & Gravy

2 pounds venison
1 onion cut in half
Flour
Crisco
1 can cream of mushroom soup

In pressure cooker, cover deer meat with water. Sprinkle with seasoning and lay onions on top. Cook until tender. It makes its own broth. In frying pan put desired amount of Crisco for gravy, add flour for thickening, salt and pepper. Brown flour. Remove onion from meat and add meat broth only to browned flour mix. After gravy thickens, add soup and meat and simmer 5 to 10 minutes.

— *Jeff Greene, Lenoir, N.C.*

Venison Burger Soup

1-2 pounds ground venison
2 16-ounce cans of tomatoes, cut up
2 medium onions, chopped
2 stalks of celery, chopped
⅓ cup of peak barley
¼ cup ketchup

1 tablespoon bouillon
2 teaspoons seasoned salt
1 teaspoon dried basil
2-3 cups shredded cabbage
5 cups of water

In a large saucepan, brown venison and drain off fat. Stir in remaining ingredients. Bring to a boil. Reduce heat, cover and simmer for 1 hour. Season to taste with salt and pepper.

— *Charles Barker, Eagle, Mich.*

Five-Hour Venison Stew

Into Dutch oven pour:
3 cups tomato juice
½ teaspoon lemon and pepper seasoning
Add 2 pounds venison cubes and submerge.

2 tablespoons sugar
4 tablespoons tapioca

Add chunks of the following vegetables:
6 carrots
3 potatoes

5 stalks celery
1 large onion

Cover tightly and bake 5 hours at 250 degrees. NO PEEKING!

— *Lorraine Wegner, West Bend, Wis.*

Deer Stew

2 pounds deer meat
1 can tomato sauce
1½ cups water

3 tablespoons oil
1 onion

3 potatoes, chopped
6 carrots
5 medium onions
Salt and pepper to taste

Brown onion and meat in oil. Add tomato sauce and water. Simmer for hour. Add carrots, potatoes and more water if needed. Add seasonings and cook until vegetables are cooked.

— *Everitt Chesser,*
  Springfield, Ky.

Venison Soup

1 large shank bone, cut into three pieces
2 pounds shank meat
2 beef bouillon cubes
2 bay leaves
½ teaspoon savory
1 tablespoon peppercorns
1 onion sliced

Several celery leaves
1 onion, diced
3 carrots, diced
2 celery ribs, sliced
3 medium potatoes, diced
2 pounds canned tomatoes
Salt

Place bone and meat in a large pot with enough water to cover. Add bouillon, bay leaves, savory, peppercorns, onion slice and celery leaves. Place over high heat and bring to a boil. Cover and simmer for 4 hours. Remove meat and bones. Strain broth to remove bay leaves and vegetables. If there is any fat on top, skim it off. Pour the broth back in the large pot and add tomatoes, diced onion and sliced celery. Cook for 15 minutes. Add carrots and cook 10 more minutes. Add potatoes and parsley and cook for another 10 minutes. Check seasoning and add salt if necessary. Serves 6.

Venison Sausage-Vegetable Chowder

2 tablespoons butter
2 tablespoons all purpose flour
1 teaspoon salt
1 teaspoon onion powder
¼ teaspoon dried dill weed
4 cups milk

1 large package frozen vegetables, partially thawed (beans, peas and carrots or broccoli)
1 16-ounce can whole kernel corn, drained
½ pound venison sausage, sliced

In a large saucepan melt butter over low heat. Blend in flour, salt, onion powder, dill weed and pepper. Add milk all at once. Cook over medium heat, stirring constantly until thickened and bubbly. Stir the vegetables, corn and sausage into the soup. Cover and simmer for 10-15 minutes or until vegetables are done. Makes 6 servings.

Venison Chili

- 3 pounds ground venison
1 garlic clove, chopped
3 teaspoons salt
1 tablespoon red pepper
2 cans of kidney beans
½ pound shredded cheddar cheese

1 bag of nacho chips
2 onions, chopped
1 teaspoon paprika
2 tablespoons chili powder
2 cans of pork and beans
1 can tomato sauce

In a large pot, brown meat over medium heat.
Add onions, garlic, salt, red pepper, paprika, and chili powder; stirring constantly.
Once meat is cooked, stir in cans of kidney beans and pork and beans along with tomato sauce.
Lower heat; stirring occasionally.
Cook for 1 hour. Serve in bowls, top chili with shredded cheddar cheese. Add nacho chips on the side.

— *Joe Bontke*
Long Valley, N.J.

Purist Chili

2 pounds ground venison
4 strips bacon, chopped
1 medium onion, chopped
1 large clove garlic, minced
Finely slivered peel of 1 orange
1-2 tablespoons chili powder

2 tablespoons ground cumin

¼ teaspoon ground black pepper
1 cup beef broth
2 teaspoons hot paprika
3 canned jalapeno peppers, finely chopped

Saute the bacon in a 2 quart enamel saucepan until crisp. Add the onion, garlic and orange peel. Cook, stirring occasionally, 5 minutes. Add the meat and cook until light brown in color, about 4 minutes. Stir in the remaining ingredients. Heat to boiling; reduce the heat. Cook uncovered, stirring occasionally, until chili has thickened, about 1 hour and 15 minutes. Serves 4.

Adirondack Chili

3 pounds ground venison
¾ pound ground beef (chuck)
2 medium onions, diced
2 tablespoons dehydrated pepper flakes
½ stick butter or margarine
2 tablespoons garlic powder
4 tablespoons seasoned salt
4 tablespoons chili powder
3 tablespoons ground cumin
3 tablespoons black pepper (coarse ground)
4 tablespoons red-hot sauce

2 tablespoons Worcestershire sauce
1 tablespoon hot, dijon or deli mustard
½ teaspoon oregano
1 tablespoon salt
¼ teaspoon crushed red pepper
1 29-ounce can tomato puree
1 15-ounce can tomato sauce
1 6-ounce can tomato paste
2 15-ounce cans chili beans
2 15-ounce cans stewed tomatoes

Saute butter and onions. Brown meat, put in Crock pot, add seasonings, puree, paste and sauce.

Cook on high 1-2 hours, stirring occasionally, covered.
Add chili beans, cook 1 hour, add more tomato sauce if needed.

— *Robert J. Clark*
Batavia, N.Y.

Hot Tomatoed Venison

2-3 pounds ground venison or loin
1 quart tomatoes
1 quart hot sauce
2 tablespoons Worcestershire sauce

1 teaspoon marjoram
2 teaspoons fresh basil
Creole seasonings (add amount according to your taste)

Brown thinly sliced or chunked venison in butter or margarine for 1-2 minutes. Combine all the ingredients in a Crock-Pot and cook for 2-3 hours. You can serve alone or over noodles, rice or mashed potatoes.

— Hal Featherman
   Mumford, N.Y.

Buck Bourguignon

2 pounds venison (2 inch cubes)
½ pound fresh mushrooms
¼ pound bacon, smoked slab
½ pound whole small white onions, cooked
½ pound baby carrots, cooked
2 cups red wine
¼ teaspoon thyme
1 bay leaf
1 tablespoon fresh parsley, chopped
3 tablespoons flour
¼ teaspoon fresh ground pepper
¼ teaspoon salt
2 tablespoons butter
1 cup venison stock (beef stock can be used)

Slice mushrooms; saute in margarine. Set aside.
In a large pot, fry diced bacon until crisp. Remove and set aside. Drain bacon grease; place 3 tablespoons back in large pot. Put flour in a paper bag, add cubed venison and shake. Remove venison from bag, place in pot and brown well.
Add wine, thyme, salt, pepper, bay leaf, venison stock and parsley
Cover pot and simmer for 1 hour or until tender.

Add all other ingredients; simmer additional 10 minutes. Serve over egg noodles or rice.

— Joseph Yesalonis, Commack, N.Y.

Hunter's Burgoo

1½ pounds venison (stew meat, ¾-inch cubes)
16 ounce tomato sauce
3 tablespoons cooking oil
1 14½ ounce can French style green beans
1¼ cup onions, chopped
2 cloves garlic, chopped

1 cup celery, chopped -
2 4-ounce cans mild green chiles, chopped
1 10-ounce package frozen okra
1 tablespoon sugar
Pinch of Old Bay seasoning
1 teaspoon Mrs. Dash's original blend seasoning

Brown venison with one clove garlic and ¼ cup onion in cooking oil in a
Dutch oven. Add remaining ingredients except sugar, Old Bay and Mrs.
Dash's. Slow simmer until okra is cooked or desired consistency is attained.
1-2 hours. Stir in sugar, Old Bay and Mrs. Dash's and simmer 5 minutes.

— *Herb Conner, West Union, W. Va.*

Cajun Fried Backstrap

Seasoning Mix:
1½ tablespoons salt
½ teaspoon cayenne pepper
½ teaspoon white pepper
¼ teaspoon black pepper
¼ teaspoon garlic powder
¼ teaspoon onion powder
¼ teaspoon celery salt
¼ teaspoon oregano
¼ teaspoon thyme

Ingredients:
1 pound backstrap
1 egg
2 cups buttermilk
½ cup milk

½ cup flour
½ cup bread crumbs
1 cup peanut oil

Day before: Prepare seasoning mix and set aside. Slice backstrap in ½-
inch medallions. Pound to ¼ inch thick and season with 1 teaspoon of
seasoning mix. Place meat in large zip-lock bag and add the 2 cups
buttermilk. Place in refrigerator for 24 hours, turning bag occasionally.
Preparation: Mix egg and milk in large bowl and set aside.
Mix 1 teaspoon seasoning mix with flour and spread on baking sheet.
(Leftover seasoning mix may be stored and used in any meat dish).
Remove meat from buttermilk, drain and pat dry with paper towel. Dredge
in flour, then in milk and egg mixture, (shaking off excess). Dip in bread
crumbs, coating well and patting down so that crumbs adhere to meat.
Heat oil in heavy skillet on medium high heat. Fry until golden brown on
both sides — do not overcook. Serve hot with french fries, green salad
and hot buttered french bread. Serves 4.

Gyros Meat Loaf

2 pounds ground venison
1 8 oz. can tomato sauce
1 cup onion, minced
½ cup fine dry bread crumbs
2 large eggs
¼ cup mint leaves, chopped

2 teaspoons each, pepper, dry oregano and dry basil
1 teaspoon dry rosemary
2 cloves garlic, minced
Salt

In a bowl, combine meat, tomato sauce, onion, bell pepper, bread crumbs, eggs, mint pepper, oregano, basil, rosemary, garlic and ½ teaspoon salt. Squeeze mixture with your hands to mix very well. Firmly press meat into loaf pan. Bake, uncovered, in a 350-degree oven until well browned on top, about 1½ hours. Let stand until warm. Strain off juices. Invert loaf onto a plate and turn brown side up. Serve warm or cold. If made ahead, cover and chill. To make sandwiches, wrap meat slices in pocket bread and add condiments.

Venison Meat Loaf

1 pound ground venison
1 egg
1 cup bread crumbs
½ cup onions, chopped

1 cup milk
1 strip bacon
Ketchup

Preheat oven to 350 degrees. Mix bread crumbs and milk together. Add venison, egg and onion, mix thoroughly. Shape into a loaf. Put strip of bacon on top and then ketchup. Put about ½ cup water in baking dish or pan and bake for 1 hour uncovered. If a larger meat loaf is made, you may have to cover it the least 30 minutes if it gets too brown. If in a hurry put it into muffin tins and bake 30 minutes.

Venison Hot Dish

1 pound ground
1 onion
1 package cream cheese (8 ounces)
1 can cream of chicken soup

¼ cup milk
¼ cup ketchup
Pillsbury biscuits

Mix all ingredients together in large oven-proof bowl. Bake at 350 degrees for 10 minutes. Top with biscuits and bake for another 20-25 minutes.

Venison Sausage Meatballs

1½ pounds ground venison
½ pound sweet sausage
1 egg beaten
1 teaspoon salt
2 tablespoons dry onion

1 tablespoon parsley
1 cup dry bread crumbs
½ teaspoon pepper
½ teaspoon brown sugar
½ cup of bacon drippings

Combine all ingredients except bacon drippings. Mix well. Shape into 1-inch balls. Fry in bacon fat over medium heat, evenly browning all sides. Blot meatballs with paper towel. Arrange on platter and serve. Yields 4 dozen.

— *Joe Bontke, Long Valley, N.J.*

Creamed Deer Burger with Potatoes

1 pound of deer burger
2 tablespoons milk
1½ teaspoon flour
1 can cream of mushroom soup
1 4-ounce can mushrooms (optional)

1 can of beef broth or 2 cups water with 3 bouillon cubes
4 medium potatoes, cut in chunks
½ teaspoon salt
¼ teaspoon pepper

Make patties in usual size, then dip each in milk and then flour.
Brown both sides until burgers are just about done.
Add rest of ingredients and cover and cook slowly over low heat till potatoes are done. Serves 4.

Venison Meat Loaf

1½ pounds deer burger
1 cup crushed cracker crumbs
2 eggs, beaten
1 8-ounce can tomato sauce
½ cup onions, chopped
Dash of marjoram
2 or 3 tablespoons green pepper chopped
1½ teaspoon salt
1 medium bay leaf, crumbled or ½ teaspoon dry bay leaf

In bowl, combine all ingredients and knead well. Shape and place in a bread pan. Bake at 350 degrees for about 1 hour. Serves 6.

— *Fran Anderson, Thief River Falls, Minn.*

Dry Bones

Usually bare bones just denote death. Deer hunters revel in the exception. Go and hear the pop of dry bones, see the glint from polished tines, and imbibe the magic of the antler.

■ *Al Cornell*

In 1892, Francis Parkman wrote of the millions of bison, "...nothing is left but bones..."

Likely they were similar to the bones of a prophet's vision, "...and lo, they were very dry." The bison's bones symbolized the West's transition, and they symbolized death. Usually bare bones just denote death. Deer hunters revel in the exception.

Members of the deer family tote bared and drying bones, ones exterior to the body. Outside the flesh and veins. Dry, dead bones, becoming bleached. Yet sutured to the living. Unique in the world of bones.

If nothing living wore dry bones, in what manner would we imagine them? Absolutely weird, practically unimaginable, grotesque? Certainly grotesque, and subject for a modern cartoon.

But bones do grow outside the body. They live and grow, then die and dry. Still firmly attached to the living, they dry and shrink and bleach. Antlers are unique.

If something living wore dry bones, how would we view them? Trophies, pieces of art, elegant? Certainly elegant. Worthy of the mantle.

Again, if there were no bone growth forming an exterior appendage protruding from the head, how would we imagine it grew? We might envision a similarity to horn, continuing to grow from the base so that more mature animals would tote larger appendages. Nature is conservative and rarely expends energy in the manner associated with the annual renewal of antlers.

We might well ponder their existence. Are bones as deciduous as a maple leaf? Both are firmly attached until the time is right. Then they lose the grip with the death of one layer of cells.

Both shed quickly at the proper time. As with the tooth-edged structure, so it is with the tined appendage. One is cast away as the pedicle lets go, the other as the pedicle undoes its hold. Come May, beneath a branch of swelling buds, bulbous masses begin their regrowth.

Late spring paints abundance into the landscape. Yet, the doe's ribs show as her body pours energy into the rapid development of the newborn. Bucks use this luxury of plenty to produce an extravagant structure of new bone. All other mammals, from the least to the greatest, lack the ability to regenerate an appendage. It happens only on the frontal bone of the cranium in members of the deer family. Velvet, that thin, fine-haired skin, can quickly grow to amazing dimensions as it supplies most of the calcium, phosphorous, protein, and other essentials to the antler.

Veins shrink; velvet dries and sloughs. The new appendage retains no characteristic of continued life. A layer of living cells bonds this dead bone to the skull.

Regular visitors to the deer woods begin to perceive messages from these dead and drying bones. Antlers, attached or cast, communicate by their shape and

> *Nature is conservative and rarely expends energy in the manner associated with the annual renewal of antler.*

dimensions. First, they answer the species question, and then they go beyond to address individual matters. A yearling's antlers will often clearly telegraph the age, but not always. While this set of antlers tells little about genetics, it can reveal more about nutrition and winter severity. Large antlers might broadcast a combination of traits, such as maturity, genetics, nutrition and social status. Antlers with similar shapes and oddities, found over a few-year period, might announce the continued survival of a particular individual.

Yet, beyond those normal messages from this strange appendage there is more. You have to be there to grasp it. The doe perceives it. Hunters share in the spell.

Go and hear the pop of dry bones, see the glint from polished tines, and imbibe the magic of the antler.

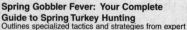